Contents

ABSOLUTE HONESTY

**Building a Corporate Culture
That Values Straight Talk and
Rewards Integrity**

Larry Johnson
&
Bob Phillips

AMACOM
American Management Association

New York • Atlanta • Brussels • Buenos Aires • Chicago • London • Mexico City
San Francisco • Shanghai • Tokyo • Toronto • Washington, D.C.

Special discounts on bulk quantities of AMACOM books are available to corporations, professional associations, and other organizations. For details, contact Special Sales Department, AMACOM, a division of American Management Association, 1601 Broadway, New York, NY 10019.
Tel.: 212-903-8316. Fax: 212-903-8083.
Web site: www.amacombooks.org

This publication is designed to provide accurate and authoritative information in regard to the subject matter covered. It is sold with the understanding that the publisher is not engaged in rendering legal, accounting, or other professional service. If legal advice or other expert assistance is required, the services of a competent professional person should be sought.

Library of Congress Cataloging-in-Publication Data

Johnson, Larry, 1947–
> *Absolute honesty : building a corporate culture that values straight talk and rewards integrity / Larry Johnson and Bob Phillips.*
>> *p.   cm.*
> *Includes index.*
> *ISBN 978-0-8144-3480-2*
> *ISBN 978-0-8144-0781-3*
> *1. Corporate culture–Moral and ethical aspects.   2. Communication in organizations–Moral and ethical aspects.   3. Corporations–Moral and ethical aspects.   4. Business ethics.   5. Honesty.   I. Phillips, Bob, 1947–   II. Title.*

HD58.7.J612   2003
174'.4–dc21

2002155806

Printing number

10   9   8   7   6   5   4   3   2   1

Moving from "Attack and Defend" to "Discuss
  and Solve"   165
Minimizing Defensiveness in Others   168
Removing the Great Wall   174

**Chapter 7 Absolute Honesty Law #5:
             Reward the Messenger   176**
Blatant Retribution   178
Intentional but Subtle Retribution   179
Unintentional Retribution   181
Disconfirming Messages   184
Perception Can Be Reality   189
Sleazy, Wacko, Bizarre Management Practices   190
Manager's Code of Conduct   192
Truth on a Napkin   201

**Chapter 8 Absolute Honesty Law #6:
             Build a Platform of
             Integrity   203**
Focus on What's Important   208
It Starts with Leadership   209
Leadership Obsession = Organizational
  Infection   213
Create a Platform of Integrity   214
Build Your Platform on Ethical Tenets   217
Noninstrumental Ethics   219
Why Noninstrumental Ethics?   220
Establish an Ethical Foundation   224
Applying the Five Tenets to Up-Selling   227
No Easy Answers   228
Create and Stick to a Platform of Integrity   229
Base Your Platform of Integrity on Solid Ethics   230
Live by Your Platform of Integrity   233
Developing the Tenets and the Platform   235

Acknowledgments

MANY PEOPLE HELPED US WITH THIS BOOK, STARTING WITH OUR spouses, CJ Johnson and Lisa Phillips. CJ contributed innumerable ideas and examples to the book's content. She also read and proofed it so many times since its conception in 1996, it's a miracle she can look at it now without gagging. Lisa provided stories, ideas, and editing throughout. She then mastered the enormous task of acquiring all the citation permissions and formatting the manuscript for submission to AMACOM—all the while enduring myriad last-minute changes, mostly from Larry, who couldn't leave it alone. Most of all, we thank both CJ and Lisa for practicing what this book preaches by giving us the absolute honesty we needed, no matter how painful, to make this book something we hope you will find valuable.

We also want to thank Mike Snell, our agent, for hammering on us until we created a viable proposal; Steve George, Dana Huebler, and Sam Horn for editing our work; Tom Short for his thoughts about how IBM manages to run an ethical ship; Andrea Gold for her perspectives on how she runs an ethical company (Gold Stars Speakers Bureau of Tucson, Arizona); Sheila Paxton for sharing her approach to listening to her employees; Chip Clark for her insight into the impact communication styles have on how people work together; Jan Vessa of Intel Corporation for validating our thoughts about absolute honesty; Tim Thorsteinson, CEO of Grass Valley Group, who has served as a model of ethical and honest leadership for Bob; and Hanna Kuenn, Larry's eleven-year-old niece, whose feedback helped us make the book more readable.

On a personal note, Bob extends thanks to a few special people in his life who have given him inspiration: Bill Phillips, his father, who was a role model in speaking up and telling people how he felt even when it cost him in his chosen profession; Fred Moore, his seventh-grade teacher, who taught him that there is more to life than just sports; Don Baker, his high school football coach, who taught him the importance of setting reachable goals, providing the proper coaching, and when to apply situational leadership; Cal Udall, a great mentor, who opened his life to the world of business and taught him how not to take yourself too seriously when you are successful; Dick Renckly, director of human resources at U-Haul Corporation, who directed him into a career in human resources; and Larry Johnson, who asked him to cowrite this book and then bugged him until he agreed.

Larry extends thanks to some special people as well: Ruth Boggs, his grandmother, who taught him the importance of doing the right thing, even when it's hard to do; Hannah Schwitzer, his seventh-grade teacher, who encouraged Larry to use his talents of persuasion and presentation to change people's lives (seventh grade was a good year for both Bob and Larry); Meagan Johnson, Larry's daughter, who, despite her father's parental faults, has become one of the most accomplished practitioners of absolute honesty and ethical living we know; CJ Johnson, who, for thirty-two years of marriage, has helped him grow into the person their dogs think he is; and Bob Phillips, whose wealth of experience and corporate wisdom added immeasurable richness to this book's message.

Finally, we want to thank the unethical corporate officers who contributed to the 2002 Crisis of Ethics in Business USA. They, along with several other undesirable corporate miscreants we know, served as perfect models for what *not* to do when demonstrating absolute honesty in the workplace.

AUTHORS' NOTE

To bring the principles of absolute honesty to life, we used many examples and stories of good and bad practitioners of those principles. Some of these people are well-known, or at least have been written about in the public domain. We refer to them by first and last name, and as a courtesy to readers, have tried to cite the sources of our information.

Some of the examples are about people we have interviewed or know personally. Where appropriate, we refer to them by first and last name, and where appropriate, we keep their identities confidential, using fictitious first names only. In a few situations, we offer case studies that are not based on any real person but reflect situations we have observed or know about. In those cases, we have used first names only.

With regard to our own names, to avoid the self-referencing awkwardness inherent in a book with more than one author, we refer to ourselves simply as Larry and Bob.

If reading this book brings to mind an example or situation that you would like to share with us, we want to hear it! Please e-mail it to *stories@absolutehonesty.com*.

PART 1

THE CHALLENGE

CHAPTER 1

The Naked Truth

"The good I stand on is my truth and honesty."

—WILLIAM SHAKESPEARE, HENRY VIII

WORLDCOM. ENRON. DOZENS OF DOT-COMS. TYCO. ARTHUR Andersen. Adelphia. AOL TimeWarner. The 2002 Crisis of Ethics in Business USA sent us all reeling with shocking revelations of dishonesty, manipulation, and silent complicity. The really bad news was the cost of this dishonesty to the U.S. economy, which ran into trillions of dollars. In addition, it diminished the faith the rest of the world has in the way we do business. Clearly, dishonesty does not pay.

We will show you that honesty *does* pay and that creating a culture of straight talk and integrity not only keeps the media at bay but also makes an organization more competitive in the global economy and better trusted by customers, employees, and shareholders. To do this, we attack the sort of passivity at both the personal and organizational levels that allows little lies to grow into giant disasters.

THE KUMBAYA SYNDROME

The seeds of this passivity were sown, ironically, in the 1980s, when companies across the nation rushed to embrace a management model that focused on the benefits of teamwork and its ability to empower organizations. In general, this approach resulted in tremendous increases in productivity and improved employee morale—so we are firm supporters. (In fact, in our consulting practices we have worked with several companies to help maintain their team systems.) That said, many organizational cultures built on the team/empowerment model have often preached a subtle (and sometimes not-so-subtle) mantra that says, "For the company to function as one big happy team, we all must be 'nice' to each other."

Of course, there is nothing wrong with being "nice" per se, but one frustrated engineer described this misguided organizational niceness this way: "No matter how stupid or unethical a decision my team or my manager makes, we are all expected to embrace the stupidity, never argue, and start singing 'Kumbaya.'"

As organizational consultants, we have talked to hundreds of executives, managers, and employees in various industries, and many have expressed this same frustration with what we call the *Kumbaya Syndrome*. They complain that being "nice" often translates into being cooperative rather than confrontational, going along to get along, accepting less than stellar results when accountability is called for, or simply not telling the truth when doing so would be either politically inconvenient or professional suicide.

We see this fear of confrontation and lack of truthfulness as the organizational equivalent of the fairy tale "The Emperor's New Clothes." Most people know the story. An unscrupulous tailor with a gift for salesmanship convinces a vain and somewhat stupid emperor to pay a large sum of gold for a suit of clothes made from a thread so exquisite and fine that only the most intelligent and sophisticated will be able to see it. The guileless emperor buys this fantasy and, when the tailor "presents" him with his new suit, he proudly parades through the streets stark naked. Of course, none of the townspeople dare to point out that their emperor has no clothes on, preferring to support his deluded fantasy rather than risk being punished. It takes a young boy who doesn't know any better to shout out the truth that is obvious to all and finally give the emperor the honest feedback he so desperately needs.

If managers can't get honest feedback from their employees, they, like the naked emperor, will make foolish decisions. Instead of telling an "emperor" how wonderful he looks in his new suit, employees should be encouraged, if not required, to speak their minds and go to the mat for what they believe in, even if it means disapproval from their managers or colleagues. Without such honesty, an organization exposes itself to fallout from bad decisions based on bad information, much like an emperor without clothes.

This book speaks to an urgent need to reestablish a standard of communication that encourages open discussions and healthy debate; tells the truth; doesn't mince words; and, most of all, is guided by a moral and ethical sense of right and wrong. We call this communication style *absolute honesty.*

When we think of absolute honesty, we think of Mrs. Edna Lever, Larry's eighth-grade teacher. Mrs. Lever was known throughout the school as a taskmaster, a strict disciplinarian, and a bit of a grouch. With a glare and a stern word, Mrs. Lever would never hesitate to tell you when you did something wrong and how to correct it. On the other hand, with a smile and a brief comment, she would always let you know when you did something right and that it pleased her. No matter what, you knew that she would always tell you the truth, and you sensed that her intentions were always in your best interests.

Consequently, Mrs. Lever's students always scored highest on the annual achievement tests. Parents competed to get their children into her class. By midyear, Mrs. Lever's students universally loved her. (It took time for some of them to warm up to her gruffness.) Mrs. Lever was a superb practitioner of absolute honesty. She told the truth when the truth needed to be told, she was clear in how she told it, and her focus was always on doing the right thing for the right reason (her students' welfare).

We believe there need to be more Mrs. Levers practicing absolute honesty in organizational life today.

Don't get us wrong. We don't think you have to be a grouch to practice absolute honesty. In fact, we believe that common courtesy and a sincere concern for other people are highly desirable traits. Absolute honesty is *not* about attacking others nor is it about winning just to prove you're better than someone else. It's about using the truth to achieve higher, nobler goals. What made Mrs. Lever effective was not her grouchiness. We all know grouches who are just that— grouches. What made her great was her willingness to be straight with you and to do it in a way that showed you how to be a better person.

Absolute honesty is also about doing the right thing for the right reasons. It is recognizing when decisions and actions either are un-wise or are not within the bounds of ethical and moral standards— and it's about having the courage to voice your opinions about those decisions so they can be corrected.

This doesn't mean that we advocate insubordination or arguing endlessly against decisions made by your manager or your company— quite the opposite! At the core of absolute honesty is the practice of "disagree and commit," which means that if you don't agree with a decision or action, you should be free to express your feelings openly and without fear of being punished for doing so. Once that's done, however, you are expected to support whatever decision your man-agement decides to follow, unless it is ethically wrong to do so. We discuss the "disagree and commit" concept further in Chapter 5 and the topic of ethics in Chapter 8.

Not surprisingly, some corporate giants have long known the value of straight talk and no-nonsense communication. Intel inte-grates expectations of straight talk and truthfulness into employee performance reviews and trains its people in the effective use of confrontation to solve difficult issues. Based on the practices we've observed and helped implement in such companies as American Express, Harley-Davidson, Sequent Computers, Tektronix, and Intel, we show you how to practice absolute honesty and to communicate more courageously with your colleagues, customers, friends, and family. We also show you how to build a culture that encourages and nurtures the practice of absolute honesty.

IT AIN'T EASY

We are not so naive as to think candor and truth telling don't include risk. Our guess is that if any subordinate of Tyco CEO Dennis Kozlowski had objected to Kozlowski's alleged misappropriation of millions from the company's coffers, that employee would soon have been an ex-employee. As an old Turkish proverb says, "If you tell the truth, have one foot in the stirrup." Yet there are times when telling the truth is the right thing to do, even if the odds are stacked against you.

Consider Sherron Watkins, Enron's vice president of corporate development. In August 2001, she wrote an e-mail to Chairman Ken Lay outlining her concerns about the company's financial dealings[1] that said in part:

> Dear Mr. Lay,
> Has Enron become a risky place to work? For those of us who didn't get rich over the last few years, can we afford to stay?

The memo went on to describe her concerns about two questionable deals, Condor and Raptor) that Enron had engaged in to hide its losses. She concluded with:

I am incredibly nervous that we will implode in a wave of accounting scandals. My eight years of Enron work history will be worth nothing on my resume, the business world will consider the past successes as nothing but an elaborate accounting hoax. Skilling [Enron's then CEO] is resigning now for 'personal reasons' but I would think he wasn't having fun, looked down the road and knew this stuff was unfixable and would rather abandon ship now than resign in shame in two years.

What do we do? I know this question cannot be addressed in the all-employee meeting, but can you give some assurances that you and Causey will sit down and take a good hard objective look at what is going to happen to Condor and Raptor in 2002 and 2003?[2]

Six months later, Enron was in bankruptcy, its employees out of work and without retirement funds, its accounting partner, Arthur Andersen, headed toward ruin. The only bright spot was Sherron Watkins. Her courage made her a recognized celebrity hero on the streets of Houston.[3]

Perhaps it was a case of too little, too late, but nevertheless, Ms. Watkins's forthrightness and candor are to be applauded. We believe there need to be more Sherron Watkinses walking the halls of corporations.

This book shows you how to build an organizational culture that supports and encourages people of candor and courage. The benefits of such a culture are enormous. Organizations that value doing the right thing, telling the truth, promoting no-nonsense communication, and confronting difficult issues move ahead in their industries and markets by creating:

▲ Cultures of integrity
▲ Compelling brands

- ▲ Competitive advantages
- ▲ Productive workforces
- ▲ Consistent leadership
- ▲ Positive morale

In addition, the organizations that do the right thing can expect to avoid negative press and keep their officers out of jail more often than those that don't.

CULTURES OF INTEGRITY

Arthur Andersen once had a reputation for honesty. That reputation was decimated when Andersen's role in the Enron debacle was exposed. To many in the accounting world, however, this came as no surprise. Two months before the Enron story broke, Andersen agreed to pay $217 million to settle a suit against it for its role in the Baptist Foundation of Arizona (BFA), duping 13,000 elderly investors out of their life savings.[4] According to an article published in Salon.com, an online news agency,[5] Andersen was accused of practices at BFA that have a hauntingly familiar, Enron-like ring:

- ▲ Ignoring or failing to thoroughly investigate shell companies created by insiders who grotesquely enriched themselves while hiding BFA's mounting debt in "off-balance sheet companies"
- ▲ Ignoring knowledgeable whistle-blowers
- ▲ Altering documents
- ▲ Ignoring well-known accounting industry "red flags" that indicated white-collar fraud was taking place

Andersen's name has also cropped up in the investigations of Qwest, WorldCom, and Peregrine Systems[6]—all subjects of investigations for wrongdoing. Gee, is there a pattern here? Perhaps it's just a coincidence, but it appears likely that the "unusual" accounting practices Andersen applied at Enron were more than just isolated incidents.

We believe that when lying, dishonesty, and unethical behavior are accepted in one part of a company's culture, those standards of behavior will migrate throughout the entire organization. Nothing occurs in a vacuum. When the culture authorizes aberrant behavior, aberrant behavior becomes the norm, and a culture of integrity ceases to exist.

COMPELLING BRANDS

In 1982, seven people in the Chicago area died after ingesting Tylenol® Extra Strength capsules that had been laced with deadly cyanide. A subsequent investigation found that someone had intentionally contaminated the capsules after the shipment had left the factory.

Most experts in marketing and advertising at the time agreed that Johnson & Johnson, the parent company of Tylenol's manufacturer, McNeil Consumer Products, would never recover from the public relations disaster. Advertising guru Jerry Della Femina said shortly after the crisis broke: "I don't think they can ever sell another product under that name. . . . There may be an advertising person who thinks he can solve this and if they find him, I want to hire him, because then I want him to turn our water cooler into a wine cooler."[7]

Johnson & Johnson proved Della Femina wrong.[8] Almost immediately, the company truthfully admitted to the public that there was a potential health risk to anyone taking Tylenol. It stopped the production of Tylenol capsules across the country and pulled all remaining Tylenol capsules from the shelves throughout Illinois.

The result: Johnson & Johnson was praised in the media for its forthright and responsible reaction to the crisis. An article in the *Washington Post*, titled "Tylenol's Maker Shows How to Respond to Crisis," said, "Through the hysteria and frustration generated by random murder, Johnson & Johnson has effectively demonstrated how a major business ought to handle a disaster. . . . There has been no Nixonian 'modified limited hangout' at the J&J headquarters in New Brunswick, New Jersey." The article went on to compare Johnson & Johnson's response with that of Firestone Tire and Rubber Company, whose officials tried to pretend that nothing was wrong when Firestone 500 tires were disintegrating. It pointed out that, unlike Firestone, Johnson & Johnson was willing to do the right thing, regardless of the fact that pulling more than 22 million bottles of Tylenol from the shelves cost the company more than $80 million and that it would very likely lose most of its 40 percent market and the $400 million in revenue Tylenol produced for the company. The article wrapped up by saying:

> From the day the deaths were linked to the poisoned Tylenol until the recall on Thursday, Johnson & Johnson has succeeded in portraying itself to the public as the company willing to do what's right, regardless of cost.
>
> Serving the public interest has simultaneously saved the company's reputation. That lesson in public responsibility—and public relations—will survive at Johnson & Johnson regardless of what happens to Tylenol.[9]

Of course, Tylenol did survive, and today it is once again one of the top-selling pain relievers in the world.

Compare Johnson & Johnson's reaction to the Tylenol scare with Jack in the Box's reaction when faced with a similar crisis. From December 1992 through January 1993, lethal food poisoning became a national issue when contaminated beef served at various Jack in the Box restaurants in California, Nevada, Idaho, and Washington poisoned more than 700 people. Four children died and thirty-five developed hemolytic uremic syndrome, which often causes kidney failure later in adulthood.[10]

Government scientists at the Centers for Disease Control in Atlanta studied, traced, and identified the pathogen *E. coli* 0157 as the source of contamination originating from tainted meat—meat that had not been sufficiently cooked by Jack in the Box restaurants.[11]

On January 15, 1993, the Washington State Health Department alerted Jack in the Box that the outbreak was linked to its hamburgers. Jack in the Box immediately denied responsibility for the crisis, pointing to the fact that many of the victims had eaten at other restaurants before becoming ill.[12]

Six days passed before president Robert Nugent admitted that Jack in the Box had been the source of the tainted hamburgers. Simultaneously, however, he attacked the Washington State Health Department for not distributing current meat-handling regulations in a timely manner. This resulted in a massively negative public response.[13] Newspapers were full of editorials criticizing Jack in the Box for shirking its responsibilities. By the end of March 1993, the *E. coli* crisis had cost Jack in the Box more than $30 million in lost revenues. Liability damages eventually exceeded $100 million.[14]

COMPETITIVE ADVANTAGES

In the midseventies, Xerox set up a team of highly talented scientists in a state-of-the-art facility in Palo Alto, California; allocated a huge budget for their use; and gave them the mandate to invent better copiers. These folks went well beyond Xerox's expectations, eventually coming up with the idea that if you could make a desktop computer user-friendly, you could eliminate the need for paper—and for better copiers in the office. The dominant operating system for desktop computers at that time was MS DOS, which was anything but user-friendly. To overcome this problem, the researchers developed an operating system that mimicked a real desktop by using something they called graphical user interface (GUI). This enabled users to point at icons, click, and open files. BINGO! They had a user-friendly system.

With great excitement, they presented their idea to Xerox's top management. The leaders of a copier company were not thrilled with the concept of a "paperless office" and sent the researchers packing back to Palo Alto.

A few years later, one of the researchers conducted a tour of the Xerox Palo Alto facility for the CEO of a company located just down the street. That CEO was Steve Jobs of Apple Computer. He saw the potential and immediately adapted the idea to the Macintosh operating system. Years later, Microsoft also "adapted" the concept (Apple called it stealing), and now 99 percent of the computing world uses some form of GUI, in either Windows or Macintosh format—and Microsoft has grown to be one of the largest and most successful companies on earth. Meanwhile, Xerox has struggled to survive—a plight it might have avoided if ninety-nine percent of all computers on earth were using a Xerox operating system.[15]

If the executives at Xerox had been more open to hearing the thoughts and concepts of their people, would they have been able to see past their own biases and adopt the new idea? If the Palo Alto researchers had been more effective in presenting their idea, is it possible they would have convinced the executives to try it out? We will never know, but one thing is certain: The chance of answering the questions positively would have improved if openness and the ability to confront disagreement had been attributes of the culture at Xerox.

PRODUCTIVE WORKFORCES

If you grew up in the United States in the 1950s and 1960s and watched any television at all, you will remember the *I Love Lucy* show. The essential plot of every episode revolved around Lucy pulling the wool over her husband Ricky's eyes to get something she wanted, or Ricky fooling Lucy to get something he wanted. Neighbors Fred and Ethel usually helped out in the deception. In one classic scam, Lucy, who wanted to get into show business, faked a nervous breakdown to convince Ricky that denying her a part in his nightclub act was driving her crazy. It was amusing to watch, but it was also sad. Call us curmudgeons, but in real life, such shenanigans can seriously damage the trust level in any relationship.

Rosemary, an acquaintance of ours, told us this story. Her eight-year-old son desperately wanted a dog, and Rosemary wanted to get one for him; she had had a dog as a child and loved it. Rosemary's husband, Sam, hated dogs, and immediately put his foot down, saying there would be no dog and no further discussion on the matter. After several arguments, they dropped the issue. On Christmas morning, without Sam's consent, Rosemary gave their son a dog as a "gift from Mom and Dad." Under the circumstances, Sam couldn't say much without coming across as Ebenezer Scrooge, but "open and honest" communication was never practiced again in that household.

You may or may not find Rosemary's dishonesty in this situation as distasteful as we did—we hope you do. After all, what kind of marriage can be truly healthy when such deceptive manipulation is standard practice between spouses?

Of course, there are two sides to every story. When we asked Rosemary why she pulled this trick, she said that Sam was often selfish and dictatorial. Taking the "indirect" (or deceitful) approach was the only way she could exert any power in the relationship. On the other hand, when we asked Sam about his relationship with Rosemary, he said that he loved her but she couldn't be trusted with money or practical matters. Therefore, his strategy was to just say "no" to everything. Was this relationship ever built on absolute honesty? We think not.

By the way, they kept the dog but divorced two years later.

In business, this kind of dysfunctional game playing can cause enormous losses of productivity and profitability. If you are an account manager who needs to know if a production order is on track, you must be able to trust that what the production manager tells you about the order is true. If you manage an employee who is not performing to expectations, but you don't have the courage to give her feedback, she will never improve because she believes she's doing okay. When you finally decide to dismiss her, you'll find yourself in court trying to explain why you were never honest with her about her performance. If you are a manager who fails to listen to people's concerns about their budgets being too tight to meet project goals, and you blindly insist they perform under threat of dismissal, you can expect them to make you think they're progressing satisfactorily when they are not. If, as a manager, you play favorites with your subordinates, basing that favoritism on whom you like, rather than on who produces, you can expect that people are going to lie and present false faces to you so you will like them rather than judge them on the results of their work. They may even get Fred and Ethel to help out.

Each example reeks of wasted effort. To remain viable, an organization must apply as much time, energy, and personpower as possible to the business it conducts. It must spend the majority of its resources producing and selling products or services. It must also spend a large chunk of those resources maintaining a healthy environment where the producing and selling can take place. It can ill afford to have its people waste time and energy playing destructive politics, protecting rear ends, defending turf, and working around dysfunctional relationships.

Psychologist Abraham Maslow's studies on motivation in the workplace[16] tell us that people will always attend to their own survival before worrying about the welfare of the organization. "How am I doing?" "Am I succeeding?" "Is my future secure?" "Am I contributing?" "Can I trust what I'm seeing or hearing, or is there unseen danger here?" These are questions that run through people's minds as they size up the work environment. When the answers are clear, and their sense of danger is low, people can apply all their energy and time to doing their jobs well.

When the answers are unclear, or indicate danger, the number of e-mails, phone conversations, and water cooler meetings about the "family dynamics" of work will rise, while concern about the actual work being done will fall.

We propose that when absolute honesty is the norm in an organization, and is actually practiced in the workplace, it is easier for people to focus on their work and not be distracted by "family dynamics." When you know your boss will be candid with you if your performance is lacking, you don't have to worry about interpreting hidden meanings, innuendoes, or nonverbal language to decide if he's unhappy with your work or just grouchy that day. When you trust that you will be told the truth if there is something you need to know about the state of the business, you can focus on your work and not worry about it. When you know that your CEO would never encourage you to buy more company stock for your 401(k) when, at the same time, she's selling all hers because the stock is poised to take a dive, you can buy it and go back to work. With that kind of trust in the working environment, you can spend your time doing what you're paid to do rather than wasting company time and your time looking over your shoulder, protecting your assets.

CONSISTENT LEADERSHIP

When Bob Phillips worked at Intel during the 1970s and 1980s, he had an opportunity to sit in on many of the manager meetings and operational reviews conducted by Andrew (Andy) Grove, Intel's COO at that time. Grove had (and still has) a well-deserved reputation for being a tough and demanding manager. The sheer power of his intellectual skills and his industry knowledge, combined with his willingness to challenge and question what he perceived to be inaccurate or false assumptions, could make the bravest of department managers quake in their boots as they stood before him to present a business issue or strategic plan.

One of Grove's direct reports recalls being chastised during a presentation when Grove interrupted and said, "If this isn't going to get more interesting, you might want to stop right there and come back next week with a better story."[17]

Bob says of his days with Grove, "After you have worked with Andy for years, nothing can intimidate you because you have been challenged by the best." That may sound like criticism, but Bob means it as a compliment. All of Grove's confrontations focused on getting at the truth, not at getting the person. When Grove asked questions, he treated everyone equally to a piercing examination of the facts and assumptions being discussed, regardless of the person's position in the company—which to the person being questioned often felt like a brutal grilling. If you did not know an answer to one of his questions, it was always better to admit it than to try to bluff your way through. Grove always sought straight and truthful answers that were in the company's best interests, not what people thought he wanted to hear.

This was the environment that Grove established at Intel when he became head of operations in the 1970s, and his legacy continues to this day. It's an environment where honesty is rigorously pursued. It's a tough place where there is little countenance for inaccuracy, sloppy thinking, or distortions of the truth. It is also a place where you know what's expected of you and you can perform accordingly. As a result, it's a place where you can focus more energy on your work and less on the political process and the "family dynamics" of the organization.

Of course, nothing's perfect. You can bet there are Intel employees who, upon reading this, will laugh and retort that Intel has plenty of politics, backstabbing, kissing up to the boss, Kumbaya Syndrome, and dishonesty. And they would be right. Any organization of Intel's size (80,000 plus employees) will have its share of family dysfunction. But we have observed that at Intel, less time and energy is spent on these issues than at similarly sized companies, and that's a direct result of working in an environment that encourages brutal honesty, straight talk, and integrity. Judging from Intel's incredible growth during the 1980s and 1990s and its absolute world domination of the PC chip market, it obviously has put its energies in the right place.

It's also interesting to note that during the 2002 Crisis of Ethics in Business USA, neither Andy Grove nor Craig Barrett, Intel's CEO in 2002, was ever mentioned in the media for engaging in unethical or illegal activities. Meanwhile, Enron CEO Jeffrey Skilling, Tyco CEO Dennis Kozlowski, Adelphia CEO John Rigas, and a host of others hit the headlines facing charges of dishonesty and deceit in their business practices.

It's not that practicing absolute honesty as an organization will guarantee that people won't engage in illegal or immoral activities, but it lowers the odds. As a leader, practicing absolute honesty may force you to admit that your company, your department, or your team did not perform to the level expected—and you may therefore have to suffer the consequences your stockholders choose to inflict on you. On the other hand, absolute honesty will rarely land you in front of a congressional committee or a trial judge.

POSITIVE MORALE

Tim, an inspector for a state agency that licenses nursing homes, told us this story. His job is to inspect facilities to make sure they meet state and federal guidelines for quality of care, health, and safety standards. If a home doesn't pass an inspection, it's usually given a period of time to correct the problem or problems before another inspection is conducted. Then, if the problem is not corrected, the inspector can impose fines, suspend the home's license, and/or shut the place down for good. It all depends on the severity of the infractions.

Tim had put a particular nursing home on probation for failure to correct several deficiencies in delivering and documenting adequate care to its residents. The place was also cited for being dirty and having a urine smell. When he returned to do a follow-up inspection, things appeared to have improved. The place was cleaner, and the problems that had caused the probation seemed to have been corrected. As Tim was preparing to leave, a staff nurse took him aside and told him to check out Mrs. Jones's chart, where he found some glaring discrepancies. While he was doing this, an aide leaned over his shoulder and said, "If you think that's bad, check out the condition of Mr. Smith's catheter in room 4B." While he was checking this out, another aide told him to look at Mrs. Thompson's untreated bedsores and compare them to what was in the chart. And while he was on his way to do that, the maintenance man suggested that he take a look at the dreadful condition of the facility's plumbing.

After closing the place down permanently, Tim asked staff members why they had been willing to "snitch" on their own employer and put themselves out of a job. It turned out that, in its effort to cut costs, the corporate office of this chain had set up a contest for the administrators of each facility. Those who could cut spending on nursing pool help by 50 percent would earn a free trip to Hawaii. (Nursing pools are temporary personnel agencies that specialize in supplying nurses and nurses' aides to the health care industry. The cost of hiring a temporary nurse from a pool is two to three times that of a nurse's normal salary and benefits, so nursing homes use them reluctantly.)

In his desire to win the trip, the administrator of this facility had told the staff that there was no money for pool personnel. Consequently, if they were short staffed, they would have to work with fewer people, which would increase their already immense workload, and they would have to work more double shifts, which were burning them out at a rapid rate.

Fortunately (or unfortunately, depending on how you look at it), the staff got wind of the administrator's motives. It was just then that our friend Tim showed up for the follow-up inspection, and staff members took their revenge.

No one likes to be lied to or used, and when employees feel as if their management has not been truthful with them, or is engaged in wrongdoing, they can, and usually will, try to even the score. It may not be as severe as it was with the folks in this nursing home, but at the minimum, an air of cynicism and subtle hostility toward management and the company will develop that can be very difficult to undo. Think of the waiter who will tell you *not* to eat the meatloaf because the cook's in a bad mood, or the disgruntled service rep who berates her own company's charges on your bill. In our travels as consultants, we had a hotel employee tell us that we could get a nicer room, at a better price, with a competitor down the street. Obviously, he had some kind of ax to grind with his management.

Creating a standard of behavior that says that everyone, including executives and managers, will tell the truth regardless of the consequences doesn't guarantee that your employees will not commit this kind of sabotage, but it does lower the odds that employees will feel deceived and used.

Honesty *does* pay, especially when it is an integral part of the culture. Chapter 2 shows you how to set the right tone and direction so that your organization stays out of trouble and prospers by doing the right things for the right reasons. Chapters 3 through 8 describe the Six Laws of Absolute Honesty, laws that, when practiced by everyone in the organization, serve to make this culture a reality. Chapter 9 explains how to create an infrastructure that encourages integrity, honesty, and ethical behavior. Chapter 10 provides a review of the book so you can quickly reference the key points covered.

Organizations, like big families, brim with a wide range of personalities, diverse roles, countless interpersonal relationships, and endless opportunities for joy and pain. While there are many reasons why one company thrives and another struggles, we believe absolute honesty is essential to the health and well-being of the people who make a company successful. Absolute honesty improves morale and supports a productive workforce. It promotes ethical behavior within a culture of integrity. It communicates the right message to customers and shareholders, enhancing the brand and building competitive advantage.

Dana Commercial Credit proved this to be true when, in the 1990s, its leadership decided that a strong ethical culture would help distinguish it from its lease financing competitors. The company's leaders chose to stop doing business with companies that made promises they couldn't keep and that delivered less than the best quality and service. They began distributing an ethics card with ten "Dos and Don'ts" to all new employees. As a result of these and many other proactive decisions, the dollar volume of the company's leases more than tripled in four years, while rates of return on equity and assets increased more than 45 percent.

Executive vice president and chief financial officer Rod Filcek explained: "The leasing industry has not always had the best reputation. Our culture and reputation have given us an advantage. We have a level of trust with clients that they haven't experienced before."[18]

Trust—among employees, customers, shareholders, and the community—is a powerful reason for your organization to pursue a culture of absolute honesty.

CHAPTER 2

A Culture of Absolute Honesty

"What upsets me is not that you lied to me; it is that from now on, I can no longer believe you."

—FREDERICK NIETZSCHE

ON FEBRUARY 9, 2001, WHILE CONDUCTING A SPECIAL TOUR FOR a group of civilians off the coast of Hawaii, the nuclear submarine *USS Greenville* launched an "emergency blow," rapidly rising from the ocean depths and breaking through the surface like a whale playing in the waves. The crew wanted to show the visiting civilians what the submarine could do and, according to testimony, "give them a bit of a thrill." Unfortunately, the rapidly emerging submarine collided with the *Ehime Maru,* a Japanese fishing vessel, sinking the small boat and leaving nine of the thirty-five people on board dead.

A subsequent U.S. naval inquiry uncovered many mistakes made by the Greenville's captain, Commander Scott Waddle, and his crew that contributed to the deadly accident. Not the least was the failure of the fire control technician (FCT) to warn Commander Waddle that the sonar display had identified a ship in the area. During the inquiry, Rear Admiral Charles Griffiths, Jr., who conducted the prehearing investigation, testified, "The fire control technician should have heard Waddle's assessment of the situation and questioned it . . . he should clearly have forcibly told the captain and the officer of the deck."[1]

In a subsequent interview, Navy Captain Conrad Donahue, who has commanded two nuclear submarines during his twenty-seven-year career, stated, "On this particular ship, and on a lot of ships in the navy, the crew has so much trust in the skipper's abilities that they don't question him when they should. The FCT had a ship on the display but he saw the captain looking through the periscope. He probably assumed that if the skipper didn't see it . . . it wasn't there."[2]

This looks like a case of "The Emperor's New Clothes." How often does it happen in an organization that, for one reason or another, no one tells the manager what the manager needs to know and, as a result, the manager or the company blunders into a disaster? Perhaps an account manager spots serious flaws in a marketing strategy but, because she's new in the position, feels timid about speaking up. Maybe someone from the management team has a bad feeling about entering into a risky business deal but says nothing because everyone else is so gung ho about it. Or perhaps all the people in one department voice no complaints about an unqualified, nonperforming employee in a key position because they are reluctant to question their manager's hiring choice. "She's the boss," they reason, "she must know what she's doing." Even worse, they keep silent because they are afraid of retribution for appearing disloyal, perhaps with good reason: If she has punished other bearers of bad news, why would anyone volunteer to be the next victim?

Managers don't need to be as vain and stupid as the naked emperor to make bad decisions. Sometimes, the brightest and best simply have limited perspectives. (After all, no less than a U.S.

president, Rutherford B. Hayes, told Alexander Graham Bell he had "an amazing invention, but who would ever want to use one of them?"[3] Thomas Watson, the man who led IBM from the age of typewriters to the beginning of the computer era, said in 1943, "I think there is a world market for maybe five computers.") Whether they're out of touch with current trends, sensitive about not having all the answers, or simply misinformed, all managers rely on honest feedback from their employees. Otherwise, they, like the naked emperor, are destined to make and support poor decisions. But for managers to trust the feedback they receive and get the information they need, it helps if the corporate culture supports open communication and healthy debate.

WHAT IS CORPORATE CULTURE?

We'll answer that question with a story. When Larry was in college, he shared a dorm room with a student who raised tropical fish. Halfway through the spring semester, the roommate dropped out of school to join the army, and since he couldn't take the fish to basic training, he left them to Larry as a "gift." Larry, a lifelong dog person, had no experience caring for fish, but he did his best to follow the feeding instructions his roommate had left behind. For a while, the fish did fine, but after several months of Larry's fish-ignorant, college-distracted care, the tank became so clouded with algae and used fish food you could hardly see the little guys swimming around.

So, with the best of intentions, Larry set out to clean the aquarium. After transferring the fish to a small container, he dumped the dirty water from the aquarium, scrubbed the glass inside and out with Windex, and then rinsed and refilled the aquarium. Finally, he put the fish back into their sparkling clean home and watched proudly as they swam back and forth across the tank. This happy display didn't last long, however; within an hour, all the fish were dead.

A friend who knew something about tropical fish guessed that the fish had died from either the shock of the change in water temperature, the residue of Windex that may have been on the glass, or both. In other words, to paraphrase James Carville's famous statement about the economy during the 1992 presidential election, "It was the environment, stupid!" that killed the fish.

In organizations, we call the social and political environment in which people work the "corporate culture." Like the water in the fish tank, corporate culture is the medium in which the business of the company takes place. It's reflected in everything that occurs in the organization—from the way people greet each other in the morning to the way they behave in meetings to the way decisions are made—and it affects every aspect of the business. Fail to attend to it and algae-like strands of indifference and inertia will grow, making the atmosphere murky and inhospitable. Introduce a toxic presence, and it will cause the spirit of the company to sicken, and even die. Change it too abruptly, and it will throw everyone into a shock from which the business may never recover.

Before you transform your own organizational culture into one of absolute honesty, it is helpful to have a clear and complete picture of the culture currently in place. You can form that picture by observing and analyzing your organization from three perspectives: (1) common behavior patterns, (2) organizational values and beliefs, and (3) personal attitudes and assumptions. As we look at each of these components in detail, we provide some questions to ask that should help you with your analysis.

COMMON BEHAVIOR PATTERNS

In every organization, the existing culture encourages, or at least tolerates, certain behaviors that the majority of its members consistently exhibit. For example, in one company, employees are required to wear dresses or suits, while in another they come to work in jeans and sweatshirts. In some offices, employees call their bosses by their first names; in others, as Mr. or Ms. So-and-So. Some offices are as quiet as libraries whereas others sound like a party in full swing. Such behaviors might emerge from any number of factors, including the nature of the business, the stated directives or unstated ideals of upper management, or the size or location of the business.

In our consulting practice, we conduct leadership seminars for many different companies and we've found that, depending on the organization, the majority of attendees will arrive either early or right on time, and a few will drift in up to ten minutes late. At one large financial institution, however, no one ever arrives until ten minutes after the starting time, and stragglers sometimes wander in a half hour or even forty-five minutes late.

Initially, we assumed that these variations in tardiness, or lack thereof, came from how people felt about our seminar: If they liked it and considered it valuable, they would make the effort to arrive on time, but if they didn't like it and deemed it a waste of their time, they would consistently arrive late. Based on the evaluations we ask participants to complete after each seminar, however, a whopping 99 percent report that they enjoy the seminars and see great value in them. Amazingly, the highest evaluations have come from the financial institution where everyone is so consistently tardy.

Over the years, we've come to realize that the promptness or tardiness we see in different companies has more to do with a common behavior pattern than with employees' feelings about participating in our seminars. Not surprisingly, when we attend business meetings at any of these companies, we notice that the arrival patterns to the meetings tend to match the arrival patterns at our seminars. Once again, we have to remind ourselves, "It's the culture, stupid."

Incidentally, this particular behavior pattern paints a telling picture of a company's culture regarding time. By observing the pattern, we can expect to answer a number of questions. For example: Is discipline lax or tight? Does time drive the completion of work? Are deadlines meaningful?

In the same way, consistent behavior patterns can tell us how a particular culture views honesty and healthy debate. Bob remembers that when he worked at Intel Corporation during the 1970s and 1980s, he would walk down the halls and hear heated discussions emanating from office cubicles and conference rooms. In meetings, people would passionately express their points of view, sometimes late into the night, in order to resolve differences of opinion. Such behavior patterns served as constant reminders that the company actively supported and encouraged a culture of absolute honesty, a practice that began with Intel's inception in 1969 and continues to this day.

Andy Grove, Intel's president and chief operating officer at that time, considered it essential for people to confront each other in a healthy, constructive way, so that differences of opinion could be aired and addressed quickly. For this reason, all Intel employees still complete formal training in the techniques of confronting others in a straightforward, positive manner. Grove told Bob that if people don't feel comfortable speaking up or contributing their ideas, especially when those ideas are unpopular or go against the status quo, then the best decisions won't emerge in the shortest amount of time. In a fast-moving, competitive market like semiconductor manufacturing, this could kill a company's competitive advantage.

With a culture that supports, if not demands, honesty and healthy debate, Intel has long enjoyed a reputation for being a place where people express their opinions freely and assertively—and the company has profited handsomely as a result. Again, it's the culture . . . well, you know the rest.

Assessing Behavior Patterns for Absolute Honesty

You can assess the degree of open communication and healthy debate in your company by asking some simple questions:

▲ When differences of opinion on business issues arise, are people in your company likely to express those differences openly, or do they tend to wait and see which way the wind is blowing?

▲ If an employee is asked by her manager to do something immoral or illegal, would she object or refuse? Would she be likely to report it to the appropriate person or department in your organization?

▲ When a team member has a habit that bothers others—such as holding the floor during meetings, interrupting frequently, or consistently failing to meet deadlines—does someone on the team usually confront him, or do people just wish he would change while complaining to others about his behavior?

▲ When the boss expresses an opinion that others disagree with, do people respond by falling into an uncomfortable silence and discreetly rolling their eyes, or do they enter into a lively discussion and debate?

▲ When an employee is underperforming, is she likely to be informed by her supervisor as problems arise, or will she get broadsided with the news at her next performance review?

▲ When an employee sees a colleague engaging in an illegal or unethical act, is she likely to mention it to her manager?

▲ When a work process is flawed, do people make suggestions for improvement, or do they just gripe to their coworkers about the company's "stupidity" for doing things that way?

▲ Do suggestion boxes collect complaints and innovative ideas, or do they fill up with candy wrappers and clutter?

▲ Do people let their supervisors know when they don't like a new policy, or do they gather in the break room to moan about what "they" (i.e., management) are going to do next?

▲ In meetings, do people with strong personalities always hold the floor and get their way, or does everyone get a chance to speak, with all positions considered?

ORGANIZATIONAL VALUES AND BELIEFS

A company's culture tends to reflect the values that guide the company's actions. Intel's honest discussions and healthy debate were adopted early in its history. The directive to communicate straightforwardly and to confront conflict openly was presented in new employee orientations, published on the walls in "values posters," listed in the employee handbook, and inscribed on employees' laminated ID cards. In these ways, management left no doubt that the company expected employees to live up to this policy in all their interactions.

Of course, Intel managers also had to model these values in their behavior; otherwise, the message would have been meaningless. Remember, when we use the word *values,* we're talking about the organization's "real" values, which may or may not match the values printed in the mission statement or the employee handbook. You can always tell what an organization's real values are by observing the behavior of its management, especially in times of crisis.

We know of a company whose founder did not believe in layoffs. From its inception in the 1940s, management held this value as official policy—and more important, rigorously adhered to it. During business downturns, the company would go to great lengths to avoid releasing employees—even having executives and professional staff sweep parking lots to keep them busy until business improved. Not surprisingly, the employees were fiercely loyal to the company, and turnover was consistently low.

When the founder died, his son took over as CEO and promised to maintain his father's benevolent personnel policies. However, when the business took a downturn a few years later, he quickly laid off 20 percent of the workforce. This large and unexpected layoff resulted in plummeting productivity and souring morale; not surprisingly, when the economy turned around, talented employees left in droves. Eventually, a competitor took over the debilitated company, which by then was only a shell of its former self.

How does a viable organization with nearly a half-century of history crumble to nothing in less than a decade? Although the son had promised to uphold his father's values, he did not "walk the talk," as his father had done, and the shift in the organization's real values helped bring down the company. When employees realized from their new president's actions that the "real values" of the company meant putting profits before people, they adjusted their behavior to fit the new paradigm. Once they knew their hard work and loyalty meant little in terms of job security, they wisely decided to jump ship.

Management behavior is an indicator of company values, and employee behavior will always be a reflection of those values, whether they are the stated values or the real values. It comes down to trust and, as our parents told us, trust must be earned. If there is congruence between what you, as a manager, say and what you do, people will trust what you say. If what you say and what you do don't match, employees will soon see the discrepancy and punish you for it.

Employees base their beliefs about organizational values on what they see and hear rather than on what management tells them. If you, as a leader, want to create a culture where people feel free to speak their minds and act with integrity, you'd be wise to repeatedly declare your beliefs regarding those values and, more important, behave in a manner that reflects them.

For example, John, the CFO of a company we work with told us about Randy, a young accountant he'd recently hired. The first quarterly report Randy submitted showed that revenues and profits were in line with the projections top management had supplied to the Wall Street analysts who followed the company. As Randy prepared his second quarterly report, he told John that profits were going to fall far short of expectations and asked what he should do.

"What do you mean? 'What should you do?'" John asked.

"Well," said Randy, "Should I transfer some expenses to restructuring, or capitalize the development software we expensed, or what? How would you like me to handle it?"

"I want you to report the truth," John responded. "Anything else would fly in the face of our company values of honesty and integrity. Frankly, I'm surprised you would even suggest taking another tact. Didn't we cover this stuff during your orientation?"

Bewildered, Randy replied, "Well, yes—several times. But at the last two companies I worked for they talked ethics all the time but at the end of the quarter we were still expected to do whatever it took to make the numbers match projections. In fact, that's why I eventually left them both. I didn't like the pressure to be dishonest."

John told us that this conversation was a lesson for him that regardless of how many sermons you preach about company values, employees will apply their own prejudices and perceptions to what they hear—and it's only when your values are backed up with action that the message sinks in.

Establishing a Value System of Absolute Honesty

To establish or change the values of a culture, leaders must first clarify what those values are and then publicly declare their belief in them. From that point on, they must consistently behave according to those values. This can be especially challenging when an organization proclaims honest communication and healthy debate as key values. As we've said, leaders and managers must be willing to model the behavior themselves and encourage it in their employees. Keep in mind that employees will need a great deal of encouragement and support: Few acts are more daunting than arguing for an unpopular cause, confronting one's coworker, or disagreeing with one's boss. For honest communication and healthy debate to occur, employees must trust that the environment is safe to express themselves. If a manager tells people to speak up and then "executes" someone for doing just that, employees will trust what they see, not what they hear, and they will act accordingly.

We recently witnessed a healthy display of speaking up at a weekly staff meeting for one of our clients. While the group discussed a particularly difficult customer, Tom, the manager, joked, "Don't worry, if he gives us too much trouble, we'll just sic Lisa on him." Lisa's job involved approving or denying computer system changes requested by internal customers and her tough, no-nonsense attitude has earned her such nicknames as the "System Cop" and, not so kindly, the "Wicked Witch of the West."

When Tom made the offhand remark, Lisa responded in a clear, nonaggressive, but very firm voice. "Wait a minute, Tom. When you refer to me like that, even jokingly here in the group, it really puts me in a difficult position. You and I have talked about customers perceiving me to be a 'witch,' and comments like that only make it worse."

For a few awkward seconds, no one said anything, then the group continued with its discussion, although a heavy tension hung over the room. Then Tom, much to his credit, interrupted. "Just a minute, everyone. Before we go any further, I'd like to address what Lisa just said." He turned to Lisa. "You're right—we did talk about the issue of you being perceived negatively by customers. My comment was out of line. I apologize."

Instantly, the tension dissolved, and the group moved on to the business at hand. Afterward, in our role as consultants/observers, we discussed what had happened. When we asked Lisa why she felt comfortable confronting Tom, the rest of the team laughed. "That's Lisa's style!" someone volunteered. "She'll speak up to anyone, at any time, about anything—even her boss." (Small wonder that she is cast in the role of the "cop" who delivers bad news to customers!)

Lisa, however, gave Tom credit for creating an atmosphere where team members feel free to speak their minds without fear of retribution. Even with her naturally forthright manner, she said that she had worked for other managers to whom she would *never* have spoken up about *anything*. In other words, if Tom had been a less open manager and prone to punishing employees for their honesty, Lisa would have kept her mouth shut. (Of course, her resentment toward Tom would have festered and manifested itself as indirect complaints to coworkers or a Dilbertesque attitude of cynicism and mistrust.)

After hearing Lisa's explanation, we complimented Tom for his willingness to admit he was wrong. We asked him if his response to Lisa was part of an intentional effort to maintain the open atmosphere he aspired to. "I suppose," Tom modestly replied. "But mostly, I apologized to Lisa because I *was* wrong, and the apology was appropriate." He then also pointed out: "Had I truly felt I was right, I would have told Lisa so with the same forthrightness she had used with me." If he always apologized, or said he was wrong, even when he believed he was right, Tom knew his graciousness would be perceived as weakness. "The key to nurturing an open culture," he explained, "is to simply express your views honestly and respect everyone else's right to do the same."

In the final analysis, employee behavior reflects company values, but managerial behavior creates those values. In other words, it's what you *do* to model, reinforce, and reward open communication and healthy debate that really counts.

Values in Action at GE and in the U.S. Army

In 1989, General Electric CEO Jack Welch created an organizational practice he called Work-Out. Consisting of mandatory monthly meetings between groups of employees and managers, the program provided an open forum where employees could discuss problems, inefficiencies, and ineffective practices with their managers. According to Welch, the intent of the innovative practice was both practical and intellectual:

The practical goal is to get rid of thousands of bad habits accumulated since the creation of General Electric. . . . The intellectual part begins by putting the leaders of each business in front of a hundred or so of their people, eight to ten times a year, to let them hear what their people think. . . . Ultimately, we're talking about redefining the relationship between boss and subordinate. I want to get to the point where people challenge their bosses every day.[4]

Of course, the success of any program depends on more than a simple mandate, even under a leader as dynamic and powerful as Jack Welch. To ensure Work-Out's success, Welch launched the program by participating in numerous sessions where he modeled the principle—openly sharing information and engaging in lively give-and-take discussions with employees. In the process, by allowing himself to be vulnerable to confrontation and criticism in front of others, he conveyed an important message: If the boss is doing it, it must be okay for me to do it.

Another organization that has made remarkable progress toward creating a culture of open discussion and truth telling is, believe it or not, the U.S. Army. In the 1970s the army's National Training Center introduced AARs (After Action Reviews) as a way to capture lessons learned from real and simulated battles. The sole purpose of the practice, which became institutionalized during the Gulf War, was to figure out how to "do it better" the next time. Here's how it works. After an event or battle, the officer in charge leads a discussion focusing on four questions:

▲ What did we set out to do?
▲ What actually happened?
▲ Why did it happen?
▲ What are we going to do next time?

The ensuing discussion adheres to a firm set of ground rules:

▲ There is to be absolute honesty.

▲ There is no finger pointing or blaming.

▲ Discussions stay in-house with no tattling to bosses.

▲ Mistakes admitted to or uncovered during AARs cannot be held against a soldier later.

As you can imagine, once soldiers see that these ground rules will not be violated—that it truly is okay to "tell it like they see it"—a wealth of valuable information emerges. For example, AARs held during the 1994 police action in Haiti resolved a number of problems, from the simple to the complex. Because so many vehicles got stuck in the sand, some troops included the need to pack a tow bar in their report. Troops in Port-au-Prince, after being unexpectedly called upon to help deliver babies, quickly wrote up an AAR to provide medics with obstetrics training. Also, while carrying out the dangerous task of disarming the population, soldiers discovered that they encountered far less opposition when they approached people in their homes, rather than on the street; consequently, they recommended switching from street sweeps to house-to-house searches.

Clearly, soldiers discussing mistakes made by their superior officers is a huge departure from military tradition. Soldiers have always done this, but always out of earshot of the officers involved. Now it is officially condoned and done in an open forum so lessons can be learned from the discussions. The practice also means that soldiers will often disagree with their superiors in public, once a major military no-no. But, as General Gordon Sullivan, the army's former chief of staff, points out, that's okay because "disagreement is not disrespect."[5]

One of the goals of this book is to provide you with some practical approaches you can take to make open, honest communication an attribute of your organization's culture. Start by asking yourself some questions about your company's values and, more specifically, how those values apply to open communication and healthy debate.

Your Organization's Values

- ▲ Does your organization have a set of values or behavioral norms that is published and displayed?
- ▲ Does your own behavior and that of other employees reflect those values?
- ▲ Does your organization have a written code of ethics based on stated values that influences or drives decisions?
- ▲ Do you have a code of conduct based on your code of ethics that if violated could lead to termination?

We discuss codes of ethics and conduct in Chapters 8 and 9.

The Extent of Open Communication and Healthy Debate

- ▲ Does top management publicly support the honest expression of ideas?
- ▲ Do top managers' actions reflect these values? That is, do they openly express themselves and encourage others to do the same?
- ▲ Are suggestions for changing the status quo actively solicited from employees and responded to openly and quickly?
- ▲ Are people punished for expressing unpopular views or disagreeing with superiors?
- ▲ Does the organization tend to hire people who are outspoken and opinionated?

▲ Has management installed systems to establish and reward
the practice of open communication and healthy debate?

▲ If the situation with Lisa and Tom had played out with your
team, would the person in question have confronted you as
Lisa did with Tom? Would your reaction have been as gracious as Tom's? How would the team have reacted?

PERSONAL ATTITUDES AND ASSUMPTIONS

This aspect of corporate culture refers to the values and accompanying behaviors that individuals in the organization find acceptable or
unacceptable. In other words, at the risk of stereotyping, it refers to
the *kinds of people* who work in your organization. Depending on the
nature of your business, there may be a great deal of homogeneity or
diversity in terms of the types of people and their individual values
and behaviors.

For example, Bob worked with a Christian product company
where, not surprisingly, the majority of employees shared a fairly
uniform worldview. Almost all belonged to the Christian faith,
tended to dress conservatively, voted Republican, opposed abortion,
and believed that one should forgive the sins of fellow human beings.
Homogeneity was a hallmark of their culture.

Another homogeneous company Larry worked with provided
treatment programs for troubled children and adolescents. The majority of these employees, as counselors, social workers, and psychologists, based their livelihood on being understanding, tolerant, and
sympathetic to others. Their CEO, a no-nonsense Harvard MBA with
a background in overseeing business turnarounds, had no problem
telling people what he thought. If something didn't make economic
sense, he did not hesitate to question it. He told Larry that one of
his biggest frustrations was that almost everyone in the organization
tended to communicate indirectly and generally shied away from

confrontation. Worst of all, he complained, "They are so nice that when I need a straight answer about performance, or ideas for change, if there is the least chance that what they say sounds like criticism of *anyone*, they button their lips. It drives me crazy."

It is not surprising that two companies with such narrow focuses employ so many similar and like-minded people. In organizations that provide specific services or products, this kind of homogeneity often prevails. A graphics firm will usually have more "creative types," an accounting firm will be filled with people who want "just the facts, ma'am," and a sales organization will overflow with extroverts. When such homogeneity exists, you may find it easier to build a culture of absolute honesty, straight talk, and integrity because you will know where to focus your efforts. For example, if you employ many extroverted salespeople, you probably won't have to worry too much about teaching them to speak their minds, but you may have to address the tendency to "stretch the truth." And while you can probably rely on number crunchers to speak truthfully and plainly, you may have to encourage them to speak *up*. The Christian product company and therapists mentioned earlier probably won't need any lessons in honesty but might benefit from training in assertiveness and constructive confrontation.

Of course, most organizations have a more general focus, and individual assumptions and personality types will be far more diverse. In that case, cultivating a culture of honesty may prove more challenging because you'll be working with more variables. As you assess individual attitudes toward open expression and the accompanying behaviors, you'll find some people like Lisa (the system cop who challenged her boss Tom's offhand remark), who will tell you what she thinks, no matter what the consequences. Others will only tell you what they think when you ask them directly. And some will only tell you what they think you want to hear, regardless of the truth.

In addition, individual attitudes toward honesty can vary widely.

When Larry's daughter, Meagan, was a young sales manager, she learned this unsettling truth when, at a team meeting, one of the aggressive salesmen on her team proudly announced that he'd earned an extra $15.00 at lunch. After paying a $4.50 tab with a $5 bill, the waitress gave him change for a $20 bill, and he happily stuffed the money into his wallet without pointing out her mistake. The salesman's story led to a discussion within the group about the ethical issue of keeping the change. To Meagan's surprise, the group's reaction was mixed. One-third of the team saw nothing wrong with the salesman's action, one-third thought he should return the money, and one-third had no opinion.

How do you cultivate a culture of honesty and openness when dealing with a mixture of people with diverse attitudes, varying abilities to candidly speak their minds, and different definitions of honesty? It all comes back to values—not individual values, but the values of the organization. By clearly defining, establishing, and proclaiming values that promote honesty and healthy debate and then building a culture that supports them, you increase your chances of either attracting individuals who uphold those values or encouraging employees to cultivate them.

Southwest Airlines, for example, presents itself as an airline where you can pay a low fare for a no-frills flight but have a fun experience and get great customer service. Anyone who flies Southwest can tell you that its employees have internalized the organizational values of fun and great customer service: They all seem to be having a blast working together to serve their customers. The fact that Southwest hires, trains, rewards, and promotes people based on how well they demonstrate these values raises the odds that they will get people to act that way.

Here are some questions to help you identify the individual assumptions or personality types among your employees and to determine whether homogeneity or diversity exists:

The Nature of Your People

▲ Does your organization have a specific focus that naturally draws people from certain backgrounds or professions or with certain worldviews?

▲ Do the majority of people in your organization fall into a certain age group (twenty-something, over forty)? If so, what attitudes or behaviors can you attribute to that group?

▲ If homogeneity in personal attitudes and behaviors exists, which aspects of those attitudes and behaviors support a culture of honesty and which detract from it?

▲ If more diversity exists in terms of individual attitudes and behaviors, are you presenting your organization's value system in such a way that employees can internalize and cultivate the key values within themselves?

EMBARKING ON THE TRANSFORMATION

Considering the ingredients that make up your corporate culture, how do you go about transforming it into one of absolute honesty, where open discussion and healthy debate are the norm? Before you start, remember this: Change takes time. In his book *Leading Change,* John Kotter points out that companies undergoing major changes in systems or culture generally take a minimum of about eighteen months to complete the transformation.[6] In an article in the *Harvard Business Review*, Commander D. Michael Abrashoff described how, in the course of eighteen months, he managed to convert one of the worst-operating ships in the navy, the *USS Benfold,* into an award-winning centerpiece of the navy's top performers.[7] Changing a large company, of course, may take longer.

Jumping too quickly into a major change usually leads to disaster. (Remember how the fish reacted when Larry changed their water?)

XYZ Technologies, a manufacturing company, struggled to contend with a competitor that was bringing products to market faster than it could. After an intensive recruiting process, XYZ hired Ken as its new chief operating officer to help improve its product time to market. In his previous position at a Fortune 100 company, Ken had successfully implemented and oversaw a crossfunctional program that dramatically reduced product development cycle times. Within his first month at XYZ, Ken determined that the company needed the same kind of program.

He presented the idea to his management team and, although everyone had reservations about the plan, they all nodded in agreement. They considered it a radical departure from their normal modus operandi, but no one felt comfortable confronting the new boss over something he was so obviously excited about. Later that day, Ken instructed Juanita, the HR manager, to set up a training program and begin scheduling managers and employees to be trained immediately in the new methodology.

Juanita, speaking one-on-one with the new COO, felt more comfortable in voicing her concerns. "I'm not sure how this will go over," she told Ken. "It's going to require a great deal of interdepartmental cooperation, and we've never operated that way. The different departments have always functioned like independent fiefdoms under strong directors." Not only was communication limited between departments, Juanita explained, but interdepartmental wars were not uncommon—and this lack of departmental cooperation was a major contributor to XYZ's slow product development cycle. "It's a huge problem and it certainly needs fixing," Juanita acknowledged. "I just don't think people are ready to jump into such a big change without some preliminary work."

Ken listened respectfully to Juanita's wise words, but instead of heeding the warning, he moved ahead with his program. Over the next year, product development cycle times not only failed to improve, they took longer to complete. Customer complaints about product quality rose, warrantee costs skyrocketed, employee turnover jumped 20 percent, and, worst of all, the company's competitor captured a major piece of XYZ's market share.

As he cleared out his desk on his last day, Ken wondered why a program that had met with such success at his previous company would fail so miserably at XYZ. What else can we say but "it's the culture, stupid."

It is little wonder Ken failed. Instead of taking the time to gain the respect and trust of his new management team before introducing his idea, he tried to force them to adapt to a radically different "aquarium" with radically different water conditions. Many organizations make the same mistake. They try new programs or the latest management fad with little or no thought to its compatibility with their organization. When it fails, they blame the program or their managers or the general employee population.

To create a corporate culture that encourages open communication and healthy debate, it's essential to first assess the culture's readiness, especially if such openness is not the norm, and then move slowly. Take the time to discuss the issue with your management team. Ask them for their thoughts on the subject of open communication. Suggest that they survey their respective departments using the questions in this chapter to get a clear sense of the level of non-communication and confrontation avoidance that exists in the different departments.

Once you've armed your team with the data, involve them in identifying ways to move the organization to a more open culture. Their ideas might be better than any you'll find in this book, but don't hesitate to offer what you've gleaned here as discussion starters and guidelines. Whatever you do, remember to go slowly. You don't want to "change the water" in the aquarium so quickly that you end up with dead fish.

THE FORMULA FOR EFFECTIVE CHANGE

A friend of Larry's recently complained that he was having difficulty getting his management team to embrace and implement a much-needed strategy to expand and diversify the company's product offerings. Eight months earlier, he had assembled the team and asked them to come up with some ideas and work out a viable plan. Priding himself on being a true believer in participative decision making, he left the meeting feeling a sense of accomplishment. He waited eagerly to see some results, but months passed with no action from the team. In meeting after meeting, they discussed and debated the pros and cons of different strategies but never arrived at a consensus.

Obviously distressed, the friend turned to Larry for help. "Why," he asked, "is nothing getting done?"

Larry had to hold back from saying, "Welcome to the real world," because this is a classic example of how difficult it can be to initiate change. No matter what the situation, it's always a struggle for people to change, even when they have a hand in developing the direction of the change and can see the benefits of it. After all, the unknown is scarier than the known, or as Harles Cone, one of our heroes in the world of consulting, says, "We always prefer the certainty of misery to the misery of uncertainty."

In the early 1990s, employees at IBM suffered through the misery of uncertainty under the powerful leadership of a new and demanding CEO. After floating comfortably for years on an unchanging but losing course, the company struggled through a challenging upheaval to transform itself from a dying behemoth into one of the most vibrant companies in today's marketplace. Most observers attributed the incredible turnaround to Lou Gerstner, who took over as CEO in 1993.[8] His predecessor, John Akers, believed that networked personal computers would be the wave of the future and had set about dismantling the company's mainframe business. By the time Gerstner arrived, Aker's strategy had become conventional wisdom, and even though sales and stock prices were spiraling downward, everyone stayed the course without question.

They had no idea of the sea of change they faced when Gerstner stepped up to the helm. Direct, brusque, and unafraid to confront conventional wisdom, the new CEO questioned everything IBM was doing. He pushed to revitalize mainframes, taking the position that the company must once again serve as the source of business computing solutions and that mainframes should be a part of those solutions. He also demanded accountability for performance, something that had not been emphasized under Akers. According to one long-time IBMer, "Meetings in the pre-Gerstner days were congenial and pleasant whether anything was accomplished or not. . . . Meetings with Gerstner are anything but pleasant now. He insists that excuses be replaced with results, and that if something isn't working, it's either fixed or it's scrapped immediately."[9] Ultimately, Gerstner's aggressive, hard-nosed strategy worked. IBM's stock rebounded, profits rose, morale improved, and the company rose up to once again become an industry leader.

Whether it's transforming IBM back into a corporate giant, restructuring a department, or changing to a culture of absolute honesty, most changes, even those with positive goals, are painful and difficult. In observing the process of change in his own life and the businesses he consults for, Larry has identified three aspects of the pain involved in change, which he calls P1, P2, and P3. Understanding these elements can help managers implement change more effectively in their companies.

P1: The Pain of Continuing with the Status Quo

Have you ever owned an old, reliable, anonymous-looking car that you simply could not get rid of? As long as it ran well, looked halfway decent, and got you where you wanted to go, you were happy to hold onto it. In other words, you experienced very little P1, the pain of continuing with the old way. However, when old faithful started to run poorly, broke down with increasing frequency, and embarrassed you with the pitiful looks it inspired, your P1 started to grow. Slowly, you began to hate the car and dream of buying a new one. Before you knew it, your P1 (the pain of continuing with the status quo) had become too strong to ignore.

P2: The Pain of Not Having What You Need or Want

As your P1 became almost unbearable, you began to notice all the new cars cruising past you on the way to work, and you lusted after their shiny exteriors and stylish modeling. When a car commercial aired on television, you actually paid attention, picturing yourself behind the wheel of whatever model was being advertised. A new car would stretch your budget, and your old car was still getting you where you needed to go, but as your P2 (the pain of the desire you feel when you see something you want but don't yet have) grew, you felt that you simply *must* have a more powerful, plusher model that oozed prestige and luxury.

P3: The Pain of Actually Going Through the Change

P3 was the price you had to pay for the newer, more expensive car: the dollars it cost, the concessions you made to your spouse, the hassle you endured negotiating at the dealership, the depreciation in the car's value as you drove it off the lot, etc.

Ultimately, when the pain of driving your old car plus the pain of wanting the new one outweighed the pain of buying the new one, you bought the new one. Think of it as an algebraic formula:

When P1 + P2 > P3, change will occur

When the pain of continuing with the "old way" (P1) plus the pain of the unfulfilled desire for the "new way" (P2) becomes greater than the pain of changing to the "new way" (P3), people will change.

In the case of IBM, employees obviously needed a good dose of P1 to let go of conventional wisdom, and Gerstner, with his tough-as-nails approach, provided that dose. For Larry's friend who wanted to motivate his management team, our advice was to raise the P2 by setting some hard deadlines for implementing changes and promising worthwhile rewards for meeting them. At the same time, he lowered P3 by attending the planning sessions and helping the team work out a viable strategy.

As you work to transform your company's culture to one of honesty, straight talk, and integrity, you can manipulate these variables to help stimulate the change. By increasing the pain of P1 and P2 and lowering the anticipated pain of P3, you increase the odds that change will occur. For example, by insisting that people be outspoken and honest—and being ready to create discomfort for those who refuse to do so—you increase P1 (the pain of continuing with the old way) in the company. Then, by promoting the virtues of honesty, creating a safe environment in which to express it, and practicing it yourself, you help to raise P2 (the pain of desire to do it). Finally, by providing infrastructure, training, and institutionalization for the practice of absolute honesty, you lower P3 (the pain of getting there).

THE TRANSFORMATION PROCESS

With an understanding of the culture that currently exists in your organization and the challenges you'll face changing it, you're ready to begin the transformation. In the following chapters, we guide you through the process and give you handy tools to help you along the way, but for now, here are some ground rules to get you running:

▲ *Create and publish a set of conduct guidelines and ethical standards that are clear to everyone and are practiced rigorously by you and your management team.*

▲ *When hiring new people, consider assertiveness and a willingness to speak up as positive attributes.* We're not suggesting that you make outspokenness a major hiring criterion or seek only to hire applicants who emulate Johnny Cochran with an "in-your-face" verbal confrontation style. However, if you want to cultivate a working environment where people will tell the truth when the truth needs to be told, make it a hiring practice to view outspokenness and plain speaking as valuable assets.

▲ *Clearly state and publish what you want.* If you want people to be candid and forthright, let them know—and remind them often that such behavior is condoned and desired. Follow Intel's example and be sure to publicize company values and the expectations supporting cultural honesty through the mission statement, the employee handbook, bulletin boards, and other appropriate venues.

▲ *Open your ears and aggressively listen to people.* If you want people to express their opinions, ask for them. Nothing will encourage openness and truth telling like a sincere interest in people's ideas and opinions. Remember Commander Abrashoff, who transformed the *USS Benfold* into one of the navy's top-performing ships? When he took command, there was poor crew performance, and the ship's turnover rate was one of the highest of any ship in the navy. Abrashoff spent his first days wandering among the crew asking them to tell him what they thought was wrong and to offer suggestions for fixing problems. After listening carefully, he assigned teams to develop and implement those suggestions for improvement. According to Commander Abrashoff, he tackled the problem in this way because he really had no idea what to do, and he figured the only logical approach was to ask the crew for advice since they were closest to the problems. The simple act of listening not only gave him the answers he needed but also, he later realized, inadvertently stimulated the spectacular turnaround in morale and performance. "Once they knew I was truly interested in what they thought, the suggestions and ideas started rolling in and the morale started shooting up."[10]

▲ *Take people seriously, even if you think they are crazy.* The key to encouraging people to speak up and open up is to listen to all opinions with the same sincere interest. Even if you know an idea won't work or if it sounds crazy, listen to everyone's ideas with the same respect and show people you take them seriously. When he took over as CEO at Avis Corporation, Robert Townsend, author of *Up the Organization*, set up "Breakfast with Bob" meetings so employees at any level could come in early, get a free breakfast, and tell him what they thought. Avis's extremely successful "We Try Harder" campaign can be traced to these discussions. Of course, people brainstormed numerous ideas, ranging from the ridiculous to the unworkable, before coming up with this winner. According to Townsend, once employees know you respect their opinions and aren't going to punish them for expressing themselves, they'll tell you what they think. What's more, he says, "Once they know you respect them and truly take them seriously, you can tell them to go to hell if you want, and it will be OK."[11]

▲ *Create an infrastructure to support open communication, confrontation, and ethical behavior.* An old saying claims that "the farmer's shadow makes the best fertilizer," meaning plants attended to have an advantage over those neglected. Nothing happens in a vacuum, and the same goes for creating a culture of honesty. Setting up an official platform for honest discussions, like Work-Outs at GE or AARs in the army, is an excellent first step to filling that vacuum. It also helps to include new behavior expectations in employee performance goals, annual reviews, and overall evaluations. In addition, offering regularly scheduled, formal training that focuses on topics like business ethics, constructive confrontation, and the forthright expression of opinions demonstrates that the company actively encourages their practice.

▲ *Establish, publish, reward, and practice the Six Laws of Absolute Honesty.* These rules are the hinge points for creating an open culture. We discuss each in detail in the following chapters, but here's a quick summary.

THE SIX LAWS OF ABSOLUTE HONESTY

Absolute Honesty Law #1: Tell the Truth

Your ability to lead others depends on their trusting you. By consistently telling the truth you not only earn that trust but also create a psychological obligation that compels others to do the same for you. The downside, of course, is that telling the truth can be inconvenient, embarrassing, and painful. As we explore this fundamental rule, we show you how to avoid the pitfalls and difficulties of building a corporate culture where telling the truth is sacrosanct.

Absolute Honesty Law #2: Tackle the Problem

Learning to confront tough issues in a healthy and straightforward manner can enable people to quickly resolve differences of opinion while maintaining their dignity and mutual respect. Abiding by this law includes practicing constructive confrontation, a technique for resolving differences that emphasizes solving problems and making decisions by focusing on the best possible outcome for the organization while avoiding damage to the relationships of those involved.

Absolute Honesty Law #3: Disagree and Commit

We've all been to meetings where everyone appeared to agree to a decision but then, once the meeting was over, immediately started criticizing it; lobbying for their own positions; or, worst of all, sabotaging the meeting's action plan. The Law of Disagree and Commit requires everyone in the organization to agree to express their opinions openly and clearly even if those opinions go against the grain of the group; however, once everyone has reached consensus on a particular decision or course of action, all are expected to commit their wholehearted support to the decision. The exception to this law is when the group or your management has made a decision that is morally, ethically, or legally wrong. We address this issue in Chapter 5.

Absolute Honesty Law #4: Welcome the Truth

Responding to criticism defensively and attacking when we feel attacked are such instinctive behaviors that they are daunting to overcome. A culture of honesty depends on being able to criticize and accept criticism in an open, healthy, and nondestructive way. By drawing on specific tools and techniques, people can learn how to avoid reacting defensively and lashing out when criticized, as well as how to offer criticism using a respectful and useful approach.

Absolute Honesty Law #5: Reward the Messenger

Rewarding the messenger for delivering bad news or contrary opinions is not the norm in most companies. Often, those who speak up, disagree with the status quo, complain about a decision, or object to the ethical soundness of a decision become the victims of subtle, and sometimes not-so-subtle, forms of retribution. Nothing will kill the spirit of open communication and honest debate in an organization faster than retribution. Remember, it was fear of retribution that kept the townspeople from telling the emperor he was naked as he paraded through the town. If managers punish people for expressing their opinions, those opinions will simply go underground, reappearing as cynical e-mail jokes and hushed conversations in the lunchroom. For this reason, managers must vigilantly guard against this practice. Complicating their task, however, is the fact that even when actual retribution is not present, the perception that it exists can produce the same effect. Incorporating this rule in your company, then, means identifying and eliminating not only practices of retribution, but also any perceptions that it exists.

Absolute Honesty Law #6: Build a Platform of Integrity

A culture of honesty and integrity must be based on a foundation of honesty and ethical practice. The two go hand in hand. If you want people to speak up when wrongdoing occurs, it helps to clarify what qualifies as wrongdoing and what people should do when it occurs. That expectation provides a platform of integrity upon which the person can act. Without it, expressing opinions about what is wrong can be risky indeed.

In the next six chapters of this book, we explore these laws in depth, examining how you can apply them to yourself and to your organization. We alert you to the most common roadblocks to absolute honesty and tell you how to recognize and remove them. We give you strategies and techniques you can implement to drive the transformation to a culture that celebrates honesty, encourages straight talk, and rewards integrity.

At the beginning of this chapter, we described the tragedy of the *USS Greenville,* a blunder that could have been averted if open, honest communication had been encouraged. Later in the chapter we introduced the U.S. Army's AARs, where open, honest discussion after key events helps the Army learn from mistakes and duplicate successes. What was the difference?

In both cases, the culture dictated the result—nothing stupid about it.

PART 2

THE SIX LAWS OF

ABSOLUTE HONESTY

CHAPTER 3

Absolute Honesty Law #1:
Tell the Truth

"To be creditable, we must be truthful."

—*EDWARD R. MURROW*

WHEN CONGRESSIONAL INTERN CHANDRA LEVY DISAPPEARED IN the spring of 2001, Congressman Gary Condit at first refused to discuss the case. When he eventually talked, he claimed that his relationship with the young political intern had been strictly platonic. Of course, as anyone who followed the news now knows, Condit was lying. Not surprisingly, once his deceit was exposed, everything he said about Levy's disappearance came under close scrutiny. He had an airtight alibi on the day of Levy's disappearance and was not considered a suspect, but his dishonesty generated mistrust and a desire on the part of many to see him punished. And punish him they did: His constituents overwhelmingly rejected his bid for reelection, leaving no doubts about *their* opinions of his veracity.

As our parents and teachers told us, the worst truth is always better than the best lie. That doesn't mean that telling the truth is easy or won't have negative consequences. It simply means that when faced with a choice of telling the truth, postponing its telling, or lying, we think telling the truth is the best choice because when you do, you:

- Create trust.
- Do the right thing.
- Discover it's rarely as painful as you think.
- Pay a higher price for lying.
- Get it behind you.
- Keep things simple.

And, of course, you avoid damaging your relationships.

TELL THE TRUTH: YOU CREATE TRUST

Several years ago, Larry bought a used sports utility vehicle. One morning it started making horrible grinding noises while it lurched and shuddered down the street. Larry was able to drive it as far as Greg's Auto Repair, a local garage where he expected to pay thousands for what he worried might be a blown front-end differential. To make matters worse, he feared being gouged because he had never used this garage or mechanic before. That afternoon Greg called with the good news: A bolt had fallen out of the brake caliper and was jammed between the brake pad and the rotor. Total cost: $50.

Larry now takes all of his auto business to Greg, including warranty work on his new car—work that would normally be done at the dealership. That's right! Larry *pays* this fellow for work he could have done for *free* simply because he trusts him completely. Such is the nature of trust.

Social-psychological research has shown that people are most likely to trust a person when they are in a vulnerable position and the person chooses to treat them truthfully and honorably. For leaders, the lesson is obvious: If you are always straight with people, they will learn to trust you.

The president and founder of a medium-size publishing company, put it this way: "I always tell the truth, no matter what the situation or circumstance. That way, no one is ever taken by surprise by my behavior or responses. My staff tells me it is the reason they like working for my company. And since our staff turnover is never more than 1 or 2 percent per year, it must be working."

TELL THE TRUTH: YOU DO THE RIGHT THING

In Chapter 1, we used Jack in the Box as an example of how *not* to respond to a crisis. That's only part of its story. According to Gene Vosberg, president of the Washington Restaurant Association, Jack in the Box recovered from initially fumbling its response to the E-coli crisis and redeemed itself by showing remarkable devotion to improving food safety. The chain adopted a food-handling program that had been developed by NASA in the 1960s and championed its use throughout the industry.[1] It finally told the truth and then did the right thing. As a result of Jack in the Box's leadership on this issue, we are all safer when we eat fast food, regardless of the restaurant in which we are eating.

The action helped Jack in the Box grow as well. When the crisis struck, Jack in the Box had approximately 800 stores. Today, the chain owns more than 1800.[2]

We don't mean to imply that telling the truth is easy or that it automatically produces better results. There is a scene in the movie

A League of Their Own that we love. The film is about the formation of the first professional female baseball league during World War II. In the scene, pitcher Dotie Hinson (played by Geena Davis) whines to her coach, Jimmy Dugan (played by Tom Hanks), that reaching the level of play he wants her to reach is hard. His reply is classic:

"Hard? Hard? Well, of course it's hard. That's why it's worth doing."

Telling the truth can be easy when it has no repercussions. When we might offend someone, need to tell someone something they don't want to hear, or might incur negative consequences for telling the truth, our mettle is truly tested.

TELL THE TRUTH: YOU DISCOVER IT'S RARELY AS PAINFUL AS YOU THINK

Dan is a talented author and professional speaker. He signed a contract with Marlene at A-One Speakers Bureau to handle all his business exclusively with the hope that A-One's marketing experience would increase his bookings. After two years, Dan's bookings had declined rather than increased, and he wanted to end the exclusive arrangement. However, he was hesitant to tell Marlene the truth about how he felt because he was afraid she would never book him again. Since, at that point, A-One represented 100 percent of Dan's bookings, he would have lost a significant amount of business until he could establish himself with other bureaus. That Dan and his wife were close friends with Marlene and her husband only complicated the situation.

For several months Dan did nothing about the situation, not wanting to be honest with Marlene but resenting the fact that he was paying her bureau for services he wasn't receiving. Finally, after some urging from his spouse, he set up a meeting. As it approached, Dan's worry accelerated. He had trouble sleeping and began to engage in what author Meagan Johnson calls "catastrophic chaining."[3] That is, you imagine a difficult situation you are facing and then blow it out of proportion, one "chain link" at a time. Dan's catastrophic chaining went something like this:

> We'll start the meeting with some pleasantries and then I'll ask her to end the exclusive relationship. Before I can list the rational reasons for the change, she'll tune me out and start getting upset, thinking that I don't appreciate all she's done for me. As I continue to explain, she'll think that I'm rejecting her personally, and react like a "woman scorned." Then she'll curtly reply, "Fine," and end the meeting, saying that it won't make a difference in our relationship—but I know it will, and I'll never hear from her again. Then she'll tell her staff to take me off their booking lists, and she'll call all her competitors and tell them that they shouldn't do business with me because I'm unappreciative, ungrateful, and can't be trusted. I'll never get another booking from *any* bureau, and my business will fail. I'll eventually go bankrupt, lose my house and my family, and be the pity of all my friends. It's possible that I could end up on skid row, and suicide would be my only option.

Dan was ready to cancel the meeting and continue the unsatisfactory relationship with Marlene when he ran into Bob. Dan explained the situation and asked for some advice. Bob asked him why he'd chosen to do business with Marlene and her company in the first place.

After thinking a moment, Dan explained that he had the highest regard for Marlene, that Marlene had always been ethical, was a straight shooter, and that he liked her personally. At that point, Bob asked, "Then why are you worried about all this crazy scorned woman stuff? It sounds like Marlene is a professional, stable, competent, ethical businesswoman, and, after all, Dan, this is only business. It seems to me that you ought to trust the instincts that led you to do business with her in the first place and level with her. She certainly deserves that much from you."

The next day, Dan met with Marlene and nervously explained what he wanted to do. She smiled, said that she agreed, that the arrangement wasn't working for either of them, and that she had planned to suggest changing it herself. She assured him that he would always be one of her favorite speakers to book and that they would remain good friends—all of which has proved to be true.

So often we put off telling the truth because we exaggerate the potential negative results of doing so. Then, when we finally face the situation, we discover that our fears were out of proportion to the actual outcome. Meanwhile, we've lost sleep, bred ulcers, and alienated others while fretting about it. Worse, we sometimes never get around to telling the truth at all—and that can cost us dearly.

TELL THE TRUTH: YOU PAY A HIGHER PRICE FOR LYING

Della was working the telephone help desk when she answered a call from a customer who was obviously angry. He said that Joe, the outside sales representative handling his account, had promised to call him before the end of business the previous day but had failed to do so. Della couldn't transfer the call to Joe because he was on an airplane to Europe. As an inside service representative, her job was to support the outside reps, so she did her best to calm the customer down.

Meanwhile, Della cursed Joe under her breath. This wasn't the first time she had had to clean up one of his messes. Not that Joe was the only rep who made mistakes or left problems for her to fix. Many others were just as guilty. What bothered her was that she knew Joe would deny any responsibility for the problem. He would blame the voice mail system, claim the customer misunderstood, or whine that he couldn't get through or that he'd left a message with someone at the customer's office who didn't pass the message along. In other words, based on Joe's past behavior, Della knew that Joe would lie in order to avoid blame. Nothing was ever Joe's fault, and she disliked him intensely for it.

When Della told us this story, she admitted that she had, on occasion, intentionally failed to cover for Joe just to get him. She also confessed to complaining about him to anyone who would listen. She had even made not-so-subtle comments to Joe's boss, such as, "Well, I couldn't find Joe again, so I went ahead and took care of his customer."

All of us make mistakes. Lying about those mistakes almost always makes the situation worse, not better. It not only impeaches our credibility, but it insults those to whom we have lied.

History is full of political examples of this axiom. It was both stupid and wrong of Richard Nixon to approve illegal break-ins into the offices of Daniel Ellsberg's psychiatrist and the Democratic Party at the Watergate Hotel. Given his overwhelming popularity in the polls, it probably would not have undermined his presidency if he had admitted his complicity when the burglars were first caught. Instead, his lying about having no knowledge of the events, combined with his willingness to sacrifice the people he'd ordered to commit illegal acts, turned public opinion against him and eventually forced his resignation. Almost every political commentator and pundit of the time said that had Nixon admitted his sins and "taken his medicine like a man," the nation would have forgiven him and moved on.

Bill Clinton discovered a similar backlash when he looked into the camera and told us he had *not* had sex with Monica Lewinsky. He survived impeachment, but his legacy as the President who oversaw the greatest economic boom in this country's history will forever be tainted by the perception that he is a liar and philanderer.

Faced with embarrassing failures, leaders who choose honesty limit the damage to themselves and their organizations. In the spring of 2002 the media reported that a multistate crime ring had rigged McDonald's "Who Wants to Be a Millionaire?" game. McDonald's responded with extraordinary straightforwardness and honesty. Its president immediately admitted that there had been a fraud, made a public apology, and initiated a new game. According to Chris Ryan, who heads Ryan and Associates, a Phoenix-based crisis management firm, McDonald's minimized the damage from the fraud because:

> They were not playing a waiting game. You cannot get into that corporate mentality where you run it up and down the flagpole twenty times. From what I saw, McDonald's moved very quickly, and the public was willing to forgive them quickly. And if you think about it, it wasn't in the news very long. They dealt with it and moved on.[4]

Whatever your religious or cultural background, you were probably raised with a list of rights and wrongs firmly planted in your head. "It's right to be trustworthy; it's wrong to cheat. It's right to pay your own way; it's wrong to steal. It's right to be faithful to your spouse; it's wrong to mess around. It's right to be nonviolent; it's wrong to hurt others." Included in this list for most of us is, "It's right to tell the truth; it's wrong to lie." Not that any of us have never lied. It's just that most of us consider it wrong to do so, and therefore we often judge those who do harshly. Those who lie to us, especially if they are in positions of leadership, risk their standings as trustworthy leaders. The nicknames "Tricky Dick" and "Slick Willy" say it all.

TELL THE TRUTH: YOU GET IT BEHIND YOU

Sandy was the administrative assistant to Barry, the president of a product sales and distribution company. Sandy was extremely well organized and competent. She was dedicated to her job and willing to work very hard. Her only fault was having difficulty saying "no." She would do whatever was asked of her, whether it was in her job description or not. When Barry asked her to do special projects, she did them. When someone was needed to stay late to meet a customer, she stayed. When the marketing director quit and Barry asked her to take over some of the marketing director's duties until he could find a replacement, Sandy did so. When field managers asked her to research information for their reports, she willingly complied. In fact, Sandy agreed to so much work that she routinely had to come in at 7:00 A.M. and stay past 7:00 P.M. She spent every Saturday and half of Sunday in the office just trying to catch up. Most days she ate lunch at her desk while working.

Sandy was well on her way to a physical and psychological meltdown when, late one afternoon, Barry chastised her for an error he'd found on a document she had typed. Immediately she snapped at him that if he wasn't always dumping work on her, she could take the time to do it right. She started to cry, screaming that she couldn't stand him, that she hated the job, and that she wanted out *now!* She stormed out the door and never came back.

When we were told about the incident, we checked out Sandy's work history and discovered that this was not the first time she had left a job because she felt overworked. No big surprise. Sandy is one of those people who have a strong need to please others and an equally strong fear of confrontation. Consequently, as work piled on beyond what was reasonable, she was unable to push back and speak the truth. She could have said, "Wait a minute, Barry, I'd be glad to do this project, but I'll need some help on routine document prep while I'm working on it." She also could have suggested a change, "I'm spending every weekend here and I can't do that forever. How about we bring in some clerical help so I can focus on the important stuff?" Instead, she continued to let herself be used beyond her capacities. Like gas building up in a corked champagne bottle, when the pressure got to be too much, Sandy exploded.

We're not saying that Barry didn't own some of the fault here. A manager as insensitive to his employees' stress and strife as Barry was deserves to lose them. If he had intervened, he could have given Sandy the opportunity to express her frustrations, and things might have changed. Our guess is that Barry's obtuseness to her plight sent a not-so-subtle message that said, "I don't want to hear anything about you not being able to get the job done. Just keep working." Sandy, who naturally played the martyr, continued to take on more and more until she could take no more.

The message for managers is this: If you want to know the truth, you must be willing to seek out and listen to truths you may not want to hear.

If you tend to be like Sandy, the message for you is to practice some absolute honesty with the Barrys in your life by negotiating a set of operating rules that serve both your interests. Additionally, you would be well served to deal with each increment of the work overload as it happens so the gas in your bottle doesn't build to the point of explosion. We call this real-time honesty. It means addressing issues as they occur so they don't linger and grow out of proportion to their importance. Dan, the speaker, was guilty of not practicing real-time honesty. By the time he spoke to Marlene about changing his contract, he had worked himself up into such a tizzy that he almost imploded rather than exploded.

Practicing real-time honesty is easier said than done, especially if you're not used to doing it. It requires vigilance and a willingness to speak up quickly. Too often, issues we should address slip by us like drops leaking from a pipe in the ceiling. It's only when the ceiling caves in that we realize we should have acted when we first saw the water stain growing in the corner.

For example, a manager notices that an employee comes in a few minutes late. He might think to himself, "Hmm, I ought to say something to him," but the moment passes. When it happens a few more times, the manager makes a mental note to say something soon but fails to do so because the employee is so productive otherwise, and such conversations are uncomfortable. Finally, the manager's assistant mentions to him that other employees resent the fact that "Jeff" can come in any old time he wants, while they are required to be punctual. Saved by the assistant! He will now actually go talk to Jeff. However, if he had been vigilant and applied real-time honesty as the problem occurred, it wouldn't have grown into a potential teamwide, flood-from-the-ceiling morale problem.

Or consider the director of a medical facility who suspects that her accounting manager is overbilling the government for Medicaid reimbursement. She knows she should question the accounting manager about some of the suspicious charges she sees, but hesitates to do so because profits are down and she's under a great deal of pressure from her superiors to show a rosy bottom line. So she says nothing, rationalizing that it's probably not all that flagrant, and besides, if she starts digging, she might open a Pandora's box that can't be closed.

Meanwhile, the accounting manager notes that when the director reviews the billing reports, she never questions billings that push the legal limit for allowable charges, so he assumes that doing so must be okay with her. He may even perceive that she *wants* him to do it, but can't say so openly for fear of appearing unethical. So he pushes the envelope a little more with each billing, and she continues to say nothing.

Soon, their silent complicity has expanded to downright bilking of the government. Had the director had the moral insight and the intestinal fortitude to call foul early in the game, she would have taught the accounting manager the limits of her toleration for these risky billing practices. He would have adjusted his behavior accordingly, and a crime would never have occurred.

TELL THE TRUTH: YOU KEEP THINGS SIMPLE

Abraham Lincoln once said, "No man has a good enough memory to be a successful liar." If you always tell the truth, you never have to conjure up excuses or backpedal on your explanations about why your company didn't make its numbers. You never have to create stories about what happened to a customer's order. Best of all, you never have to remember both the lie and the truth because you know that whatever you said, it will always match the way things really happened.

By keeping things simple and honest, you free yourself of the worry about being caught in a lie and the consequences when you are. You create trust among those around you. You strengthen relationships. You reap the benefits of doing the right thing. You discover that the discomfort of being honest is rarely as unpleasant as the pain caused by deceit. You avoid paying a high price for lying. Through the practice of real-time honesty you live and work in the present, neither haunted by lies told in the past nor fearful of having to "pay the piper" in the future. Those are the benefits of telling the truth.

EIGHT GREAT FEARS OF TELLING THE TRUTH

It would be naïve to advise you to always tell the truth without acknowledging the barriers that make this difficult. We have identified the *Eight Great Fears of Telling the Truth*:

1. Fear of retribution
2. Fear of hurting other people's feelings
3. Fear of change
4. Fear of being disliked
5. Fear of losing support
6. Fear of paying the price

7. Fear of losing competitive advantage

8. Fear of losing face

Fear of Retribution

People often worry that if they say what's on their minds, someone will cause them pain for doing so. This may be realistic. Consider the plight of Dr. Jeffrey Wigand, a former staff scientist and corporate executive with Brown and Williamson Tobacco Company. Wigand had first-hand knowledge of the company's deliberate efforts to get and keep smokers hooked on nicotine. After he revealed what he knew to *60 Minutes* producer Lowell Bergman, he was fired for "poor communication skills," endured lawsuits, was smeared in the media, and even had death threats leveled against him and his family.[5]

The good news was that it saved lives by helping the government force Brown and Williamson to alter the carcinogenic ingredients in its products. It also led to an eventual $236 billion settlement against Big Tobacco. According to David Kessler, then commissioner of the Food and Drug Administration (FDA), "Dr. Wigand's assistance was central to the FDA's investigation into the role and effect of nicotine in tobacco products."[6]

Dr. Wigand survived the ordeal to do even greater good. He became an award-winning high school teacher, was the recipient of numerous awards for his courage in exposing the tobacco industry's misdeeds, and developed a nonprofit organization called Smoke Free Kids, Inc. to help reduce teen tobacco use. *The Insider*, an Academy Award–nominated movie about his experiences, was released in 1999.

Of course, not all whistleblowers fare as well as Dr. Wigand. Many are fired and never heard from again, so the danger of retribution remains a very real barrier to telling the truth. In Chapter 7, "Reward the Messenger," we examine both sides of the issue: how to avoid becoming the victim of truth retribution, and how to make sure you don't practice truth retribution yourself.

Fear of Hurting Other People's Feelings

People say "the truth hurts" because sometimes it really does. Larry's brother-in-law Kernan was a baseball star all through grade school, high school, and college. He was drafted by the San Francisco Giants and spent the next six years working his way through the team's farm system until he finally reached AAA (the level just below the big leagues). After jus⁺ one season at this level, his manager told him he wasn't good enough to play in the majors and released him. Kernan will be the first to tell you that the truth can hurt a lot.

On the other hand, what if the manager never told players who were not cutting it that they had to go and why because he didn't want to hurt their feelings? It's too ludicrous to imagine. The manager's job is to weed out the inferior players and promote the superior ones. If it hurts people's feeling, too bad. It comes with the territory. Of course, if he's a decent person, he does it in a way that minimizes the hurt. For example, instead of saying, "You just can't cut it so you're out of here," he might say, "You're a talented ballplayer [which was the truth] and we appreciate your efforts. It's just that we have people who are more talented [also the truth], so we'll have to let you go." Both messages are painful, and both are the truth. The difference is in the degree of collateral damage inflicted. The bottom line, however, is that the manager does not shrink from being honest.

We are not saying that you should go around telling people what you think of them or what their faults are just because you think it's "the truth." Silence is golden when there is no reason to tell them or when it is none of your business. However, how often do we shirk from telling another person the truth when we *have* good reason to tell them and it *is* our business, because we don't want to hurt their feelings or offend them?

For example, suppose you notice that a colleague inflates the numbers on his sales reports to make himself look good and increase his commissions. You know that if you say something to him or to your boss, you risk the chance that he will be offended. And what if you're wrong? How embarrassing. So you say nothing, telling yourself that it's none of your business. Meanwhile, his larceny continues, and perhaps expands. How many of the scandals that made up the 2002 Crisis of Ethics in Business USA started with such passivity? We will probably never know, but rarely does evil appear in full bloom. It usually starts small and grows, feeding on the fear of others to make a fuss or stand in its way.

Fear of Change

Remember our friend the psychologist who said, "People always prefer the certainty of misery over the misery of uncertainty."[7] It's always easier to stay where we are than to move somewhere else, especially if where we are is working well for us and "somewhere else" is unknown. Speaking the truth often means admitting that what worked before is now obsolete—and that's a scary thought.

Consider the Tudor Ice Company, founded by Fredrick Tudor[8] in 1803. Convinced that he could make a profit by cutting ice from lakes in the northeast U.S. and sailing it to customers in warmer climes, he sent his first shipment to Martinique in the West Indies. Unfortunately, given the length of the trip and the unsophisticated methods of insulation, his anticipated profits quickly melted away.

But Tudor was persistent. He worked to improve his cutting, insulating, and shipping techniques and by the time of his death in 1866, his company was the number-one ice company in the world, shipping millions of tons of ice per year to markets as far away as India.[9]

By the 1880s, however, Tudor Ice Company's reign of the business was in rapid decline. By the turn of the century, Tudor was out of business—done in by competition that used the newly invented process of refrigeration to produce ice at a fraction of the cost of cutting it.

Ironically, all Tudor had to do to stay in the game was to replace its cutting operations with refrigerated manufacturing. It already had the storage, shipping, and marketing capacity in place. But that never came to pass. Tudor Ice Company trudged forward, cutting ice while competitors redefined the business by producing it mechanically.

It's hard to imagine that the company's managers couldn't see that refrigeration was the superior option, but to accept this truth would have meant abandoning what had worked so well for decades. Such is the strength of the blinders produced by complacency and the fear of change. Consequently, the truth that was so vital to Tudor's survival was most likely never uttered in its board rooms or its planning sessions. In the end, *none* of the companies that cut ice were able to make the transition to manufacturing it.[10]

To be candid and truthful we have to be willing to embrace the changes that will occur when we speak the truth. Fear of those changes will lead us to keep our mouths shut or, worse, to distort the truth so we never have to consider other ways of producing ice until it is too late.

Fear of Being Disliked

The philosopher William James once said, "No more fiendish punishment can be devised, were such a thing physically possible, than that one should be turned loose in society and remain absolutely unnoticed by all the members thereof."[11] We all have the need be liked, accepted, and valued by others. And to a certain degree, it's healthy. For our ancestors, being accepted and valued by the tribe was essential to survival. If you weren't, you were ostracized and faced almost certain death, alone and unsupported in a hostile environment. In today's team-oriented world, if our coworkers, subordinates, and superiors do not accept us, it's hard to get anything done.

On the other hand, as we mentioned in Chapter 1, there is such a thing as too much getting along, which we call the *Kumbaya Syndrome*. It is often easier not to disagree or express an unpopular opinion when there is pressure from others to "join the crowd and start singing 'Kumbaya'." This pressure may be real, as it was with the engineer we mentioned whose company was so team oriented that disagreement was actively discouraged. In most cases, however, the pressure is internally generated. We "go along to get along" because it's easier, it's safer, or we just don't want to risk being at odds with others. We hate to be considered the "wet blanket."

Christina is the head of payroll and finance for a small manufacturing company. She's been on the job for four weeks. She described this dilemma to us:

During her first week, Dick, the head of sales, mentioned at a meeting of the management team (of which Christina is a member) that a substantial order from a large client had closed that day. Until the previous day Jack, a sales rep Dick disliked, had handled the account. Jack had resigned to work for another company in a different industry. Dick was glad to see Jack go and had replaced him with Dana, an up-and-coming rep for whom Dick had great hopes. Technically, the commission for the sale, which was substantial, should have gone to Jack, but Dick had decided to give it to Dana instead. Everyone at the meeting, including the owner of the company, shrugged in agreement, and they continued with other business.

Christina was in a quandary. She thought that the company would be at legal risk if Dick pursued his plan. She also felt that it was just plain wrong. On the other hand, she was new to the position, and she didn't want to draw negative attention to herself. She told us that she sat through the rest of the meeting churning inside, wondering what to do. After a sleepless night, she went to Dick and explained how she could understand why he didn't want to pay Jack the commission, but after thinking about it, she felt that the company would be at risk and that he might want to reconsider. He thought a moment and said she was probably right and that he would have the commission check sent to Jack, even though it galled him to do so. Since then, Dick and Christina have become friends.

Of course, not all endings are so happy, and you do risk offending others when you tell them truths they do not want to hear. You can lower that risk in a number of ways that we will address in Chapter 4, "Tackle the Problem." For now, here are three steps you can take:

1. *Lower the emotional temperature.* When Christina talked to Dick, she described the effect his action would have on the company. She delayed expressing her own personal feelings about its rightness or wrongness. This tactic lowered the "emotional temperature" of the conversation so Dick would not feel personally attacked or feel the need to defend his own values.

2. *Give the other person an out.* Christina very wisely did this by explaining that she had been thinking about it overnight, and it had occurred to her that not paying Jack the commission could cause a problem. It was as if this was something that was easy to miss during the meeting. This allowed Dick to back out gracefully by saying, "Gee, I hadn't thought about that either."

3. *Do it in private.* Confrontations, and that's what this was, usually go better when conducted without an audience. Neither party has to worry about the embarrassment of appearing wrong or losing a battle in front of others.

Fear of Losing Support

Sally, a veteran accounting manager, worked for a progressive software company located in the northeast United States for fifteen years before moving to the Sunbelt to get away from cold winters. Unable to find a position in the private sector, she took a job managing a division of the tax department of a large municipal government. She soon noticed that the work of one of her direct reports, Jim, was extremely substandard. She started asking Jim to redo his work, which he would do but would frequently repeat the same mistakes. He also missed deadlines, spent too much time away from the office on noncity business, and tended to have a sour disposition that led to citizen complaints.

Jim's personnel record showed that his reviews from past supervisors had all been rated "above average," which puzzled Sally. Had this fellow performed well for others but not her? Was she the problem? She suspected this wasn't the case when she noticed that, during his twelve-year tenure with the city, Jim had held fourteen different positions, all lateral moves.

A little investigation proved her suspicions correct. Jim's performance had always been substandard, but no previous manager had been brave enough to give him the feedback he needed to change or to take the initiative to dismiss him. He was simply shuffled from one department to the next like a bad penny.

Since it was time for Jim's annual review, Sally decided to give him a less-than-satisfactory rating and to deny his annual salary increase. Jim, of course, filed a grievance with the city's personnel board, which ended up supporting him rather than her. The board's position was that if no one had been honest with him about his performance for twelve years, it was unfair to expect him to change overnight. They accompanied this absurd rationale with an insistence that Sally change Jim's rating to "satisfactory" and approve his raise.

Sally now understood why Jim's previous supervisors had chosen to pass him along rather than deal with him. If they had to fight this kind of bureaucratic lunacy, their best option was to pass him to some other unsuspecting department. To this day, Jim remains at the city, still doing substandard work. Sally left to find a job in a small company where she wouldn't have to fight bureaucracy to effectively manage her operations.

You may be asking, "What could these previous managers have done, given the obstacles they faced?" But our question is this: Is it not a manager's job to do what's best for the organization? Did their passing Jim from one department to another not make the organization worse?

Additionally, what kind of example did they set for their subordinates to emulate? By virtue of their position, managers are always in the spotlight, watched by an audience of subordinates who are very perceptive. Employees always know who among their colleagues performs well and who doesn't. Imagine the effect each manager's passivity had on Jim's coworkers as they watched their manager do nothing about his incompetence. Even if it meant fighting a losing battle with a misguided HR department, the mere attempt to do something would have set a positive model for their subordinates to witness.

Of course, that would have been hard, but as the coach in *A League of Their Own* said, that's why it's worth doing.

Fear of Paying the Price

When Congress questioned former executives Ken Lay and Jeffrey Skilling about their roles in Enron's collapse, they both claimed their Fifth Amendment rights to not incriminate themselves. They had that right, but what a shame that they chose to invoke it. If Enron had not defrauded its investors by hiding losses in shady partnerships and illegal activities, Lay and Skilling would have had nothing to take the Fifth about. It reminds us of the adage: "If you can't do the time, don't do the crime."

Our guess is that Lay and Skilling have never thought of themselves as crooks. Competitive businessmen? Yes. Common criminals? Never. But where do you draw the line? In a survey commissioned by Starwood Hotels & Resorts, 82 percent of 401 high-ranking corporate executives admit to routinely cheating at golf.[12] The author of the study attributes this high percentage to the competitive nature of executives. But if they will cheat at golf, how many would cheat in their business practices as well? Let's hope not many. We certainly don't mean to beat up CEOs and business executives; in our experience the overwhelming majority of the many we've worked with are honest and ethical. But for those caught in the 2002 Crisis of Ethics in Business USA, cheating at golf, we suspect, would be just one small indicator of a much larger pattern.

More accurately, perhaps, it would be one small step down a very dark path. In his treatise on the nature of evil, *People of the Lie,*[13] psychiatrist and author M. Scott Peck makes the point that people are seldom born evil or become so all at once. More often it is a gradual journey where one step toward darkness is followed by another until there is no turning back.

It would not be surprising to learn that Lay and Skilling, along with many of the 2002 gang of CEOs who were accused of wrongdoing, had slipped down similar slopes. The question for all of us to ask ourselves is, "Am I on any kind of slope that would lead me to want to claim my Fifth Amendment rights?"

Fear of Losing Competitive Advantage

In business, there are many reasons to keep secrets, such as the desire to keep competitors from learning the details of your upcoming marketing plan or the design of your newest product. Companies that aren't careful to guard such information can face a huge disadvantage in the marketplace. A bit of paranoia can be healthy.

On the other hand, many executives and managers carry this paranoia too far, fearing that if they share anything about the business with their employees, the information will leak to competitors or be used by the employees themselves against the company. Ironically, the opposite is often true.

Harley-Davidson Motor Company is a case in point. Its partnering philosophy encourages collaboration and joint decision making between the company and its unions. At its Kansas City Plant, for example, the president of the union and the plant manager share an office. Many key decisions are made jointly regarding anything from production to budgeting or from staffing to overtime. The plant manager will usually consult with the union president before making the decision.

The same principle applies at the department level. Shop stewards and department managers share workspaces and will often collaborate on decisions relevant to their departments. Additionally, every employee is on a team that gets a daily update on the production numbers and financials of the plant. Quarterly, the plant manager and the union president present the quarter's results to all the employees in a plant-wide general meeting, where they entertain suggestions and questions in a fashion similar to the Work-Out meetings at General Electric.

Harley-Davidson exemplifies a growing movement among American companies to openly share pertinent information with employees. Those companies are discovering that telling the truth actually empowers people, which helps create a competitive advantage quite the opposite of what many leaders fear.

Fear of Losing Face

We all have a need to appear competent, responsible, and successful to others, to have others think we are okay. To that degree, we worry about what other people think of us. When this worry becomes too great, it can keep us from telling the truth or cause us to lie in order to save face and appear competent. The costs can be high.

The president of an accounting firm told us about Tammy, one of her auditors. Tammy had made a mistake on a due diligence report for a client after the audit had been submitted to an institutional investor. Instead of admitting her mistake when she discovered it, which would have involved contacting the investor and making the correction—embarrassing but not the end of the world—she pulled the original documents and altered them. Later, an unrelated problem with the audit caused the investor to request another copy, which was made from the original document. The client noticed the disparity and questioned the accuracy of the entire audit. The client ended up losing the investor, the firm ended up losing the client, and Tammy ended up losing her job. Tammy's desire to save face produced disastrous consequences, especially considering how easily the entire thing could have been fixed.

According to a study by Professor Stella Ting-Toomey of Simon Fraser University, cultural differences can exacerbate the issue of saving face, especially when those of European descent work with those of Asian descent.[14]

Bob confirmed Ting-Toomey's findings when he was vice president of human resources for Tektronix. Bob was involved in offering the Tektronix country manager in Taiwan, Mr. Wong, a significant promotion to a regional manager's position that included more than a 50 percent increase in his total compensation package. After some consideration, Mr. Wong called Bob to say that he had decided to not accept the position and that he would be leaving the company.

Shocked, Bob asked him, "Why?"

Mr. Wong replied that although the new position was a good position, if the company did not have enough faith in him to do his current job, he would lose face with his customers and employees and he would be unable to perform effectively in the new role. He would rather leave the company than suffer the embarrassment caused by his lack of effectiveness.

It seems to us that this was carrying modesty and a concern for appearances to absurd extremes, but with names like Johnson and Phillips, you can guess that we are not of Asian decent, so we probably, at times, lack sufficient sensitivity to understand Mr. Wong's position. Additionally, Mr. Wong may have misinterpreted the offer as being a subtle demotion rather than a promotion, since it would take him farther from the action of dealing with customers and being involved in the business. Also, Mr. Wong himself may not have chosen to take the position for fear of failing with the increased job responsibilities.

Whatever the real reason for Mr. Wong's behavior, it serves any manager well to be alert to the fact that the possibility of losing face can be a powerful reason people shy away from expressing themselves openly or telling the truth. If doing so will place them in an unflattering light, don't expect them to leap into center stage.

FEAR KILLS THE SOUL

Mahatma Gandhi once said: "Fear is a disease worse than any other. Disease kills the body, fear kills the soul." But just as a disease can be cured, our fears can be overcome. You probably remember an experience from your childhood that taught you this truth. Perhaps it was the first time you dove off the high diving board at the local swimming pool. Before you climbed the ladder, you looked at it for the longest time, procrastinating as you envisioned the frightening plunge down into the water.

Then, one by one, you ascended what seemed to be a countless number of steps to finally arrive at the back end of the board. As you looked down, your heart, which had been fluttering, began to race as you saw the world from this breathtakingly scary perch. Step by painful step, you approached the end of the board. From its end, the water seemed miles below. You considered turning around and backing down the ladder. This wasn't worth it. You'd try it some other day. But somewhere in the background you could hear your friends egging you on, and you knew that if you retreated you would suffer their derision. So, with a burst of courage you never thought possible, you stepped off the end of the board and descended into what you were sure would be certain death.

And then you were in the water and swimming to the edge of the pool, having conquered this challenge and ready to climb the ladder again, this time with the courage and confidence of an Olympic champion.

In those brief moments you learned a vital life lesson: There is only one way to conquer fear and that is to do the very thing you fear. If the management of Tudor Ice Company had done so, it would have embraced the truth about its changing industry—and your refrigerator today might be a Tudormatic. If Gary Condit had done so and told the truth about his relationship with Chandra Levy, searchers might have found her sooner and he might still be in office. If more people at Enron had blown the whistle early on, perhaps Enron might be a viable business today.

Because in every case, the worst truth beats the best lie.

NO EXCUSE FOR ABUSE

Robert is an electrical engineer in a company that has implemented the absolute honesty approach. When Robert doesn't get his way, he often throws a temper tantrum. If coworkers disagree with him, he calls them "ignorant" or "misinformed," and if someone makes a mistake that affects one of his projects, he shouts obscenities at the person loud enough to be heard several cubicles away. After fielding more than a few complaints about Robert, Joanne, his manager, confronted him about his behavior. "Hey," Robert replied, almost proudly, "I'm just practicing that honesty stuff you guys are always preaching."

Our name for this gross distortion of the absolute honesty principle is honesty abuse. Obviously, Robert has other issues on his agenda that he's angry about and is using absolute honesty to express them inappropriately. Or maybe Robert's just a jerk. Either way, there's no excuse for his behavior.

We believe that absolute honesty should never be used as an excuse for tactlessness, pointless cruelty, or inflicting harm, but should be restricted to getting at the truth and solving problems. For example, Larry's wife hired a man who was inexperienced but looked promising during the interview to work at the mortgage company she runs; he had passed all the tests with flying colors. When it came to actually learning the new job, however, he couldn't master the complexity of the work. She finally had to dismiss him.

Telling him that she was letting him go because he wasn't able to master the work was an act of absolute honesty. It got at the truth, it solved the problem, and it wasn't tactless or mean. Telling him she was firing him because he was "too stupid to cut it," however, would have been an act of pointless cruelty.

FEAR NO TRUTH

The premise of this chapter is that, in the long run, the truth is always better than a lie, even if it is more painful at the time. Thomas Jefferson once said, "The man who fears no truth has nothing to fear from lies." Lies inevitably get us into more trouble than telling the truth, even when the truth is painful. Ironically, our fears keep us from such honesty. In this chapter we examined some of those fears and concluded that there is no "trick" or "technique" for overcoming them except to face them and to act. When you do so, we believe that, no matter how painful the truth and how great your fear of telling it, it's rarely as bad as you think and often produces unimagined benefits.

For example, doctors and medical institutions who make a mistake rarely apologize for any pain or suffering they might have caused because later it can be used as ammunition against them in court. But in a 1994 study of British medical malpractice patients, 37 percent said they wouldn't have brought suit had the doctor provided them with an explanation and an apology.[15]

On the other hand, choosing to do otherwise can exact painful consequences. For example, in 1991 four senior executives at Salomon Brothers failed to take appropriate action when they learned of unlawful activities on the government trading desk. Although there was no law obligating them to disclose the improprieties, their failure to do so caused a crisis of confidence among employees, creditors, shareholders, and customers. They were forced to resign, and their ethical lapse compounded the trading desk's legal offenses immeasurably. The company ended up losing more than $1 billion in the scandal. According to Lynn Sharp Paine, author of *Cases in Leadership, Ethics, and Organizational Integrity: A Strategic Perspective*, had the executives simply come forward and told the truth, regardless of what the law required them to do, the cost of the disaster could have been minimized.[16]

CHAPTER 4

Absolute Honesty Law #2:

Tackle the Problem

"The aim of argument or of discussion should not be victory, but
progress."

—*JOSEPH JOUBERT*

AS MANAGING EDITOR FOR A WOMEN'S FASHION MAGAZINE,
Marisa had not only led the magazine from virtual obscurity to
nationwide distribution, she had also doubled subscriptions and
tripled advertising revenue. Then along came Jonathan, a hot
new art director who announced during his first editorial meeting
that he wanted to transform the magazine into something "more
twenty-first century, for the Internet generation."

Feeling defensive and struggling to keep from launching into
a verbal attack, Marisa returned to her office and spent some
time reflecting on the situation. Jonathan, she reasoned, was
young, relatively inexperienced, and in spite of his bravado, probably nervous about making a good impression. The next day,

she met with Jonathan to discuss the issue, gently but firmly explaining that the readers were professional women in their thirties and the magazine had to reflect their tastes and sophistication level. After some discussion, Jonathan agreed to tailor his new design to the magazine's readers, and Marisa agreed to give him the freedom he needed to create an innovative and appropriate design.

This story illustrates the fine art of constructive confrontation: confronting others when you disagree with them, but doing it in a way that achieves the best resolution to the problem at hand and, ideally, strengthens the relationship between the confronting parties.

We call the methodology constructive confrontation. The term has been used at Intel since the 1970s and lies at the heart of Intel's culture of honesty and open communication. It is a communication process designed to resolve problems and difficult issues.

The key to constructive confrontation is remembering to attack problems, not people, and to search for solutions that best serve the organization, not individuals. It sounds deceptively simple. However, since it involves the interaction of human beings who are infinitely complex, implementing the process can be tricky. We have trained thousands of people in this methodology in our consulting and training business. Our approach consists of six basic steps:

1. Do your homework.
2. Open the debate.
3. Open your ears.
4. Open your mouth.
5. Open your mind.
6. Close the deal.

STEP 1: DO YOUR HOMEWORK

Any lawyer will tell you that trials are not won in the courtroom but in the law library, preparing for the case. The same goes for a work-related discussion, especially where disagreement is involved. If you've studied the facts of the matter at hand, there is a greater chance that your case will be heard and the best solution discovered. In the example above, if Jonathan had researched the market more thoroughly, he might have presented a better argument to Marisa that the magazine's fans preferred a hipper focus. The outcome of the initial discussion might have been different if he had done his homework.

Of course, if every well-researched argument won the day, life would be simple indeed. Human beings are more complicated than that. Marisa's years of experience may have blinded her to new opportunities and methods. It's also possible that she felt threatened by Jonathan's brash style and innovative approach. Perhaps Marisa just wanted to test Jonathan's resolve to see if he really knew what he was talking about. Or, as the example described, Marisa may have been right: Continuing with the magazine's present focus was the best path for the company. Each side in every confrontation can muddy the debate with personal agendas that remain undisclosed.

To raise the odds that he would be heard and taken seriously, Jonathan would have done well not only to research his facts, but to think about how he would present them to Marisa—and Marisa would benefit from doing the same.

Here are steps that will help you prepare for a confrontation:

Identify the Issue

Disagreements are often complicated by the presence of more than one issue. In the case of Marisa and Jonathan, deciding the direction of the magazine's "look" was, ostensibly, the only question under discussion. We call it the *presenting issue*.

There may also be *secondary issues* involved. Is the competition coming out with a hipper version? Is the company considering major changes like a merger or a buyout? How is the market changing?

Additionally, there may be emotional or hidden issues in play.

Has Jonathan earned the right within the group's social structure to make such a radical suggestion? Was Jonathan showboating rather than presenting a valid, well-conceived idea? Did Marisa feel threatened by Jonathan's aggressiveness? Was this meeting the proper place to start a discussion of this magnitude?

We call these *under-the-table issues.* Under-the-table issues can exert enormous influence on the discussion of the presenting and secondary issues. This often happens to married couples with a history of bitter battles over unresolved conflicts. A discussion about who will do the dishes can escalate into a fight over money, lack of intimacy, unfair distribution of labor, or past sexual infidelities. Meanwhile, the dishes go unwashed.

They might even get thrown and broken.

Before launching into a full discussion about the look of the magazine, both Jonathan and Marisa would have benefited from acknowledging the under-the-table issues. This doesn't mean they should be addressed head on, but awareness of them helps each party make conscious decisions about how to deal with them before, during, and after the discussion. Such awareness also helps the parties keep the conversation focused on the presenting issue. Otherwise, it can easily be pulled off track by the magnetic forces these under-the-table issues exert.

For example, Jonathan might have prefaced his suggestion for a new look for the magazine with an acknowledgment that he may not see the big picture as well as Marisa does because he is new to the industry. Such an admission could soften Marisa's reaction that Jonathan is being a presumptive rookie who doesn't know his place.

Marisa, on the other hand, might have gone out of her way to acknowledge Jonathan's creative ideas and their potential for the future, showing that her deep commitment to the magazine's current format did not mean she wasn't open to new concepts.

We are not implying that either of them should be dissuaded from expressing their opinions in a straightforward manner. It wouldn't be constructive confrontation if that were the case. It just means that adapting one's approach to accommodate the interpersonal, under-the-table issues will raise the odds that each person's thoughts will be considered seriously by the other.

Decide If the Issue Is Worth Confronting

Not all issues need to be confronted and not all fights need to be fought. Larry hired Betty, a young Gen-Xer, to be a presenter for his training company. Betty is bright, well educated, and a terrific trainer. A day after she came aboard, there was a scheduling snafu and Larry found himself double-booked. All of his other trainers were booked as well, so Larry asked Betty to take one of the two assignments. He then called the client, for whom he'd done much training and consulting over the years, and explained that there would be a substitute. The client, accustomed to having the principal partner of the firm do its training, didn't sound happy about the arrangement, but agreed.

The catch was that all this took place on a Friday afternoon, and the program was scheduled for the following Monday morning—and Betty had never seen the material before. Larry reviewed it with her and suggested that she study it over the weekend. They agreed to meet on Sunday afternoon to review it one last time.

On Sunday, Betty mentioned that she'd been out late Saturday night partying with a new boyfriend. Larry was furious. He had trusted this inexperienced kid with a valuable client, and she had had the gall to go out dancing when she should have been burning the midnight oil.

Wisely, Larry said nothing at the time. With less than twenty-four hours before the seminar, this was not the time to talk to Betty about her preparation habits. Instead, he planned to confront her first thing Tuesday morning.

The next day Larry received a voice mail from the client, who enthusiastically thanked him for sending this terrific trainer in his place. In fact, Larry got the distinct feeling that the client liked Betty better than him.

The question we would ask at this point is: Should Larry confront Betty about her method of preparation? We would say no. It's now a nonissue the way she prepares her business. As long as it works, why fight a battle that doesn't need to be fought?

Like any communication, confrontation is expensive because it consumes the time and energy of the participants. It costs even more when it adds stress to the relationship. The old adage to "pick your battles" makes good sense.

This advice is especially relevant for those who like to battle over minutiae when there are larger issues to address. We've been at meetings where two engineers argue about how many circuits can be inscribed on the head of a pin while everyone else rolls their eyes and impatiently waits for them to finish. At many high-tech firms, this is called "rat holing." Those who are guilty of it need to learn self-awareness and self-control. For those who are its victims, interrupting with something like, "Hey, you guys are rat holing. Let's move along," usually works.

Identify the Desired Outcome

If you don't know what you want from a confrontation, you'll probably end up with something else. Defining your goals ahead of time can help you avoid confronting people just to make a point, prove yourself right, or punish the other person.

A manager who had been through our constructive confrontation training told us that he'd tried this approach with an employee who was chronically late, but it hadn't worked. We asked him to explain.

"The guy just sat there and stared at the floor. He wouldn't answer any of my questions. He wouldn't offer any ideas. He just wouldn't engage or deal with it!" We then asked, "Has this fellow continued to be late to work?" The manager thought for a moment and replied that as a matter of fact, the employee had been coming to work on time lately.

"Then it sounds like it worked," we replied. "Yes," said the manager, "but he wouldn't respond during our discussion." We then asked him, "What did you want—for him to come to work on time or for him to talk to you when you confront him?"

The manager thought for a moment and replied, "Now that you put it that way, what I really wanted from him was an apology. I went out on a limb to hire this guy. He lacked the required education for the job but he was a friend of my brother-in-law. And now he does this to me? The least he could do was say he was sorry."

This was obviously a case of the manager engaging in confrontation without being aware of an under-the-table issue of his own. It was also a case of not knowing what he wanted before he went in. Our advice to him was to let it go. He'd gotten the result he wanted. Fretting about the lack of an apology was a waste of time and energy.

Our advice to you, as you prepare for a confrontation, is to take stock of the presenting issues, the secondary issues, and the under-the-table issues prior to the confrontation, and to be crystal clear about the outcome you desire.

See the Situation from the Other Person's Perspective

Allen had been a branch manager of a social service agency for eighteen months. He was enthusiastic about his new position. He came in early and stayed late. He often worked on weekends.

Ralph, his manager, was pleased with the performance of Allen's office but was concerned that Allen was burning himself out. He suspected that Allen was not delegating enough to his people. His suspicions were confirmed when he filled in for Allen while Allen was away at a seminar.

Ralph noticed that agents would ask for help in completing certification forms that, given their time on the job, they should have been able to handle themselves. When Allen returned from vacation, Ralph watched him interact with several agents. If there was anything unusual about a certification form, Allen would say, "Let me handle that."

Ralph decided to give Allen some feedback. The conversation went like this:

Ralph: *Allen, I've noticed that you're working way too many hours. I think you should delegate more.*

Allen: *I delegate as much as I can, but there are some things only a manager can do.*

Ralph: *When I covered for you last week, I noticed that several people didn't know how to do the more difficult cert forms. If you delegated more to your people, instead of doing them yourself, it would give them the opportunity to learn how to do them. Then you could spend your time on more important things.*

Allen: *I do that, but with the workload, I'm doing the best I can. Are you saying that I'm not getting the important things done around here?*

At this point, Ralph began to wonder why Allen was getting so defensive. He thought Allen would have accepted his suggestion to delegate more without question, after which they could have discussed ways for Allen to do this. Instead, Allen was arguing with him.

We would suggest that Allen's defensiveness was natural, given Ralph's assumption that Allen had a problem with delegation (probably accurate, but not necessarily Allen's perception) and his imposing a solution when Allen had yet to acknowledge there was a problem. If Ralph had been willing to see the situation from Allen's perspective, he might have taken a different approach.

Instead of starting with the suggestion that Allen needed to delegate more, Ralph might have described what he'd observed when he filled in for Allen and pointed out that it was unacceptable for senior agents to be unable to do difficult certs. He could then have asked Allen for possible remedies for this situation.

> **Ralph:** *Allen, when I filled in for you last week, I noticed that several senior agents didn't know how to complete the more difficult cert forms. Do you have any ideas for getting them up to speed?*

In the first scenario, Ralph treated Allen like a child, assuming he, Ralph, was the all-knowing parent, and Allen just needed to be told what to do. Adults hate being told what to do. It's not surprising that Allen got defensive.

In the second scenario, Ralph respected Allen as an adult. He shared his observations of the problem with Allen and asked him for his thoughts on how it could be solved. We think that approach is more likely to lead to a discussion of possible options for making a positive change, including more delegation by Allen.

STEP 2: OPEN THE DEBATE

Like a tennis match, a constructive confrontation requires someone to serve the ball and someone to return it. Here are suggestions for opening the discussion:

Describe the Problem or Issue Specifically

In clear, concise, nonaccusatory terms, describe the presenting problem or issue. Ralph did that with Allen in the second scenario. With this approach, there is no doubt what your concern is. It's straightforward and to the point.

The management literature offers differing opinions about the best ways to open the debate when the issue involves criticism. Some authors suggest using the *sandwich approach*, where you lead off with something positive, then deliver the criticism, then end up with something positive. The thought here is that it's important to protect the person's ego while at the same time telling him what you would like him to change. Here's an example:

> "Randy, you're one of our best salespeople. The customers like you, and your closing rate on cold calls is in the top 20 percent for our sales force. I am concerned, however, that you often promise customers delivery dates that are unrealistic. We've received several complaints about it. Randy, you're so talented, I know you can get this straightened out."

Notice how the bad news is sandwiched between two pieces of good news. On the surface, this approach seems reasonable. If used sparingly, it's probably fine. The problem with it is that people aren't stupid and if you always deliver feedback in a sandwich, they start to realize that the purpose of the message is the zinger in the middle. Then they start doubting your truthfulness about any of the good things you tell them because they're always wondering when the zinger will come.

Not that there is anything wrong with acknowledging someone's strengths when giving feedback—we just think it's better to avoid making a sandwich and get to the point. We especially liked the approach our editor at AMACOM, Adrienne Hickey, used with us when she gave us feedback on our initial proposal for this book. She said, "Listen guys, I'm not going to waste time telling you what I liked about your proposal. If I didn't like it, we wouldn't be having this discussion. Now let me tell you what I don't like about it." There was enough good news there to relieve our anxiety about getting our book published, but she didn't patronize us with unneeded accolades.

Not that there is anything wrong with praise and positive feedback. Quite the opposite. Experience has shown us that, when giving criticism, the direct approach is the best as long as it's given in an environment where positive feedback is abundant. And we do mean abundant. A study by the Gallup Organization[2] found that, when employees get positive feedback about their performance at least once per week, they are likely to be more productive, serve customers better, produce higher profits for the company, and change employers less frequently. On the other hand, if all they hear is criticism and they're never told they are doing well, their performance tends to decline. That doesn't mean you shouldn't offer criticism. Everyone can benefit from corrective feedback, and it is one of the essential jobs of managers to provide it. Our contention is that it is better to serve them as separate dishes than to pile them together in a sandwich.

Assuming that Randy gets lots of positive feedback for the things he does well, the direct approach would be to say, "Randy, I just got a complaint from a customer saying she didn't get her order as promised. That's the third complaint this week. What's going on?"

It's clear, it's direct, it describes the problem, it explains the impact, and it expresses your feelings.

Some managers, fearing confrontation, take an *indirect approach* by asking questions, hoping to lead the employee to the desired answer. Consider the previous example where Ralph was concerned that Allen should delegate more. If Ralph had taken the indirect approach, the conversation might have sounded like this:

Ralph: *How are you feeling these days, Allen?*

Allen: *Fine, why do you ask?*

Ralph: *You seem to be tired. Are you getting enough sleep?*

Allen: *I think so.*

Ralph: *Do you feel like you're working too much?*

Allen: *Well, there's a lot to do right now. If we could get an increase in our budget, I could hire some extra help.*

Ralph: *Do you feel like you can't get it all done with the budget you have allotted?*

Allen: *No, I'm willing to work hard, and so are my people. It's just that there's a mighty heavy workload. With proper funding, we could do wonders here.*

As you can see, Allen isn't letting Ralph herd him in the direction Ralph wants him to go. But unlike the second scenario described earlier, where Ralph was clear that there was a problem that needed solving, this time Ralph left Allen guessing. Consequently, the conversation bogged down into a discussion of budgetary issues.

We advise against the indirect approach for two reasons: The conversation can easily get off-track, as it did here, and it's dishonest. From the beginning, Ralph's questions were not genuine. They were deceptive attempts to lead Allen down a predetermined path.

Parents do this when they ask their two-year-old, "Do you want to take a bath?" What they are really saying is, "I want you to take your bath now." If the child answers the question by saying no, they have a dilemma on their hands. Either they have to play along, hoping that the child will change his mind, or they have to insist that bath time is *now*. The child learns that the question is really a deception and that his parents are willing to be disingenuous with him.

We think it's better to be direct about the nonnegotiables of the discussion by giving the child genuine choices with a real question: "It's bath time. [DIRECT approach] Would you like a bubble bath or a regular bath? [a real question giving real choices]."

Likewise, Ralph should have said, "I had a problem with some of your staff not knowing how to handle special applicant certifications [direct]. I know that you handle a lot of the certs yourself. How are you going to get them up to speed? [a real question giving real choices]."

Use "I" Language

The goals of constructive confrontation are to solve problems, make decisions, and resolve disagreements effectively. They are not to focus on people's faults, foibles, and shortcomings. When people are accused of anything negative, their natural reaction is to become defensive. It stands to reason that any language that can minimize the chances that one or more of the participants in a confrontation will feel personally attacked will serve to keep the conversation headed in a constructive direction. Using the word *I* instead of *you* serves this purpose. It implies that you are taking responsibility for the opinions and observations you're expressing. Though you may be describing something the other person did or failed to do, your language carries no accusation when you stick to using the word *I*.

On the other hand, the word *you* in a potentially negative situation like a confrontation will almost always be interpreted as accusatory. It focuses the discussion on the other person rather than the problem.

▲ "You shouldn't lie to investors."

▲ "You didn't consider the client's changing market."

▲ "You are wrong on this."

▲ "You didn't make your numbers this quarter."

▲ "You make me sick."

They all say something personal about the other person. Now consider the impact of "I" language:

⚠ "I think it's wrong to lie to investors."

⚠ "I think we need to consider the client's changing market."

⚠ "I don't agree with those results."

⚠ "I'm disappointed to see that the quarterly numbers are off."

⚠ "I feel sick."

All say how "I" feel about the situation and don't presume to say anything about the other person.

Of course, you can carry this too far. Getting through a discussion, especially a heated one, without saying the word *you* could make you sound like an idiot. So use your best judgment. Just remember that the more times you use the word *you* when confronting or disagreeing with people, the greater the odds they will take offense.

Focus on the Present and Future

We all know that it's impossible to change the past, but that doesn't keep us from talking to others as if they have that ability. For example, the accusation "You didn't get the required signatures on the Williamson contract" implies that the speaker thinks that, somehow, this person can go back in time and erase that mistake. That's obviously impossible. What the speaker really means is: "You screwed up. You should be ashamed. Please don't let it happen again."

If constructive confrontation is truly about solving problems and not attacking people, then the only useful part of the statement is the last sentence, "Please don't let it happen again."

When a discussion dwells on events that have already occurred, there is a tendency for all involved to defend their positions and not move toward creative problem solving. This doesn't mean you should avoid discussion of past events at all costs. Again, it would make you sound like an idiot. Sometimes you must discuss the past in order to create solutions for the present and the future. Dwelling on the past, however, when there is fault to find or blame to be placed, raises the odds that the confrontation will be perceived as a personal attack rather than a problem-solving exercise.

This is especially true if it involves criticism. Because the past cannot be changed, criticism about the past puts people in the impossible position of being held accountable for what they now can do nothing about. It's like criticizing your spouse for dating a particular person before you were married. It's a great way to end up sleeping on the couch.

Not that we advocate releasing people from accountability for their past behavior. (That's what the criminal and civil justice systems are all about.) We're just saying that if your goal is to get problems resolved rather than punish people for their mistakes, the present is a more productive place to be.

Try these alternative statements:

- ▲ Instead of saying, "You never tell me when you're going to change a production run," try "In the future, I'd like to know in advance if you are going to change the production run."
- ▲ Instead of saying, "You made a mistake in your calculations," try "I don't agree with your figures."
- ▲ Instead of saying, "You didn't get the newsletter out on time," try "It's important to me that the newsletter get out on time. Can I have your commitment to making that happen?"

With these kinds of statements, the person can actually do something to solve the problem without having to defend his or her honor.

STEP 3: OPEN YOUR EARS

Listening is one of those skills for which school provides no formal training, but we are expected to be proficient at it from the day we step into the classroom. "Listen up," the teacher told us. Some of us did, some didn't. Those who did, and did it well, usually performed better in school. They gathered more facts, retained more information, and did better on tests. People usually liked them better.

But listening can be challenging. When we listen to someone who is interesting, entertaining, or sharing information that we deem important, it seems effortless and fun. However, if the person we are listening to is a poor communicator, is boring, or isn't sharing information we care about, listening can be tedious at best and painful at worst. In a confrontation where we feel strongly about our own point of view, listening becomes almost impossible.

We get so wrapped up in the rightness of our own position that we often fail to consider the merits of the other person's views. We only listen to find fault in their arguments. Meanwhile, they are doing the same thing to us. The irony, of course, is that our goal in a confrontation is to have the other person listen to us and seriously consider our point of view. Too often, that is the one courtesy we hold back.

Mutual Reciprocity

The term *mutual reciprocity*[3] refers to the give-and-take associated with any human relationship. It says that, for a relationship to be healthy, the giving and the taking must eventually balance—much like a bank statement. The *Law of Mutual Reciprocity* says that, to the degree you give others what they need, they will tend to give you what you need. If you treat people right, they will tend to treat you right. Put another way, "What goes around, comes around." In our college days we called it "karma."

But there are three catches to this law:

Catch #1: The giving and taking refers to needs, not wants. We all have needs: for respect, to be heard, to be taken seriously, to be valued. We also have a plethora of wants: to win, to dominate, to be popular, to get our way. The difference is that getting a *need* met contributes to our psychological well-being, while getting what we *want* only makes us happy for the moment. Both are important in life, but mutual reciprocity applies mostly to the mutual meeting of *needs*.

If you give people what they want, they won't necessarily give you what you want. Suppose I want to launch a new product following Plan A, and you support Plan B. We can have a great debate over the merits of both, but if you cave in and give me what I *want* because my arguments are more persuasive, because you're intimidated by me, or because I'm just plain right and you're wrong, don't expect me to necessarily give you what you *want* next time around.

On the other hand, if you give me the respect and serious consideration that I, as a human being and a professional *need*, the odds soar that I will be willing to give you a similar level of respect and consideration in return. In his landmark book, *The Seven Habits of Highly Effective People*, Stephen Covey calls this "emotional banking."[4] We see it as making a deposit in your *needs account* and getting interest back on the deposit.

Catch #2: The order of giving is critical. You must be first. Saying, "Why should I listen to him? He never listens to me." won't start the process. It starts when you make the first move. You've got to listen first, show respect first, and take the person seriously first. The odds then rise that the other person will listen to you.

Catch #3: You may have to initiate collection procedures. Since humans vary considerably, you will probably run into some lawbreakers—those who will meet their needs on your expense account but never return the favor, thus violating the Law of Mutual Reciprocity. If you have given due respect and truly listened to one of these lawbreakers in a confrontation or debate, and he fails to reciprocate, you are within your rights to collect. For example, by interrupting and saying, "Just a minute, I heard you out and showed you that I truly understood and valued your thoughts. Now it's your turn to do the same for me."

Applied to the act of constructive confrontation, the Law of Mutual Reciprocity says this: To the degree that you listen to the other person *first,* and prove to him that you truly understand and seriously consider his position, he will be likely to reciprocate by truly listening to and considering your position. It's the first step toward finding the best solution to the problem.

Besides, it is to our benefit and to that of the organization to truly listen and consider the other person's position. The point of the whole process is not to win but to find the best possible solutions. Pushing our own case to the point of winning at all costs risks doing a great disservice to the organization in which we work, especially if the other person is right and we (heaven forbid!) are wrong.

Proving You Listened

Sometimes it's hard to tell whether or not you are being listened to. The person sits there looking at you, nodding his head, and holding eye contact, but you're just not sure he's getting it. It's reassuring when he gives you some kind of signal that tells you that, indeed, he not only listened but he understood.

We were doing a large consulting and training program for a client some years ago. We asked Phil, a well-known electrical engineer/consultant whom we'd never met before, to help with the technical piece related to the client's business (integrated circuits). At our first planning meeting, each of us discussed what we would bring to the table for the job. When Larry explained his role, Phil looked thoughtful for a moment and then perfectly summarized Larry's comments, saying, "So you'll provide the participants with interpersonal tools to increase collaboration and overcome differences when they reach stalemates in their decision-making process. That is so powerful. It complements my technical piece perfectly by . . ." Larry said later that as Phil spoke, he could feel himself relax and start to trust

Phil and to like him. When we shared this with Phil, he shrugged his shoulders and said, "Shoot, all I did was listen to you."

The tip here is obvious. Listening is more than absorbing information. It's more than practicing listening skills that you learned in some seminar. It's certainly more than looking for the holes in the other person's argument so you can deliver a better counterargument. True listening is understanding what the other person said and then proving to him that you understood it and you honor it. At that point, you've made a deposit in the other person's *needs account*, and the odds increase that he will listen to you in return.

STEP 4: OPEN YOUR MOUTH

You may be saying at this point, "Wait a minute, when do I get to argue back and make my points?" You'll know when the other person gives you permission to do so. That permission appears in the form of what we call *go signals*. You'll recognize them when the person you are confronting or debating with starts agreeing that you do, indeed, understand his position. For example, Jan and Carl, owners of a chain of physical therapy clinics, were disagreeing about whether to expand their business into home health care.

It started like this:

Jan: *I think we ought to consider getting into home care.*

Carl: *I don't think so. It's too risky now. Third-party payers are in too much flux about reimbursement.*

Jan: *I think you're wrong. The opportunity is there and if we don't move now, we'll lose out.*

Carl: *You're always ready to leap without looking. We could lose our shirts.*

Jan: *But think of the opportunity. Quit being such a stick-in-the-mud.*

Carl: *I'm just trying to be sensible, unlike you.*

You may have noticed that there was little or no listening going on here and the discussion was rapidly heading toward a fight. Carl wasn't inclined to hear Jan's reasons for getting into the home care market, but then, she did nothing to show him that she had heard his concerns or that she took them seriously.

Let's listen to this conversation again, this time with Jan making an effort to put a deposit or two in Carl's *needs account*. Notice the *go signals*, which are in bold.

Jan: *I think we ought to consider getting into home care.*

Carl: *I don't think so. It's too risky now. Third-party payers are in too much flux about reimbursement.*

Jan: *So you're concerned that third-party payers won't pick up the tab?*

Carl: **That's right.** *We could lose our shirts!*

Jan: *Sounds like you feel pretty strongly about it.*

Carl: **I do.** *You remember when we got into that rehab-on-wheels fiasco. We invested the money up front without any guarantee that the insurance providers would cover that kind of care. It almost put us under.*

Jan: *You're concerned that we're going to repeat mistakes from the past.*

Carl: **Darn right I am!** *I think we should go slowly on this one.*

Jan: *Well, your cautious approach has certainly kept us out of some bad deals in the past. So if it looks like third-party* *payers are going to support it, you feel we can always get into the game later.*

Carl: **Exactly!!**

"That's right—"I do!"—"Darn right I am!"—"Exactly!"

These *go signals* tell Jan that Carl is ready to listen to her point of view on this matter because they confirm that he knows she understands his position. Until he sends them, Jan's presentation of her point of view will fall on deaf ears.

Once you hear these signals, you can proceed to offer your point of view. Here are some steps we recommend:

Claim your reality as your own.

Phrase your case in terms of the way you see it, not as if it were the "truth."

Be clear and firm about what you need.

To paraphrase Mick Jagger: You can't always get what you want, but if you try . . . you can get what you need.

Summarize the benefits.

If the other person can see the benefits for himself and/or the organization, the odds rise that he will be open to your position and concerns.

Include the drawbacks.

No proposal, plan, or position is without risks, flaws, or costs. Including the drawbacks will gain you credibility and give you a chance to deal with the problems before the other person attacks you with them.

State your feelings.

This not only conveys to the other person how you feel about the issue, but it helps you clarify your feelings about it for yourself.

Let's see how Jan expresses her point of view following our steps.

Carl, this is just my opinion on the matter, but I think we have a terrific opportunity here. The home market is just taking off and those who get in early will own the market-place. I understand the risk is high, especially with so many carriers hesitating to commit. There are a few, however, who have, and I think that if we start small and align our services to fit their requirements, we could test the market without risking too much. It doesn't matter to me if we don't start big. I just think we should get in at some level and do it quickly.

At this point, Jan may or may not have convinced Carl that this venture is the right thing to do, but that's not the point. We would guess that Carl is now much more willing to listen to her thoughts than he was in the first scenario when she told him he was wrong. And that's all you can ask for.

STEP 5: OPEN YOUR MIND

Once *go signals* have been exchanged to indicate that each side has truly heard and acknowledged the other's point of view, the conversation can move to finding a workable solution. As you apply this step, here are ways to ensure success:

▲ *Get agreement on the outcome.* Ask the other person to help you define the best possible outcome for the discussion: increased profit, reduced risk, improved quality—the list is endless. The point is to mutually agree on a goal for the discussion that rises above turf or ego issues and goes directly to the heart of what is best for the company, the community, or even the world, and then to direct the discussion to that goal.

▲ *Review the data.* It is tempting to try to reach a solution before all the facts are in. Doing so will often produce a poor decision.

▲ *Review the concerns of each.* Remember, the other person's trust comes from knowing that you respect his opinions and concerns, even though you may not agree with them.

▲ *Ask for possible solutions that address each other's concerns.* There is usually more than one way to solve any problem. By asking the other person for ideas, you increase the chances you will get a solution she can live with. Brainstorming is a good technique to use here. It requires that you list as many options as possible without editing and without discussing their pros or cons. Do this until neither of you can think of any more ideas to add to the list. Then go back and explore each one, eliminating those that have no merit.

▲ *Ask tough questions to separate the wheat from the chaff.* Asking tough questions is critical. If the discussion is occurring in a group, you may want to appoint one or more people to play devil's advocate by picking apart each solution and forcing its proponent to defend it. Chuck Knight, past CEO of Emerson Electric, had a reputation for grilling any proponent of a proposal with questions that were intentionally unsettling. Even when he agreed with the proposal, he made sure that its sponsor could defend it against extreme inquiry. Though intimidating, the practice produced profits quarter after quarter during his twenty-seven-year tenure.[5]

Let's see how Jan might apply these steps in her conversation with Carl:

Jan: *Before we go any further, are we in agreement that we both want our business to grow at least 10 percent?* [Agree on an outcome.]

Carl: *Yes, but I just want to make sure we're not jumping into some harebrained scheme.*

Jan: *And we want to minimize our risk at the same time.*

Carl: *You're darned right.* [That's a go signal.]

Jan: *So at this point, it looks like we have a couple of options.* [Review the data.] *We can stay with our present operations as they are and invest more in marketing to expand those operations. Or we can continue our present marketing efforts with our core business and direct some resources into testing out the home care market. Are there any more options we might consider?*

Carl: *Well, we could sell this whole operation and move to the Bahamas. Just kidding. No, I think that about covers it.*

Jan: *Okay, let me ask, if we venture into home health care, what happens if all the insurance companies take a stand and none of them will cover it?*

Carl: *That's just what I'm worried about. Why are you questioning your own proposal?*

Jan: *I'm just playing devil's advocate. Maybe you could do the same as it applies to* not *investing in home health care.* [Jan and Carl take turns being devil's advocate and presenting their cases, after which Jan sums it up.]

Jan: *Okay then. Let me review your concerns and mine.* [Reviews the concerns of each.] *You're worried that if we jump into* *home health care without the majority of the insurance companies committing to supporting it, the risks will be too high. So any plan we come up with needs to account for that possibility. Correct?*

Carl: *That's right.* [Another go signal.]

Jan: *And it's important to me that we get in on the ground floor of this market. Do you have any ideas for how we can do that while minimizing our risk at the level you'd like?* [Ask for possible solutions that include each other's concerns.]

Carl: *Well, we could just stay with what we have and do nothing.* [Carl hasn't read this book, so he's not playing by the rules. That's okay. Jan will simply have to persist.]

Jan: *But that doesn't address my concern, which is to get into the home care market at some level. I think we should be there to maximize our chances of meeting or exceeding our 10 percent growth target, especially down the road.*

Carl: *Hmm. Well, we could, perhaps, test the market by doing a pilot operation. But I wouldn't want to commit too much.*

Jan: *What would you be comfortable with?*

At this point, Jan and Carl can hammer out a plan.

Beware the Win/Win Approach

"Wisdom is the principle thing; therefore get wisdom. And in all your getting, get understanding."

King Solomon, Proverbs 4:7

Yolanda, vice president of sales for the Feel Good Manufacturing Company, asked the production department to adjust the specifications of an order already in process without charging the customer for the change. She felt the customer goodwill it would create would offset the costs. Brendan, the head of production, protested, complaining that the time and cost of making the changes would fall on his department. He also pointed out that this customer, like so many in their customer base, was a small operator. After hashing it out, they reached a compromise: Yolanda agreed to give up a portion of the commission on the sale to offset costs, while the company's president authorized a reduction in product margins for that customer's order. On the surface, they seemed to have arrived at a win/win solution, with Yolanda making her customer happy and Brendan not having to absorb the cost for the change. But was it really a win/win all around? NO. Each got something they wanted, but the company's margins suffered in order to pay for it.

Most conflict resolution books push a win/win approach to problem solving. WE DO NOT! Rather, we argue that the best solution is one that focuses on the greater good of the organization and society. For example, divorcing parents will often engage in bitter disputes over the custody of their children. Conventional conflict management techniques would focus the discussions on a win/win solution, perhaps where one parent gets the kids for a week, and then the other parent gets them for a week. This may be a win for both the parents, but is it the right choice for the kids?

In the above scenario, the best solution for the company might have been for Yolanda to agree to refocus the sales department's efforts on finding larger customers so margins would be higher and last-minute changes would have less impact on the bottom line. If each side of a dispute is simply wrapped up in either winning the battle or finding a win/win compromise, then the new and better answer may never be found. When the differing parties can set aside their egos and focus on what's best for the organization, winning and losing become irrelevant.

This concept of focusing on the greater good, rather than on win/lose or win/win is especially useful when questions of ethics, or doing the right thing, are at stake. Consider Cynthia Cooper, Vice President of Internal Auditing for WorldCom, who in June of 2002 told CFO Scott Sullivan that the company had fraudulently concealed almost $4 billion in losses. A win/win outcome for them both might have been to say nothing and hope the whole scandal would just blow over. That would have been a win for him because it would have given him time to find lending sources to cover the fraudulent transactions. It would have been a win (sort of) for her because she could have rationalized that she had "done her duty" by bringing the situation to his attention. But would it have been the right thing to do? Obviously not when you consider that folks like us would have continued to buy WorldCom stock, thinking it was still making a profit.

Luckily, Ms. Cooper had the intestinal fortitude to take the matter to Max Bobbitt, chairman of WorldCom's board of directors audit committee. The entire matter was eventually exposed to public scrutiny, Scott Sullivan was fired, and WorldCom became one of the villainous casualties of the 2002 Crisis of Ethics in Business USA.

STEP 6: CLOSE THE DEAL

We've all been to meetings where a problem was presented, discussion ensued, a decision was made, and the problem seemed resolved—but nothing was done. Either everyone thought someone else was going to do something, those who were charged with making it happen got sidetracked, or it just fell through the cracks of bureaucracy.

We think it's critical to make sure this doesn't happen for these reasons:

1. If there's no follow-through, the problem never gets solved and continues to plague the organization.

2. If there's no action, the time and effort that went into solving it have been squandered.

3. If people see that practicing constructive confrontation wastes time, they quickly realize that putting energy into its practice is futile, and they will stop doing it.

The steps for closing the deal are simple:

1. Summarize what has been discussed and decided.

2. Assign ARs. AR, or Action Required, has been an officially recognized term at Intel since the early 1970s. It refers to the responsibilities assigned to each person as a result of any meeting. It reflected Andy Grove's desire to impose discipline and accountability on the organization and, to this day, is a common part of any Intel employee's vocabulary.

3. Set a date for a follow-up and keep it.

Carl: *So Jan, my AR is to run a cost estimate for doing a pilot home care program. You have two ARs. First, you will research the market and identify some potential areas to stage our pilot program. Second, you'll set up a project management plan and schedule for implementation. We'll both have these assignments ready to review by next week's meeting, right?*

Jan: *Agreed.*

To become skilled at constructive confrontation, practicing the six steps described in this chapter helps. That means you must:

▲ *Do your homework.* Before the meeting or discussion, spend a few minutes identifying the disputed issues and what the acceptable outcomes of the confrontation would be.

▲ *Open the debate.* Set a positive tone for the discussion by focusing on the problem and what can be done to address it now and in the future.

▲ *Open your ears.* Listen carefully to the other person's views and summarize what you heard to show that you listened.

▲ *Open your mouth.* When you get *go signals* from the other person, be clear about your perception of reality and what you need to resolve the confrontation. Include the advantages and disadvantages of your position.

▲ *Open your mind.* Encourage an open discussion of the facts and points of view so that a solution agreeable to both sides can be reached.

▲ *Close the deal.* Follow up to make sure the selected actions have been taken and the desired results achieved.

By practicing constructive confrontation personally, and by requiring everyone else in the organization to learn and use it, the leader sets the stage for creating a culture where people will be more likely to confront difficult issues.

CHAPTER 5

Absolute Honesty Law #3:

Disagree and Commit

"Cry me a river, build me a bridge, and GET OVER IT!"

—*ANONYMOUS*

AT A MONTHLY MEETING OF THE CLINTON COUNTY SCHOOL Board, chairman Rodney Smith made a seemingly innocuous request. "From now on," he announced, "I'd like you all to keep track of every conversation you have with the public about school business, and summarize it in a written report, which I'd like you to e-mail to me at least two days before every meeting."

The group had been discussing a parent's complaint that had been misplaced and forgotten. Now the parent was angry that the board hadn't responded. The board briefly discussed what was to go into the reports, everyone seemingly agreed to complete them, and the meeting was adjourned.

It did not take long for resistance to the report to surface. In the parking lot, people grumbled about the new rule. "Where am I going to find the time to do this report? I'm just volunteering here," one complained. "Who is he to tell us what to do anyway?" said another. "Just because of one foul-up, we're supposed to change our whole routine?" said a third member. At the next meeting, only two members submitted reports, and by the following meeting the whole report idea was forgotten. Sound familiar?

The truth is, it's easy to get everyone's support for a decision or action when all they have to do is voice their support. When they must change what they're doing, resistance sets in. We call the act of giving lip service to an agreement and then sabotaging it later *lipotage.*

Intel's answer to *lipotage* is an officially sanctioned corporate norm of behavior called *disagree and commit.* Intel expects everyone in the organization to express his or her opinions openly, even if those opinions go against the grain of the group. It does not mean arguing for the sake of arguing, nor does it condone shooting from the hip without thinking through what will be said. It does mean that if you don't agree with a decision or if you have concerns about an issue, you have an obligation to speak up and tell the people who are most concerned with that decision what your concerns are and why.

Disagree and commit also means that once a decision has been made or a course of action has been selected, you are expected to support it. This doesn't mean that everyone should have input into every decision the company makes. No organization can function that way, despite what some utopian management books of the '80s and '90s implied. Nor does it mean that there must be consensus on every decision. Sometimes decision by consensus is advisable, but other times it is best for a manager to make a unilateral decision, independent of input from others.

Disagree and commit means that you are expected to speak up and contribute your opinions on those decisions in which you have input. If you have questions, you should ask them. If you have a better idea, you should share it. If you think a decision is stupid or wrong, you should say so. Then, once the decision is made, you should stand behind it.

The *lipotage* that took place in the parking lot after the Clinton County School Board meeting would not have been tolerated at Intel.

The concept of *disagree and commit* appears deceptively simple but can be tricky to practice individually and even trickier for a leader to facilitate. In this chapter we discuss the challenges of practicing *disagree and commit* and we offer some suggestions for overcoming those challenges, both for practitioners and for leaders.

SPEAK UP AND DISAGREE

In Chapter 3 we discussed eight reasons why people fear telling the truth: fear of retribution, hurting other people's feelings, change, being disliked, losing support, paying the price, losing competitive advantage, and losing face.

We made the point that overcoming fear is a matter of doing what you fear and then dealing with the consequences. We also acknowledged that overcoming fear is no small task.

Regardless of the business culture in which you work, voicing disagreement usually requires a certain amount of outspokenness. If you work in a culture that dictates that everyone "go along to get along," it can require a great deal of courage to express your opinions openly, especially if they differ significantly with those of the group or your boss. Unfortunately, most of us tend to be fairly nonassertive. We were taught to be nice, to be polite, to not hurt people's feelings, and to not cause a fuss.

Think about a restaurant experience where you were unhappy with the food. Are you the kind of person who complains to the waiter and has the food returned to the kitchen? Or are you the kind of person who says nothing, not wanting to make a fuss. Then, when the waiter asks how it was, you look him in the eye and say, "Fine."

According to a survey we conducted with several thousand of our seminar participants, if you fall into the "eat it and keep quiet category," you are in the vast majority. One respondent told us he had good reason to not send the food back because the cook would probably spit on it. So don't feel bad. Only 10 percent of all respondents say they always return the food.

If most people are hesitant to speak up in a restaurant, where they are paying for service and products, it's no surprise that they are reluctant to speak up at work, where their livelihoods depend on getting along and not making enemies. To help overcome that fear, here are some suggestions for speaking the truth about controversial subjects while minimizing the chances you'll suffer repercussions.

Express Your Feelings Offline

Let's assume you think your boss is about to make a decision that you believe to be unwise, wrongheaded, or illegal. The decision comes up for discussion during a managers' meeting, and everyone seems to agree with the boss. In a culture where absolute honesty is nurtured and encouraged, the time to voice your opinion would be right then, using the constructive confrontation techniques we discussed in Chapter 4.

If your culture doesn't encourage such honest expression of opinions or if you are the kind of person who doesn't like to make a fuss in restaurants, much less business meetings, try voicing your objection by approaching the boss one-on-one or in writing. This removes the peer pressure you may feel during the meeting to go along just to get along. It reduces the chance the boss will discount your opinions to save face in front of the group. It also minimizes the chance you will get stage fright while presenting your ideas.

Set Ground Rules for Disagreement

For the Andy Groves, Jack Welches, and Lou Gerstners of the world, lively debate and open discussions are second nature. And for you to disagree with them, as long as you've done your homework, is something they would welcome and relish.

On the other hand, your boss may not be a Grove, Welch, or Gerstner kind of person. She may find your disagreement distracting, irritating, or a sign of insubordination. As you decide how much of that behavior you are willing to tolerate before polishing up your résumé and moving on, we suggest setting some ground rules with your boss by asking, "How would you like me to disagree with you?"

She'll probably ask what you mean by the question. Point out to her that different people like to have their subordinates disagree with them in different ways. Some examples would be:

- Is it okay to disagree during a meeting with other people or would you prefer it to be in private?
- Should it only be about major issues or does she want you to correct every detail?
- Would she prefer you to practice real-time honesty and offer her your opinions as they occur, or would it be better to save them up for your weekly meeting?
- Would it be better to put your thoughts in writing or to communicate them verbally?

This discussion should accomplish four things:

1. You will get permission to disagree with her or you won't.
2. You will get some guidelines for knowing when and how to disagree with her.
3. It will bring the topic of disagreement into the open. She may want to make it the topic of the next managers' meeting.
4. It puts her on notice that you will disagree with her. That way,

she will be less likely to react punitively when you do. Knowing that, you might be more likely to speak up when it needs to be done.

Get in the Habit

Courageous acts, like any behavior, are easier when they are habits. Habits only come from repetition. You don't play the piano by learning to read music and imagining yourself playing. It takes practice and lots of it. By playing a certain piece over and over, a pianist builds pathways through her nervous system from her brain to her fingers so there is little or no conscious thought as she plays a piece.

Here are some suggestions for building pathways from your brain to your bravery muscles.

Practice Positive Cantankerousness. If you are the kind of person who never makes a fuss in a restaurant over bad food, start. When someone cuts in line at the grocery store, say something to him. Choose a political issue about which you feel strongly and debate it with those who differ. When you get an unwanted telemarketing call at dinnertime, ask to speak to the manager and engage him in a conversation about your rights to privacy. Do *anything* that will give you practice voicing unwanted opinions.

Take a Risk a Day. Do something every day that takes you out of your comfort zone. We're not suggesting that you do anything foolish like driving down the wrong side of the freeway. Just do something that flies in the face of your natural habits. For example, for Sandy, the stressed-out executive assistant we described in Chapter 3, we would suggest that she try saying "no" to at least one request every day just to get used to saying "no."

She'd probably want to do it in a way that doesn't intentionally offend the other person but that, at the same time, draws the line and says, "I'm not going to do it." Here's a four-step technique we would suggest for her:

1. Acknowledge the request.
2. Decline with a brief reason.
3. Offer an alternative.
4. Stick to your guns.

Example:

Bill: *Sandy, could you run this report for me?*

Sandy: *What's involved and when do you need it? [Step 1]*

Bill: *I need all of last year's sales figures totaled and formatted in a PowerPoint presentation for my meeting this afternoon.*

Sandy: *I'm sorry, Bill, I'm in the middle of a rush project for Dave right now that is going to take me the rest of the day. [Step 2]*

Bill: *I really need this now.*

Sandy: *Gosh, Bill, if you want to check with Dave and have him rearrange my priorities, I'll be glad to do whatever he says. He's the boss. [Step 3]*

Bill: *Oh, come on. I need it now!*

Sandy: *Bill, that's the best I can do under the circumstances. Here's Dave's cell number if you want to check with him. [Step 4]*

Sandy's normal response to Bill's request would have been to say, "Okay," and then work late to finish Dave's assignment, thus adding to her stress. Saying "no" to Bill this way gives her the practice she needs to make absolute honesty a habit while offering Bill another solution to his problem.

Create a Discussion Tree

Suppose you want to express your concerns about a decision that Michael, your boss, has made. First, imagine what you are going to say:

> "Michael, I don't agree with pushing our supplier to increase deliveries so drastically in such a short amount of time. Given his present resources, I'm concerned that it will force him to cut quality or to overpromise and then under-deliver. What's your thinking on this?"

Next, imagine the various responses Michael might make. Diagram them on a discussion tree like the one in Figure 5.1 and develop a plan for addressing each.

The discussion tree gives your position more credibility because your ideas will be more organized than if you were to simply react in the moment. It also raises the odds that you can overcome your own reluctance to confront Michael in the first place. Knowing where the land mines are makes it a lot easier to take the first steps across the minefield.

Ask Yourself: "What's the Worst That Can Happen?" As we discussed in Chapter 3, it is human nature to let our *inner voice* blow the consequences of our actions out of proportion by *catastrophic chaining*. By asking your *inner voice* what's the worst that can happen, you can use the chaining process to work in your favor.

Figure 5-1. Discussion tree.

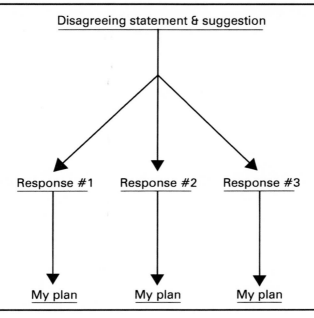

Disagreeing statement & suggestion

Response #1   Response #2   Response #3

My plan   My plan   My plan

You: *If I tell Michael I don't agree with his plan to push our vendor to double output, what's the worst that can happen?*

Inner Voice: *He could fire me?*

You: *Is that likely?*

Inner Voice: *No. But he might.*

You: *So if he fired me, would I survive? Would I go on living?*

Inner Voice: *Yes.*

You: *In fact, if he fired me for something like that, I probably don't want to work for him anyway. Right?*

Inner Voice: *Good point.*

There is no substitute for having the courage to voice your opinions, even in the face of discomfort. These suggestions simply help make the jump off that high diving board a little less daunting.

WHAT LEADERS CAN DO TO ENCOURAGE DISAGREEMENT

Assuming that you, as a leader, want your people to candidly tell you what they think, you can build an environment that nourishes and encourages such behavior. Here are some suggestions:

Insist on Candor

In an interview in the *Harvard Business Review*, Jack Welch, then CEO of General Electric, said:

> There's still not enough candor in this company. [By that] I mean facing reality, seeing the world as it is rather than as you wish it were. We've seen over and over again that businesses facing market downturns, tough competition, and more demanding customers inevitably make forecasts that are much too optimistic. This means they don't take advantage of the opportunities that change usually offers. Change in the marketplace isn't something to fear; it's an enormous opportunity to shuffle the deck, to replay the game. Candid managers—leaders—don't get paralyzed about the fragility of the organization. They tell people the truth. That doesn't scare them because they realize their people know the truth anyway.[1]

By insisting that your managers be candid with their subordinates, their peers, and you, you create a set of expectations that the truth shall prevail. It then becomes easier for people to tell the truth and harder to take revenge on those who do.

Ask Tough but Stimulating Questions

People who worked for Jack Welch described his style as argumentative and confrontational. He initiated the kinds of give-and-take discussions that exposed all sides of an issue. His tough questions were legendary, but they stimulated deeper thinking about the critical decisions being made. Welch set a standard for candid exchanges that permeated GE.

His questions were often tough because he demanded knowledgeable responses. "The one thing you can never do with Jack is wing it," said David Orselet, a retired GE executive. "If he ever catches you winging it, you're in trouble. Real trouble. You have to go in with in-depth information. Stand up for what you believe, but acknowledge what you don't know when you don't know it."[2]

Absolute honesty through tough questions and candid answers makes it hard to blur the issue with generalizations, half-baked theories, unsubstantiated arguments, and shaky assumptions. Tough, stimulating questions help you uncover and act on the facts.

Restrain Your Own Brilliance

Our guess is that you are the leader of your group, department, division, or organization for many reasons, but usually it's because you are smarter, more articulate, faster thinking, and have a more accurate view of the big picture than most of your subordinates. Additionally, as the boss, you have the unspoken power to reward and punish people who work for you. For all these reasons, you can be very intimidating to them.

If you want to encourage them to be forthright, especially those you manage, you need to control your own comments and let them speak. Keep in mind that they will often try to tailor their opinions to match yours, so if you tip your hand first, expect their "truths" to echo your own. This can lead to your becoming a naked emperor.

Bob Galvin, former CEO of Motorola, put it this way:

> The focus shifts from deciding and directing to creating and maintaining an evocative situation, stimulating an atmosphere of objective participation, keeping the goal in sight, recognizing valid consensus, inviting unequivocal recommendation, and finally vesting increasingly in others the privilege to learn through their own decisions.[3]

If your style is to "decide and direct," you will have trouble restraining yourself and creating and maintaining the evocative, stimulating atmosphere Galvin describes. The leader who is used to making decisions quickly and getting on with it must learn patience, letting others voice their opinions and having those opinions simmer in a cauldron of open discussion until a final decision emerges.

The reward will be worth the effort, however, when people speak up in the best interests of the company. It's worth it when a normally reticent sales manager mentions that the marketing campaign you're so fond of is falling on deaf ears in her region because it offends the ethnic population that lives there. It's worth it when an accountant working on your auditing team objects to categorizing certain items as investments rather than expenses. It's worth it when a vice president suggests that it would not serve the stockholders or the interests of the company for the executive team to cash in their stock options shortly before an expected downturn in business.

If you're interested in the long-term survival of your company, that kind of information is pure, twenty-four-carat gold.

Listen Intensely

Listening is the leader's way of laying out a welcome mat for the truth. As we mentioned in Chapter 2, Robert Townsend of Avis Corporation found that the key to listening to people is to "take them seriously." Intense listening sends the message that you value the truth this person is sharing with you and that it is welcome, which invites and encourages more of the same behavior.

Here are some dos and don'ts to follow in that listening process:

Do:

Allow people to finish their sentences, no matter how slowly they speak or how much difficulty they have getting to the point.

Don't:

Interrupt. Your interruption telegraphs your impatience and will dissuade them from being candid with you.

Do:

Give people your full attention.

Don't:

Allow distractions or interference. Nothing is more insulting or disheartening than engaging people in what they consider an important conversation and then taking a call. It will discourage them from being honest with you, and it's just plain rude.

Do:

Summarize their point of view. This tells them you got it and gives you a *go signal* to offer your point of view. Include in the summary a comment about how you think the person feels about the content of what he or she said: "So, Gena, you feel pretty strongly that if we force this accelerated delivery schedule on our vendor, he's going to promise us the moon, and then deliver shoddy products or miss deadlines or both."

Don't:

Assume that you understood what they said because you heard them say it. What you heard is not necessarily what they meant. Besides, if you don't summarize it, they don't know you got it, so they can't trust that you understood.

Do:

Participate nonverbally. Eye contact, nodding, encouraging "grunts," and leaning forward all say, "Tell me the truth, I really want to know." Taking notes sends a strong signal that you are listening, especially if you explain what you are doing.

Don't:

Lean back, look away, or become distracted.

Do:

Ask questions to clarify and verify their thinking.

- "What data do you have, Gena, to tell us he doesn't have the resources to do what we want and that he can't get them?"
- "What could be done to help him meet our demands?"
- "What alternatives can we explore to provide a back-up?"

Don't:

Attack the reasoning of their position or offer other solutions until their position is clarified and fleshed out with questions. Then attack only the position, never the person: "Gena, it sounds like you've thought this out very well. I'm not convinced, however, that the vendor can't perform once he understands what the cost will be if he fails. What was his performance like last year when we had all those rush shipments?"

Play the Devil's Advocate

This technique demonstrates that you are interested in considering what the person has to say, but that you want to make sure all aspects of the truth being presented have been seriously considered, analyzed, and tested. To minimize the truth teller's fear, acknowledge the merits of the proposal or thought he or she is presenting, declare that you are playing devil's advocate, and proceed:

> "Gena, you're probably right that pressuring this vendor may backfire on us, but let me play devil's advocate for a moment. Suppose we threaten to dump him altogether if his quality drops or he misses a delivery date. If you were him, what would you do?"

Create Debate Groups and Reverse Roles

You can minimize Gena's perception that she is being personally attacked and enhance the examination of her proposal by having the team debate its pros and cons. Assign Gena and those who favor her idea to argue against it, and those who are leaning against it to argue in favor. Collect the arguments on a flip chart and weigh them against each other to make a final decision.[4]

Reward Truth Tellers

Principles of behaviorism tell us that what gets rewarded gets repeated. General Electric rewards managers for their candor by including it in their performance reviews. The practice was started by former CEO Jack Welch, who said:

People said just what you said, "How can you put a number on how open people are, on how directly they face reality?" Well, they're going to have to—the best numbers they can come up with, and then we'll argue about them. We have to know if our people are open and self-confident, if they believe in honest communication and quick action, if the people we hired years ago have changed. The only way to test our progress is through regular evaluations at the top and by listening to every audience we appear before in the company.[5]

Rewarding honesty and openness can go further than a financial pat on the back in a review. Speaking the truth will have its own rewards when the speaker knows her message is heard, appreciated, and seriously considered. It is then that people get a deposit in their needs account for going out on a limb and saying what's on their minds.

Consider Ron Jensen, past director of public works for the city of Phoenix, who oversaw the turnaround of that 2,000-person department from an inefficient, problem-plagued organization into a nationally recognized model of municipal operations.

Ron's first step was to post question boxes throughout the organization where anyone could submit questions—signed or anonymous—about any topic. His promise was to publish *all* questions in the department's monthly newsletter, completely unedited (except for the deletion of obscenities), and to answer each candidly. It was sort of like Work-Outs at GE in a written, published format.

In the first month, fewer than ten questions were submitted, and half of those were hostile, often personal attacks. "Why don't you just quit? The city would be better off without you?" was an example. Ron answered them as honestly and candidly as he could. His typical answer? "You're probably right, the city might be better off, but I need the job and I'm on a mission to turn things around, so I'm not going anywhere."

Once workers realized that all questions would be posted and taken seriously, the questions became serious and started pouring in. The size of the newsletter had to be tripled to accommodate them. Along with the questions came suggestions and ideas that had never surfaced before. It was the start of a turnaround that led to the department's winning numerous national awards and being featured in a nationally televised PBS documentary, *Promoting the Common Good—Excellence in the Public Sector.*

What was the reward for all those truthful responses? Simply the courtesy of acknowledgment, the chance for employees to get straight answers, and great strides in efficiency for the department.

Forums that allow people to express their views anonymously encourage people to make suggestions for improvement without fear of retribution. And they open the door for building the trust level that makes anonymity unnecessary. In addition, they establish a stage upon which individual and organizational misdeeds can be exposed and excised. In Chapter 9 we discuss various communication systems that allow people within an organization to report unethical behavior so it can be addressed and corrected before it hits the newspapers or draws inquiry from the law.

STOP WHINING AND COMMIT

The second part of *disagree and commit* is committing. It's a pretty simple concept: Once a decision has been made, don't complain about it or badmouth it—and certainly don't commit *lipotage*. Just do it!

Carrying out the second part can be as tricky as disagreeing. What if the perceived price for disagreeing is so high that you are afraid to speak up? Does that mean you still have to commit? What if new information becomes available that makes the decision wrong? Are you still obligated to support the decision? What if, in thinking about it later, you realize that a decision was morally, ethically, or legally questionable? Are you still obliged to stand by it? What if deception occurred during the discussions—that you and your colleagues were fooled like the Arthur Andersen auditors at Enron claim they were during the 2002 Crisis of Ethics in Business USA? Are you still compelled to support the decision?

We would say "yes" to each question about your responsibilities *unless* you stay aboveboard and take a stand, explaining to the appropriate people that you will not commit and why. To do otherwise is to break your promise, implied or explicit, that you support the decision or action you were involved in creating.

Why People Renege

The reasons people renege on an implied agreement include all the questions just listed, plus some basic issues that go to the heart of the matter.

Perception of Dishonorable Intent

Bruce Nordstrom, one of the founders of the Nordstrom Department Store chain, was asked how he could support a no-questions-asked return policy, given that people would take advantage of it and it would cost the store dearly. His reply was that 95 percent of his customers were honorable people who wouldn't rip him off. He said that he refused to set his return policy to protect him from the 5 percent who would rip him off and risk offending the 95 percent who wouldn't.

We agree. Ninety-five percent of the world's population has an ingrained sense of right and wrong. When they perceive that something is crossing the line, they may not have the intestinal fortitude to stand up and disagree with it, but they will notice and often find ways to resist. Their subversive acts will be the true expression of how they feel.

Perception of Unfairness

"Life is unfair." We've heard this old adage all our lives. And it's true. Very often, life isn't fair. But most of us believe it should be.

In high school, Bob was a star athlete, excelling in football and track. In his freshman year he won enough regional and state track competitions to qualify for a varsity letter—a highly unusual accomplishment. At the end of the season, however, Bob's coach refused to award him the letter because there were upperclassmen who had not gotten a varsity letter yet. So even though none of them had as many victories as Bob, he had to wait a year for his letter in track. From Bob's perspective, this was the height of unfairness. To get even, Bob played baseball instead of running track his senior year, the year he would very likely have been a serious contender for the state championship. His track coach was furious. To this day, Bob remembers how good that felt.

Now you may be saying, "Hey, Bob, get over it! It was a long time ago. Besides, who ever said life was fair?" And you would be right. On the other hand, are there not injustices in your life that still bother you? Your little sister got a new bike and you didn't? A scoutmaster chose his favorite scout to represent the troop at a regional powwow—and it wasn't you? A coworker with inferior skills got a job you deserved? You were passed over for a promotion because of your race, gender, age, or disability—or because the boss just didn't like you? And to this day, it galls you that it ever happened.

One of life's great conundrums is that even though we *know* life isn't always fair, we cling to the notion that it *should be*—and so we expect it to be. When it proves otherwise, there is little that upsets us more. Given the chance, most of us will do something to set the scales of justice right.

In a study of nineteen companies, W. Chan and Renee Mauborgne found a direct link between perceptions of fairness and behavior. "Managers who believed the company's processes were fair displayed a high level of trust and commitment, which in turn, engendered active cooperation. Conversely, when managers felt fair process was absent, they hoarded ideas and dragged their feet." They also found that "individuals are most likely to trust and cooperate freely with

systems—whether they themselves win or lose by those systems—
when fair process is observed."[6]

These conclusions were reflected in the example we offered in
Chapter 1 of the nursing home whose staff tattled to the licensing
inspector, thus putting themselves out of a job—just to even the score
with the administrator who had treated them so unfairly in order to
cut costs. Revenge is a powerful emotion.

Compare that example with another nursing home, Scottsdale
Convalescent Plaza (SCP) in Scottsdale, Arizona. It was summer-
time, which for health care facilities in Arizona means the dreaded
summer doldrums. Occupied bed counts in hospitals, nursing homes,
and convalescent centers plummet as residents and families head for
cooler weather. For SCP it meant dealing with drastically declining
revenues and the need to cut costs.

In most organizations like this, cost cutting means limiting the
amount of extras offered to residents, reducing staffing patterns, and
laying off employees. These painful procedures are usually devised
and implemented by management—and resented and resisted by employees.

Vicki McAllister, executive director of SCP at the time, decided
to address the problem differently. She created two twenty-person
operations teams consisting of department managers, nurses, nursing
assistants, housekeepers, dietary aides, accounting personnel, maintenance people, social service staff, activities personnel, and medical
records staff. She asked them to create a plan to reduce costs by 50
percent for the summer season. She also asked that quality of care
for the residents remain at the same high level.

It was a challenge the teams embraced with relish. After much
soul searching, intensive discussion, and open sharing, the teams recommended:

- Halting the use of nursing pools
- Reducing the workday to six hours per day for all nonnursing,
  nonrespiratory departments

▲ Cutting back on nursing overtime hours

▲ Closing down treatment units and redistributing staff and residents

This last solution was remarkable because it came from the people that operated the unit to be dismantled, a longstanding team that enjoyed the highest morale and camaraderie in the organization.

According to Ms. McCallister, the results were phenomenal. The staff cooperated fully with the draconian changes recommended by the committees. Although they had resisted and grumbled about much milder measures in previous summers, this time they even volunteered to work extra shifts to make up for short staffing. For the first summer in the organization's history, SCP was able to cut costs enough to operate in the black.

When Larry asked Ms. McCallister why she thought the staff was so willing to accept the committees' recommendations, she replied that even though they couldn't all be part of the process, they had unanimously felt that it was fair.

This is not to say that every decision must be consensus by committee. Research has shown that decisions that are unilateral, autocratic, and even arbitrary will be accepted, embraced, and supported by employees if employees believe the decisions have been arrived at fairly—even if those decisions adversely affect them.[7] In our experience, the best way to ensure that perception is to be open with employees about how decisions are made, including what reasoning went into them, what the pros and cons were, and what tipped the scale in favor of the direction that was chosen.

Such openness can also lower the odds that the organization will slip into unsavory, unethical, or illegal activities. Had there been regular, open and honest discussions with all employees about company profits, losses, investments, and business practices at Adelphia Communications during the 2002 Crisis of Ethics in Business USA, maybe someone would have questioned the $2.3 billion in off-balance-sheet loans that the company granted to founder John Rigas and his family. As it was, Rigas went to jail, but not until the company had filed for Chapter Eleven bankruptcy and its stockholders had lost billions.

Perception of a Sham

Leaders have a variety of processes to choose from when making a decision—autocratic, consultative, participative, and consensual.[8] For decisions that require little more than technical expertise, the autocratic or consultative approach is usually preferable.

For example, the president of a mortgage company may choose one secondary market vendor over another, based on the rates and services provided. She may consult with her vice president of finance, but there would be no reason for her to pull her management team together to discuss it. And to create a task force of frontline loan officers to analyze the situation and produce recommendations would be an absurd waste of their time and energy.

On the other hand, she would be well advised to pull that task force together to make recommendations on changing the role and scope of duties for a loan officer. The difference is that, in the first case, she had the expertise to make the decision, and its success did not depend on capturing the hearts and minds of people who would have to carry out her decision. In the case of changing the role of a loan officer, garnering the support of those loan officers is critical to the success of the change. In that case, seeking recommendations through participation and consensus is the logical choice.

This does not mean that she has to accept the task force's recommendations for its members and their peers to accept and commit to her final choice. But if she does not, they must be able to understand her reasoning for not accepting their recommendations and know that they were seriously considered. Again, it gets back to a perception of fairness. Scholars call this "procedural justice."[9]

When people discover that the leader was simply going through the motions to appear to be asking for consensus, when all along the decision was already made, the price of noncommitment will be high. As we've said earlier, people hate to be deceived and used. It insults their intelligence and their dignity, and they will make the leader pay.

Perception of Being Powerless

Unless you are chairman of the board or CEO of your company, you will often be faced with decisions made by those above you that you do not agree with. You weren't consulted, but now you have to live with it and it ticks you off.

We recommend applying what we call the PAL approach. PAL is like a practical application of the Serenity Prayer used by Alcoholics Anonymous and other twelve-step recovery groups:

> God grant me the serenity to accept the things I
>   cannot change;
> courage to change the things I can;
> and wisdom to know the difference.

> *—Reinhold Niebuhr*

When life deals you a hand you don't like, whether it's a management decision that's unpalatable, a boss who is unethical, a spouse who nags you, or a meal that is inedible, you have three, and only three, healthy options: Positive Change, Acceptance/Embracing, or Leaving.

P   Your first option is *positive change:* Do something to change what you don't like. Take action that will effect a difference. Present a proposal that proves there's a better way for your company to go. Let your boss know you won't go along with his unethical behavior, or go to his manager and spill the beans. Refuse to accept your spouse's nagging or get the two of you into counseling. Send that meal back to the kitchen or walk out of the restaurant. Just *do* something.

A Sometimes positive change works and sometimes it doesn't. Sometimes there are things you can't change. Decisions you can't affect. People you can't influence. A spouse who won't change. A meal you have to eat because you're starving and don't have time to go anywhere else. In those cases, your next healthy choice in life is to *accept or embrace* what you don't like, understanding that there are some things in life we can't change, or we're not willing to invest the time and energy to do so.

For example, as organizational consultants, we travel a great deal. We appreciate the importance of airport security procedures, especially since 9/11. But those procedures are still a hassle we don't like to endure. Would it be worth our time and energy to try to change them? Obviously not. So we accept them (not always gracefully!) and we don't complain, even while being put through the annoyance of a pat-down and body search. It would do us no good, so why object?

You may be saying, "Hey, aren't there are some things you absolutely should never accept, even if you can't change them?" Of course there are. Some issues are worth fighting to the death over, both figuratively and actually. For example, James Alderson was a financial officer with a hospital in Whitefish, Montana, that was managed by Quorum Health Resources Inc. In 1993 he was dismissed from his job soon after refusing to follow the company's cost-reporting tactics, which he considered illegal.[10] He joined the U.S. government in a lawsuit against Quorum and its parent company, Columbia/HCA.

In October 2000, Quorum agreed to pay the government $95.5 million in civil penalties to settle two lawsuits that accused it of defrauding federal health care programs like Medicare. Columbia/HCA agreed to pay $745 million.[11] Although it cost him his job, Alderson's courage to speak up put the health care industry on notice that Medicare and Medicaid would not tolerate fraudulent billing.[12] Hats off to Mr. Alderson. We can only wish that he had been the head of the Arthur Andersen audit team at Enron back in 2002.

L If you can't or won't apply positive change to what you don't like, and if you can't or won't accept or embrace it, the only healthy option that remains is *leaving.* Sometimes this is your best way to go. Not every job situation is right for everyone. Life is too short to spend your precious time fighting battles you can't win or trying to mesh personalities that won't mesh. The relationship between employees and employers is like marriage—there are times when divorce can be therapeutic for both parties.

Our major concern is with people who, in the face of a situation they don't like or don't want, fail to choose one of these three healthy options. They're known as the whiners, the moaners, the complainers, the "lipotagers" who won't do anything constructive to resolve the source of their disgruntlement—but will talk about it to anyone who will listen. We think of them as the "people who light up a room when they leave it."

PAL—Positive Change, Acceptance/Embracing, Leaving—gives people perspective and helps them choose the battles they can win without wasting time and energy on those they are almost certain to lose. It is a tool you can offer everyone in your organization to help them overcome their own perceptions of powerlessness.

WHAT LEADERS CAN DO TO ENCOURAGE COMMITMENT

Leaders can create a culture of commitment by addressing the three major reasons people don't commit.

Perception of Dishonorable Intent

As Bob's son would have said when he was a teenager, "This one's a no-brainer." If it looks, smells, or feels unethical, dishonorable, or illegal, don't do it. The real litmus test is: Would you be proud to tell your son or daughter what you are doing? Would you want them to repeat the act?

Likewise, would you want your employees to model their behavior after yours? Do they know where you stand on issues like truth, honesty, and forthrightness so they *can* model themselves after you? Creating a published set of core values that includes these virtues is a good first step. Living and preaching those core values every day raises the odds your employees will follow the same path.

In his 1963 booklet, *A Business and Its Beliefs,* Thomas J. Watson, Jr., former IBM chief executive, said:

> I firmly believe that any organization, in order to survive and achieve success, must have a sound set of beliefs on which it premises all its policies and actions. Next, I believe that the most important single factor in corporate success is faithful adherence to those beliefs. . . . Beliefs must always come before policies, practices, and goals. The latter must always be altered if they are seen to violate fundamental beliefs.[13]

Of course, it's important that those values are worthy of your followers' respect. In 1973, Ford Motor Company became engulfed in a firestorm of lawsuits over its failure to install safety features that would keep Ford Pintos from exploding when involved in rear-end collisions. A cost-benefit analysis prepared by Ford environmental and safety engineers estimated that if left unfixed, Pintos and Ford Light Trucks would cause 180 burn deaths, 180 serious burn injuries, and 2,100 burned vehicles, which would result in $49.5 million in legal damages. They calculated that the cost of correcting the fault in the fuel system that caused the problem would be $11 per vehicle, or $137.5 million total.[14] So Ford executives decided *not* to make the repairs.

Can you imagine being one of the engineers who was privy to the

reasoning behind this decision? Assuming that you have a high regard for human life, you certainly would have been appalled to see
that your leadership was willing to sacrifice so many lives and cause
so much suffering in order to save $11 per car. You may have gone
along with the decision, fearing that if you blew the whistle, you
would suffer the fate of most other whistle-blowers. But your view of
your executives surely would have become jaded, at the least. And
the likelihood that you would enthusiastically support other management decisions? Probably poor. Your perception of their dishonorable intent would simply be too great.

So the bottom line for avoiding this perception is to have a published set of worthwhile values, and to live by them. In Chapter 8,
we suggest some. In the meantime, simply doing the right thing and
not engaging in illegal or immoral acts is a good start. Like we said,
this one's a "no-brainer." Too bad the corporate crooks of 2002
didn't get it.

Perception of Unfairness—Explain the Big Picture

Allowing people to have input into decisions through participation
and consensus raises the odds that they will feel the decisions are
fair. At the same time, autocratic and consultative decisions can also
be perceived as fair. The trick is making sure that lines of communication are open and that everyone understands the "why" of decisions as well as the "what." This means the leader must articulate
the reasons for her decisions and how those decisions support the
company's mission, goals, and objectives.

We're reminded of a scene in the movie *Saving Private Ryan.* The
platoon, led by Tom Hanks's character, has been ordered to find
Private Ryan, who is somewhere in the French countryside in the
days following D-Day. The platoon comes upon the bodies of some
GIs who were apparently ambushed by a German machine gun nest
perched at the top of a hill. When Hanks orders his men to take the

hill, some of them object, reminding him that their objective was to find Private Ryan, not to take this hill. Hanks retorts, "I thought our objective was to win the war." Then he turns and heads up the hill with his men following close behind.

When people understand the bigger picture and that the bigger picture fits with what they believe to be right and beneficial, the strongest reluctance can be overcome.

Perception of a Sham—Only Ask If You Want to Hear

Here's another "no-brainer." Obviously, the best antidote for this one is to not ask people for input unless you plan to seriously consider what they have to offer.

It's possible you may have had the best of intentions when you solicited input or sought collaboration, but for sound business reasons, you have now decided that you will take a different direction than the recommended course. In such cases, it is imperative that you take the time and spend the energy to explain to all those who participated why you've chosen to do so. Nature abhors a vacuum and, absent your explanation, people will often assume the worst and decide that your request was a sham. So beware!

Perception of Being Powerless—Promote Positive Change

Given the three healthy choices that we offered earlier (PAL), providing people with opportunities to exercise the first option, *positive change*, increases the likelihood that they will commit to what they have agreed to. One way to promote this approach is by providing a realistic picture of what can or can't be changed. Here's an exercise that you can do with your people:

> ▲ Ask your group to brainstorm a list of things about their jobs
>   that bothers them.

▲ Explain the **PAL** (Positive Change–Acceptance/Embracing–Leaving) concept.

▲ Have them put a **P** by those items they think they might be able to change. Have them put an **A** by those items they are sure they can't change and will have to accept. Have them put an **L** by those items (hopefully very few) that they will eventually quit over if things don't improve.

▲ Lead a discussion of everyone's responses. Allow people to not discuss any item on their lists, but remind them that if they don't bring it up, for whatever reason, they have made a choice to accept. And *lipotage* is not allowed. (They can also discuss it outside the meeting, in private with the person or persons best suited to help them resolve the problem, if that's more comfortable for them.)

The point here is to help people understand that there are some things that can be changed and some that can't. This seems like common sense, but if it's so common, why do so many people complain about what can't be changed and do nothing about what can?

CREATING A CULTURAL NORM OF *DISAGREE AND COMMIT*

The Law of Disagree and Commit requires everyone in the organization to express his or her opinions openly and clearly, even if those opinions contradict the group. Then, once a decision is made, all are expected to support it. When this attitude becomes common practice in an organization, whining declines and cooperation increases. To facilitate this happening, here are nine actions you, the leader, can take:

1. Clarify the ground rules for disagreement, including when it is acceptable and how best to express it. The steps for constructive confrontation described in Chapter 4 can provide a framework for these ground rules.

2. Practice "disagree and commit" yourself. Confront, challenge, and contradict as a way of exposing information that will help make a decision, making sure you follow the ground rules for disagreement. Ask tough but stimulating questions. Commit to decisions that you disagree with to model the behavior you expect from others.

3. Communicate to the organization that "disagree and commit" is the "law of the land." Establish guidelines for all meetings that promote "disagree and commit" as essential to productive dialogues. Reward the truth tellers and those who disagree.

4. Create opportunities for people to express their opinions, be heard, and be taken seriously. This includes opportunities for off-line communication through an "open-door" policy, written opinions, and other vehicles.

5. Make sure people feel that their voices are heard and taken seriously. Practice intense listening, whether one-on-one or in meetings, to validate everyone's contributions. Explain decisions that people have disagreed with to acknowledge their contributions and to explain why the decisions were made.

6. Include "disagree and commit" in new-employee recruiting and orientation. If you hire and train people to speak up when they have something to say, you will institutionalize "disagree and commit."[15]

7. Weave "disagree and commit" into your values statement. An example of how this has been done is the Leadership Code at New York Fasteners: "We give each other permission to challenge each other, even if it makes one of us uncomfortable. We are here to help, not judge."

8. Practice and preach PAL. At every opportunity, communicate the need to consider the three healthy options for moving forward. This includes verbalizing your thinking when you are weighing those options in your mind so that those you are leading can learn how to apply PAL.

9. Make the PAL principle part of the new "law of the land." By promoting PAL, you are letting people know that whining, ignoring, backstabbing, and other methods of sabotaging plans and decisions will not be tolerated.

THE BRUTAL FACTS OF GREATNESS

During the analysis of their research into how good companies became great companies, Jim Collins and his research team struggled to understand why some companies succeeded whereas others did not. One day, Collins suggested to his team that the good-to-great companies embraced what he called the Stockdale Paradox.[16]

Admiral Jim Stockdale was tortured more than twenty times in the eight years he was imprisoned during the Vietnam War. He survived by believing he would prevail, regardless of the difficulties, *and at the same time* confronting the most brutal facts of his reality. As Collins and his team discussed this paradox, they realized that it helped them understand the companies they were comparing. In each industry, two competitors believed they would prevail, but only one confronted the brutal facts of its reality. And that company became great.

The goal of disagreeing and committing is to clarify and confront reality so that the organization can prevail. Leaders like Jack Welch and Bob Galvin understood the need for tough questions, for constructive confrontation about critical issues, and for candid debates about all sides of key issues. In a complex and rapidly changing marketplace, no company can afford to ignore the brutal facts that can threaten or secure its survival. Successful leaders promote disagreement until those brutal facts are known and then commit to a course of action that helps them prevail.

As the great companies know, wishing and hoping are no substitute for knowing and acting.

CHAPTER 6

Absolute Honesty Law #4:

Welcome the Truth

"Even a paranoid can have enemies."

—*HENRY KISSINGER*

TED HAD RECENTLY COME TO WORK FOR CYBRO GAMES, WHICH
had recruited him from RST Graphics, a smaller, but very successful competitor. At RST, Ted had been the lead creative designer for a line of highly profitable products, which was why
Cybro Games recruited him so aggressively.

It was a difficult decision for Ted. He liked the special treatment that his successes earned him at RST. He could decide the
direction of most of his projects; he didn't have to follow the
usual rules to get his products approved; and best of all, he loved
the way his coworkers, his manager, and all the executives
treated him with rock star reverence.

But Cybro Games had offered him a much bigger compensation package. More important, he would have the opportu-

nity to work with advanced technology and products that RST could not offer. So he made the switch.

Ted had been with his new employer about three months when he submitted his first formal product proposal to William, the new products team leader. William wasn't Ted's direct manager, but William had almost absolute power over which products were released to market, which meant he had a great deal of influence on Ted's success at Cybro Games.

Ted had already figured out that he and William saw things differently. While Ted was a big-picture idea guy, William seemed more concerned with details and minutiae. From the first day, every time Ted ran a new idea by William, William shot it down, finding fault with Ted's logic or saying that they just weren't ready for an approach that radical.

Ted wasn't used to a negative reaction to his ideas, and after three months, he was getting frustrated. Since this was his first formal proposal, he wanted it to go well. He did extra research, making sure that his documentation was complete. He didn't want William to have anything to complain about.

A week later, William dropped the proposal on Ted's desk and said, "Sorry, guy, this just does not cut it. You should have done better research and gotten more data to support your design and marketing plan."

With blood rising in his cheeks and adrenaline coursing through his veins, Ted retorted in a caustic tone, "For your information, I spent over a month researching this product and I know it will fly. I can just feel it."

"Well," replied William, his voice rising, "we need more than just feelings to launch a new product. Market research has to support it or it's a no-go!"

"Maybe if you got your head out of your calculator, you'd see there's more to product success than numbers," Ted retorted. "You remember New Coke? All the numbers geeks like you said it would fly and it took a huge dive. But, fine, I'll rework the numbers." He made this last statement with the vocal intonation of a petulant child.

While Ted was understandably upset by William's criticism, his defensiveness, coupled with the personal attack on William, did not win him points or enhance his chances of getting his proposals approved. More important, if his proposal really was a winner, the company would suffer from Ted's failure to get it considered more seriously.

The tendency to respond to criticism defensively is an ingrained reaction that is difficult to overcome—mainly because we are genetically programmed to do it. Our ancestors learned to survive perceived danger with a flight-or-fight response. Those who froze in the presence of a saber-toothed tiger became tiger lunch. Those who fled from the tiger, or stuck the tiger with a spear, lived to pass their genes along to us. We're hardwired to defend ourselves by fighting or fleeing.

In the organizations in which we work, of course, when someone challenges or criticizes us, we can't just stick him with a spear, and running away resolves nothing. So we often resort to *symbolic spear sticking* like the barbs Ted lobbed at William when he accused William of being a numbers geek with his head in his calculator.

Of course, maybe Ted was being too sensitive. After all, it was William's job to make sure company resources were well spent. But it was also his job as a leader to bring out the best in Ted. If Ted continues to feel attacked and, in turn, continues to fight back, their relationship will quickly sour. Both of them need to change their approaches.

DEFENSIVENESS: THE ENEMY OF HONESTY

There is something I don't know that I am supposed to know.
　　I don't know *what* it is I don't know, and yet am supposed
　　to know,

and feel I look stupid
   if I seem both not to know it
   and not know *what* it is I don't know.
Therefore I pretend I know it.
   This is nerve-racking
   since I don't know what I must pretend to know.
Therefore, I pretend to know everything.

—*R.D. Laing,* Knots[1]

Psychologists have identified nine basic defense mechanisms that we use to replace the spearing and fleeing our ancestors employed.[2] Unlike our ancestors' defense mechanisms, however, these mechanisms are not designed to protect our lives so much as to protect our own sense of self-worth. Since much of our self-worth is based on how we want others to think of us,[3] those attacks that we think diminish us in the eyes of others will be the attacks we most vigorously defend against.

For example, do you know someone who has a powerful need to always be right? Have you noticed that in a heated discussion, she will argue the loudest and longest over the tiniest detail in order to prove a point, whether or not the detail is germane to the topic? Her arguments are more about maintaining her image of perfection to the outside world than making contributions to the discussion.

Or consider a person who has a powerful need to be liked. In a heated debate, he always agrees with the majority or just keeps quiet—both strategies designed to feed his need for acceptance by others. Neither strategy, however, helps the discussion move toward a fruitful outcome.

The cost of defensiveness can be high. It undermines the authenticity of our relationships and reduces the odds that truth and honesty will dominate our conversations. At the very least, it tends to derail discussions, as we saw with Ted and William. We think it's worth a closer look at these mechanisms and at changes of behavior that can produce more positive results.

In their treatise on interpersonal communication, *Looking Out, Looking In,*[4] Ronald B. Adler and Neil Towne identify nine basic defense mechanisms:

1. Verbal aggression
2. Sarcasm
3. Rationalization
4. Compensation
5. Regression
6. Avoidance
7. Repression
8. Apathy
9. Displacement

Verbal Aggression

This reaction frequently occurs during heated arguments where the gloves are off. In an executive staff meeting, the sales manager criticizes the manufacturing manager because her department botched an order. Although the criticism is valid, her immediate response is to accuse the salespeople of submitting faulty paperwork. That's *verbal aggression*. It begs the question of whether or not manufacturing owns the problem, and it postpones any efforts to solve it.

Sarcasm

Ted's sarcastic comment about William being a numbers geek only served to alienate William and distance both men from a solution to the problem. Not that all sarcasm is bad. In the give-and-take of human interactions, good-natured sarcasm can be an indicator of healthy relationships. Teams, especially all male teams, with high trust levels will often razz each other about everything from job abilities to sexual prowess—all in good fun. It's when the sarcasm is biting and hostile that it becomes a defense mechanism to avoid the truth.

Rationalization

This defense mechanism is the birth mother of excuses. It takes the blame off the person being attacked and says, "It's not my fault." If Ted had chosen *rationalization* to defend himself, he might have said, "I tried to get the data, but the information that will really tell us if our customers will buy something this radical is just not there, and probably never will be."

Compensation

Another option for the person who thinks he's being attacked is to compensate by offering other strengths in place of the weakness for which he's being criticized. "Gosh, William, you know I'm an idea guy. I come up with winners. Someone else needs to validate them."

Regression

Regression implies that we move back into a childlike, nonadult state, taking no responsibility for our part in the drama. If Ted had chosen *regression*, he would have thrown up his hands and said, "Oh, that numbers stuff. I just don't understand it. I know what I know, and what I know is that this product will fly. Let someone else worry about the numbers."

Avoidance

One way to deal with unpleasantness is to not deal with it. Examples include the CEO who knows she has a problem with employee morale but refuses to acknowledge it, the husband or wife who suspects his or her spouse is having an affair but maintains a front that nothing is wrong, the supervisor who won't act when an employee is underperforming, and the corporate board member who looks the other way while the CEO makes obscenely large loans to himself from the company's treasury.

Repression

Blocking information we don't want to hear or acknowledge to ourselves is repression. It's like taking *avoidance* to a new level. You not only avoid thinking about or dealing with some unpleasantness, you actually push it into your unconsciousness so it seems to not exist. A *Financial Times* investigation into the collapse of twenty-five large U.S. corporations found their top management amassed $3.3 billion from share sales, payoffs, and other rewards during the period from 1999 to 2001. To our knowledge, none of these individuals have admitted publicly to any wrongdoing, even though their behavior and business practices suggest that they were nothing more than common thieves who were smart enough to pull off unusually large scores. Of course, to do so would place them in legal and financial jeopardy. Failing to admit such truth to themselves, however, places them in psychological and moral jeopardy and is what repression is all about. Our guess is that in their own minds, they did nothing wrong.

Apathy

This defense mechanism is characterized by an "I don't care" response to unpleasant situations. It helps us to maintain our image of self-worth by saying, "If I don't care, then I can't really be held responsible." For example, we know a young man who has been fired from six jobs since graduating from college two years ago. His comment when we asked him about it was, "It doesn't matter. None of those jobs were what I really want to do with my career. I would have quit anyway."

Displacement

We displace criticism when we take unpleasant information about ourselves and place it on someone else. We blame others for our shortcomings. As we saw in 2002, it is not uncommon for CEO's whose companies have engaged in illegal or immoral business practices to blame their staff, their auditors, their lawyers, their partners—anyone but themselves for the actions of their companies. Ted could have practiced displacement by claiming that the marketing department hadn't given him adequate numbers or accusing William of having it in for him. *Displacement* can also include redirecting anger from the party you're mad at to someone less threatening. The manager who chews out her administrative assistant when she is angry with her boss is practicing *displacement.*

The irony of these nine defense mechanisms is that the closer the perceived criticism is to the truth, the more likely they will be used. As the psychotherapist Karen Horney once said, "We do not need confirmation for qualities of which we are certain, but we will be extremely touchy when false claims are questioned."[5] Or as Shakespeare wrote in *Hamlet,* "The lady doth protest too much, methinks."

For example, if a nurse is insecure about his ability to track medications, criticizing him for that part of his job is more likely to draw *verbal aggression* or *compensation* than would criticism of something he does well and feels secure about.

Consider Arthur Andersen CEO Joseph Berardino who, when questioned before Congress about Andersen's involvement in the collapse of the Baptist Foundation of Arizona as well as Andersen's allegedly fraudulent accounting practices at Sunbeam, Waste Management, and Asia Pulp and Paper, responded, "We are human beings, and we do not get it right all the time,"[6]—essentially saying, "It's not my fault" and "I'm not responsible." We're not psychiatrists, but this sure looks like a classic example of both *denial* and *regression* to us.

Or consider the executives at Ford who chose to not fix the Pin-to's fuel tank. To face the reality of what they were doing would have required that they admit to themselves they were behaving like monsters of the worst kind, putting them in the same category of evil as the Nazis during World War II. It's hard for us to imagine them being able to do that without engaging in some form of *repression*.

REASONS FOR DEFENSIVENESS

Since the use of defense mechanisms tends to derail or diminish the quality of tough conversations, it seems wise to keep them from creeping into our interactions as much as possible. Let's start by examining why they occur. We've found four common arenas that trigger defensiveness:

1. Power clashes
2. Colliding personal styles
3. Differing points of view
4. Actual attacks

Power Clashes

Experts have identified six basic types of power that people commonly use to influence other people and outcomes in organizations:[7]

▲ *Coercive power* is based on the followers' perception that the wielder of the power can and will cause them pain if they don't comply with his requests.

▲ *Reward power* is based on the followers' perception that the wielder can and will reward them for compliance to requests.

▲ *Legitimate power* is based on followers having decided that the wielder has the right to tell them what to do.

▲ *Referent power* is based on the followers' desire to identify
with a charismatic wielder.

▲ *Expert power* is based on the followers' acknowledgment that
the wielder has special knowledge or expertise that can be
useful to them.

▲ *Representative power* is based on the followers having demo-
cratically delegated power to the wielder to look out for their
interests.

Supervisors, managers, executives, and the specially anointed are
usually sanctioned by the organization to wield the first two, *coercive
power* and *reward power.* Everyone, on the other hand, can wield the
remaining four. For example, though he never had official authority
or sanction, Mahatma Gandhi rallied his people to expel the British
from India by wielding the *referent power* his charisma brought him
and the *legitimate power* his followers bestowed upon him.

As we've moved from an industrial/labor-driven economy to a
digital/knowledge-driven economy, the importance of these last four
powers, especially *expert power,* has grown. Today, the value of a
company lies more in the brainpower of its employees than in the
worth of its hard assets. The "boss" can no longer know everything
there is to know or make all the decisions. The work is too complicated.

Companies like Hewlett Packard, McKinsey Consulting, IBM,
and Intel have officially recognized the importance of expert power
by creating meritocracies where people are recognized and rewarded
for their expertise and their contribution to the success of the company, rather than for their ability to climb the corporate ladder.
Here's a description, taken from Intel's recruitment page on excite.-
com's career service Web site:

Intel has a very particular culture—on the one hand empha-
sizing egalitarianism and meritocracy, on the other hand

bestowing upon its insiders featureless cubicles and a healthy dose of paranoia. Insiders say "Intel is a flexible meritocracy. They increase responsibilities of people who show they can do the work and want to do more. Raises and promotions are also based on meritocracy.[8]

Intel, and most other companies that endorse the meritocracy concept, do so for two major reasons. First, it helps ensure that the best ideas rise to the top. Second, it raises the odds that its best and brightest employees will stay motivated and remain with the company, whether or not they enter the ranks of management and the specially anointed.

In companies where hierarchy rules and politics are more prevalent, this is rarely the case. When a disagreement arises between an officially sanctioned wielder of *coercive* or *reward power* versus a non-sanctioned wielder of *expert power* or *referent power*, official sanction usually wins.

That may have been the case with Ted and William. Ted may have been reacting to his perception that William was trying to lord over him with his *officially sanctioned power* at the expense of Ted's *expert power*. William could have minimized Ted's defensiveness by taking time to listen to Ted's thoughts and to validate them and Ted's expert status. He could then have explained his concerns and asked Ted for what he needed:

Ted, it looks like you've got a great idea here. It's probably just what we need to get the jump on Gizmo, Inc. You obviously know a lot about what works out there in the market and I want to work on this with you. But I'm hesitant to jump into it until we can see some more validating data, especially in the emerging retirement market. Do you have any ideas on how we could get it?

Naming the Game. To function at their best, people need to know the limitations of their freedom to act. Consultant Steve Rayner illustrates the point with an observation about a section of the Oregon coastline where a cliff drops hundreds of feet to the rocks below. Half is unfenced and unmarked. The other half has a sturdy railing along the edge to keep people from stepping over. As people approach the unfenced section, they step cautiously, never taking their eyes off the edge, focusing all their energy on making sure they don't fall. Where there is a railing, people approach the precipice without hesitation, focusing their energy on the view and getting good camera shots. Often, they will even lean over the railing to see the ocean below.

Steve makes the point that when people know the limitations of how far they can go before they will fall, they can better use their creative energies. When those limits are unclear, they waste time and energy trying to figure out where the danger zone is.

In business, this means clarifying the rules of the game. As a new employee, Ted was unfamiliar with how formal product-approval processes worked. If William had explained the purpose of the meeting and the roles each of them would play, Ted might not have expected to have *carte blanche* to launch products as he could with his previous employer. Once clued in, Ted might have been less likely to react as if he were being personally attacked.

For example, before Ted submitted his proposal, William might have said something like:

Hey Ted, I just want to prepare you. When I review your proposal, I'll probably have a lot of questions and suggestions. Please don't feel like you're being picked on. It's my job to be the detail cop, so don't feel like it's personal. It's just the way things are done around here.

Our guess is, if William had taken this approach, Ted would have responded less defensively and they could have worked together to make progress on the proposal.

Ray Zapp, past CEO of Atlas Telecom, told us that when managers with *official authority* and experts wielding *unofficial influence* butted heads in their product development meetings, heated debates would ensue, which he applauded because he felt the conflict led to greater creativity and better products. But he made sure everyone knew that at the end of the day, the "golden rule" applied; that is, "He with the gold rules—and the senior manager at the meeting had the gold." He said that clarifying this rule helped everyone know their decision-making limitations and kept the arguments in the meetings from infecting other work.

Colliding Personal Styles

Seth searched for a way to tell his boss, Diane, that one of the team's suppliers was about to miss an important delivery deadline. He knew from past experience that Diane's anger was something to avoid at all costs. He also knew that Diane would blame him for the delay, implying that if he'd been tougher and less accommodating, the supplier wouldn't have dared to be late. Dreading one of Diane's famous tirades, Seth put off telling her the news as he tried to figure out how to sweeten the story so she'd be less likely to erupt. Meanwhile, Diane had heard that something was not right with the project and intended to "kick some butt" at the afternoon meeting. She would make the members of her team understand that in this competitive business, "You've got to have a 'take no prisoners' attitude toward suppliers, or you just don't survive. If Seth doesn't have the guts to do it, I'll find someone who does."

Everyone has a style of communicating that is uniquely his or her own. Some are like Diane—direct, blunt, outspoken, and to the point—whereas others are more like Seth—indirect, circumspect, tactful, and reticent. Some people concern themselves with getting to the truth, regardless of who it hurts; others place the maintenance of relationships above all else; and still others care only about looking good.

A great deal of research and discussion on the subject exists in the literature, and many researchers have developed various models, each with a different twist.[9]

Ours is in Figures 6-1, 6-2, and 6-3. Imagine a continuum that represents how people relate to and influence others (Figure 6-1). At one end are those who tend to be low assertive in their approach to getting their way, and at the other end are those who tend to be high assertive. Low-assertive people tend to use a quiet, indirect, questioning approach to influence others. High-assertive people tend to use a more forceful, direct approach to influence.

Those who are closer to the middle of the continuum exhibit modified degrees of either characteristic.

Now imagine a continuum (Figure 6-2) that describes how people solve problems and make decisions. At one end are those who tend to rely on facts and data. We call them "fact oriented." At the other end are those who rely on intuition and feeling. We call them "feeling oriented."

Fact-oriented people will ask for data when making decisions and usually incorporate the data into whichever outcome they pick. Feeling-oriented people will go with their gut and often use data to support what they have already chosen, based on their feelings.

Where would you place yourself on each of these scales?

You can then take these two continuums and place them perpendicular to one another to create four quadrants (Figure 6-3) that

Figure 6-1. Getting One's Way.

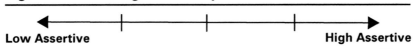

Low Assertive   High Assertive

Figure 6-2. Making Decisions.

Fact   Feeling
Oriented   Oriented

Figure 6-3. Personal Styles Grid.

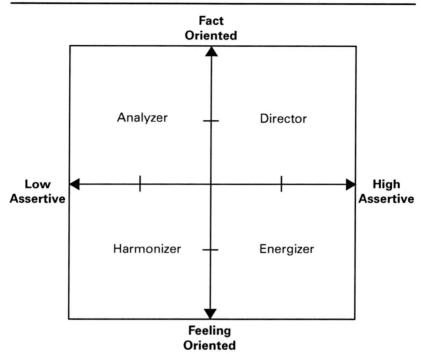

represent combinations of the two continuums. We've given these combinations the names:

▲ *Director:* Fact oriented, high assertive

▲ *Analyzer:* Fact oriented, low assertive

▲ *Harmonizer:* Feeling oriented, low assertive

▲ *Energizer:* Feeling oriented, high assertive

Directors. Directors tend to make decisions quickly based on the available facts. They often operate on the assumption that it is better to make a bad decision and fix it later than to not decide. Their work space is often utilitarian, without a lot of clutter, organized efficiently to get the work done.

Directors usually have a powerful need to be in charge and have no problem telling others what to do. While their strength lies in their can-do, take-charge approach, others might perceive them as pushy and overbearing. Directors find indecision and indirectness on the part of others to be very frustrating. They like people to get to the point and tell it straight.

Analyzers. Analyzers tend to make decisions slowly, based on as much information as possible. Their attitude is that it is better to take the time to make the right choice than to blunder into a mistake. Their work space tends to be neat and organized. They sometimes struggle with delegation because they believe, "if you want something done right, do it yourself." In lieu of doing it themselves, they are often tempted to micromanage those to whom they have delegated.

Analyzers often have a powerful need to be right. While their strength lies in their attention to detail and the superb quality of their work, others may perceive them as picky, overly analytical, and even anal. Analyzers find disorganization and lack of planning in others to be very frustrating.

Harmonizers. Harmonizers tend to make decisions by seeking inclusion and the approval of others. They often operate on the assumption that a good decision is one that everyone supports. Their work space tends to be comfortable, warm, and cozy, with lots of pictures of family and friends. They tend to be perceived as "easygoing and friendly."

Harmonizers often have a powerful need to avoid conflict and to feel that everyone is getting along. Consequently, they can delegate to and work well with others but may have trouble confronting those to whom they've delegated when there is a problem. While their strength lies in their ability to build trusting and warm relationships, others may see them as weak and easy to take advantage of. Harmonizers do not like to be pushed or bullied.

Energizers. Energizers tend to be outgoing, life-of-the-party types who love being the center of attention. They are comfortable making decisions quickly and will often base these decisions on the emotions of the moment. Their work space tends to be attractively decorated with pictures of themselves prominently displayed.

Energizers can delegate when they need to and can confront problems when they arise. Because of their tendency to operate from their feelings, if they engage in a confrontational conversation or discuss a difficult issue, they may allow the conversation to escalate into an emotional battle. While their strength lies in their ability to motivate others with their energy and enthusiasm, they can be perceived as self-centered showboaters. People who are quiet or overly critical annoy them.

In which quadrant do you find yourself? For most of us, one quadrant does not adequately cover all the approaches we take. For example, your dominant style may be that of a director, but you may also have strengths, to a lesser degree, within one or more of the other three. For most people, however, one quadrant tends to influence their behavior more than others.

If two people involved in a difficult conversation have widely varying dominant styles, the gap between their approaches can cause friction. In the case of Seth and Diane, Seth, who appears to be a harmonizer, was daunted by Diane's overbearing director style. Likewise, Diane was frustrated with Seth's failure to "kick some butt," which would be a natural reaction for her but a very unnatural response from Seth.

Likewise, Ted, who sounds like an energizer, was exasperated with William's need to have massive amounts of data in order to make a decision. William, on the other hand, probably found Ted's flamboyant, seat-of-your-pants energizer style more than a little disconcerting.

Flexing Your Style Muscles. Since people with diametrically opposed styles must work together, what can they do to make their
interaction productive? We would suggest a bit of intentional style
flexing, which means adapting your personal style to help the other
person feel less irritated and more willing to work with you.

This strategy is based on the old axiom that "birds of a feather
flock together"—which, of course, they do. Think of the people with
whom you associate. Don't most of them dress in styles similar to
yours, vote along similar party lines, and live by a set of values much
like your own?

We are comfortable with those who are similar to us. It's not a
hard and fast rule—you may have friends who are quite different from
you—but our guess is, not many, and not that different. For example,
if you are a retired, conservative Republican who's fairly prosperous,
just how many Mohawk-sporting, pierced-nose, radical left-wing anar-
chists do you count as your close friends? (Your own kids and their
friends don't count.)

Given that birds of a feather do flock together, one way to reduce
the chance of friction is to flex your style to more closely match that
of the person with whom you are disagreeing, butting heads, or simply trying to be straight.

Here are some dos and don'ts to help you adapt to each style:

Flexing to a Director

Do:	**Don't:**
1. Get to the point.	1. Engage in unnecessary chit-chat.
2. Present your ideas clearly.	
3. Use direct eye contact.	2. Ramble or appear disorganized.
4. Speak in a confident tone.	
5. Focus on results.	3. Avoid looking him or her in the eye.
	4. Hem and haw.
	5. Present problems without solutions.

Flexing to an Analyzer

Do:

1. Use data to support your case.
2. Outline the risks.
3. Give ample time to decide.
4. Prepare before engaging.
5. Match his or her speech pace.

Don't:

1. Try to fluff your way through.
2. Gloss over the downside.
3. Rush him or her.
4. Try to fake it.
5. Go faster or slower than the other person goes.

Flexing to a Harmonizer

Do:

1. Show interest in his or her family.
2. Ask for his or her input.
3. Focus on impact on others.
4. Describe feelings.
5. Match body language.

Don't:

1. Just get down to business.
2. Ride roughshod over the other person.
3. Ignore the effects on the team.
4. Just focus on the facts.
5. Go faster than the other person.

Flexing to an Energizer

Do:

1. Acknowledge his or her strengths.
2. Ask his or her opinion.
3. Express yourself.
4. Make the other person look good.
5. Use emotional words.

Don't:

1. Immediately attack his or her ideas.
2. Ignore the other person's need to talk.
3. Let him or her do *all* the talking.
4. Focus only on factual outcomes.
5. Present just data.

The idea here is to reduce the friction that differing personal styles will cause in a discussion. Less friction leaves more energy to focus on the problem at hand and reduces the chances that one or both parties are going to slip into a defensive mode.

In the conflict between Ted, the product designer, and William, the new products team leader, their difficulties, to a great degree, could be attributed to their differences in styles. While Ted seemed to fit the profile of an energizer, William was more of an analyzer. While Ted wanted to make decisions based on intuition and gut feelings, William wanted data. While Ted wanted action, William preferred caution. While Ted seemed to fly by the seat of his instincts, William liked to plan every move. No wonder they were in conflict!

Our recommendations for Ted would be to do his homework, give William the data he wants, slow down the pace of his communications, and not push William for quick answers. Our suggestions for William would be to acknowledge Ted's creative brilliance, show some excitement about Ted's ideas, speed up the pace of his own communications to better match Ted's, and give Ted a realistic time frame for when William will give him answers.

These actions may not completely close the gap between the two, but they will certainly narrow it.

Likewise, we would suggest that Seth and Diane flex their styles to close the enormous gap that keeps them from expressing absolute honesty. Seth, the harmonizer, would be well served to confront Diane more directly than he has in the past. Directors hate indirectness, and Diane is a director on steroids. Diane, on the other hand, needs to take a "chill pill" (a remedy Larry's daughter was fond of prescribing when she was a teenager). Diane needs to be aware that her blustering, "damn the torpedoes" style sends people scurrying for cover while they avoid giving her information that she doesn't want to hear but desperately needs to know.

Differing Points of View

In his book *The Living Company: Habits for Survival in a Turbulent Business Environment,*[10] Arie de Geus describes a group of British explorers at the turn of the last century who discovered an isolated, primitive jungle village high in the mountains of the Malaysian peninsula. This village had not developed beyond the Stone Age, and the inhabitants had never been exposed to any aspect of modern society, including the wheel.

As an experiment, they brought the chief of the village to Singapore to see what his impressions would be. Singapore at the time was a modern, thriving port with steamships, electric trolleys, and automobiles. After the visit, they asked the chief what impressions of Singapore were strongest in his mind. He replied that he had seen a man carrying more bananas than he had ever thought one man could carry.

In reading de Geus's story, it struck us how individual our perceptions of reality are. We are a compilation of what we have been exposed to and how we have interacted with our environment. No two of us have had exactly the same life experiences. Consequently, each of us sees the world through the perspectives of our own experiences, which can lead to entirely different views of the same scenario.

One of Larry's clients is an automobile manufacturer. While on a tour of one of the new, independently owned, megadealerships, Larry commented on how beautiful everything was, and what a great job the dealer had done in putting it together. The executive accompanying Larry, who was from the finance department of the parent company, sighed forlornly and said, "Right, and I hope he has the demographics to support this kind of luxury operation."

Two people looking at the same dealership: Larry, dazzled by the esthetics of the showroom and classy elegance of the vehicles, saw one thing, while the executive, worried about ROI and cash flow, saw something entirely different.

Stephen Covey wrote in his book *The 7 Habits of Highly Effective People*:

> Each of us tends to think we see things as they are, that we are *objective*. But this is not the case. We see the world, not as *it is*, but as *we are*—or as we are conditioned to see it.

When we open our mouths to describe what we see, we in effect describe ourselves, our perceptions, our paradigms. When other people disagree with us, we immediately think something is wrong with them.[11]

Ted and William both approached the meeting with their own points of view. Ted wanted to show his stuff by creating a "killer application"; William wanted to make sure this project wasn't a bust. As a result, they were pushing different agendas and striving for different outcomes. If they had first discussed what each wanted to accomplish, they might have been able to recognize the other person's perspective and incorporate it into their approach to one another.

For example, if Ted had understood and considered William's point of view a little better, he probably would have spent more time and energy tailoring his proposal to reassure William that there would be an adequate return on investment. On the other hand, if William had understood and considered Ted's perspective, he could have pointed out ways for Ted to create and market that "killer application."

In our consulting practices, we have observed many confrontations that could have been avoided if the session leader or the group manager had recognized how different perspectives can affect a business meeting. The leader is the critical person who can set the stage and the operating rules so discussions do not get off track. Leaders cannot be afraid to jump in during the session and clarify the perspective of each participating party.

A good leader sitting in on the meeting between Ted and William might have interrupted their conversation and said:

Just a minute, guys. Ted, it sounds like you are trying to get what you consider to be a hot source of revenue for us on the market before our competition does, right? And William, your concern is that we don't know if the ROI will be sufficient until we get more data, right?

What will it take for all this to happen?

With or without help, when differing parties can see the issue from the other person's perspective, the chance they will get defensive goes down and the odds of making a better decision go up.

Actual Attacks

If you believe that you are under personal attack, you may be right. The world is a tough place, and not everyone knows how to practice constructive confrontation. In the heat of a disagreement or during a feedback session, someone may say something that impugns your character, questions your competency, disparages your ethics, or threatens your security. Under this kind of attack, more than for any of the other arenas that trigger defensiveness, it is important that you keep a cool head and not slip into a defensive posture. Reacting defensively places the person attacking you in control of the conversation and puts you at his mercy like a puppet on a string.

For example, during an argument over a critical business decision, one of your colleagues suggests that you aren't being honest about the figures you are presenting. In essence, he's called you a liar. Your temptation would be to defend your honor by verbally attacking him, saying something like, "How dare you question my honesty? You, of all people, who can't manage your way out of a paper bag."

At this point, the discussion will probably escalate into a shouting match or disintegrate into a cold retreat on both sides, making further productive discussion impossible. Either way, you've lost control of the conversation and handed that person the power to control you.

MOVING FROM "ATTACK AND DEFEND" TO "DISCUSS AND SOLVE"

To control your own defensiveness and move conversations toward productive outcomes, consider the following steps:

1. *Take a breath and assess.* If Ted had taken a breath and thought before he spoke, he might have realized that he was getting angry because, deep down inside, he knows that attending to details has been a weakness of his since he was a child. The closer a criticism is to the truth, the more vociferous our defense will be.

2. *Apply the ABC technique.*[12] Albert Ellis, founder of Rational Emotive Therapy, tells us that environmental stimuli that move us to action can be thought of in three parts: an antecedent, (the "A" in the formula); a belief, (the "B" in the formula); and a consequence (the "C" in the formula). A colleague cracks a joke (A), you believe it is funny (B), so you laugh (C). You watch a sad movie (A), it touches you (B), so you cry (C). Your boss criticizes you (A), you believe a boss's criticism is always personal (B), so you get defensive (C).

   According to Ellis, we almost always filter the information provided by the antecedent (A) through our belief system (B), before producing the consequences (C). You laugh at the joke because your belief system tells you it's funny. You cry during the movie because your belief system tells you it's sad. You react defensively to your boss because your belief system tells you that criticism will harm you.

   The wonderful thing about our belief systems, however, is that they are open to adaptation. If they were not, we'd never learn new things and we'd never change.

   Jack Welch, General Electric's past CEO, once said, "When the rate of change on the outside exceeds the rate of change on the inside, the end is in sight." He was talking about the need for a company to keep learning and changing in response to the changing business environment, but the same principle applies to the individual. When you stop learning and changing, the end is in sight.

   Using the ABC system, we can *choose* to believe something different about an antecedent event if we take the time to do so.

We can *choose* to believe the joke is not funny because it has racist overtones. We can *choose* to believe that the movie is not really sad but is manipulating the audience with gratuitous tragedy designed to pull our heartstrings. We can *choose* to believe that our boss's criticism might serve to improve us, or that it is off base and needs correction. It's all about choice and we, as free humans, can make the choice not to react defensively but to react in a more effective manner.

3. *Ask for clarification.* You can't decide if the criticism is valid until you have information on which to base your judgment. Remember, we're talking about *your* judgment, not the criticizer's. Instead of lashing out, Ted might have said, "William, I'm puzzled. I thought I had done adequate research on this one. Could you give me some specifics on what's lacking?"

4. *Rephrase what the criticizer suggests.* This ensures that what you understood the criticizer to say is what he meant. It also gives you a chance to collect information to decide how you will respond to the criticism: "William, it sounds like you're concerned that the risk is too high, given the amount of information I've supplied so far. What would you need from me to resolve that concern?"

5. *Consider the criticism fairly.* Put yourself in the place of a knowledgeable and reasonable outsider looking in. Would this person agree with the criticism? What parts would the outsider say were valid, and with what parts would he or she disagree? Reviewing the issue in your mind from a third-party viewpoint can give you a more objective perspective to assess your own beliefs about the criticism.

6. *Acknowledge the truth.* Believe it or not, the criticizer may be *right,* partially if not completely. Acknowledge those parts of the criticism that are true. Ted would have been well served to say something like: "William, I know you and I see the research

requirements for a successful product launch differently. You've got a point about getting specific demographics on the growing retirement market. I hadn't thought about that."

7. *Describe why you don't agree with the untrue parts.* Here's your chance to make your case. Do so in a nonattacking, fact-presenting manner, and then ask for the criticizer's thoughts: "William, I don't think we should analyze this too long or we'll miss an opportunity to get the jump on the market. Several sales-people have told me that they're hearing in the marketplace that Gizmo Inc. is considering releasing a similar product. Is there a way to clarify that situation and, if it's true, fast-track this product?"

8. *Ask for and offer suggestions to resolve the situation.* "William, what if I get some rough numbers together, especially focused on the retirement market? I can have something for you by the first of next week. If the numbers are favorable, I'd like to consider at least doing a test of this product to see what happens. Would that work for you?"

Each of these steps helps move a conversation from "attack and defend" to "discuss and problem solve." Such a productive result can be possible when Ted recognizes his defensive reaction and chooses a more effective response.

MINIMIZING DEFENSIVENESS IN OTHERS

While it is true that we can't control the reactions of others, we can minimize the chances that people will react defensively in threatening situations. Communications expert Jack Gibb identified several approaches in his research that can either minimize or exacerbate defensiveness in others.[13] From his work and our own experiences, we've identified the following strategies for minimizing defensiveness in others.

Illuminate, Don't Evaluate

Larry tells the story of his parents' first visit to his college apartment. As his mother crossed the threshold, the sour look on her face spoke volumes. Somehow, he knew that the random clutter; the smell of the gym socks; the assorted beer cans; and the refrigerator; empty but for a stale slice of pizza and quart of sour milk, did not meet with her approval. Her first comment was, "How can you live like this?"

Meanwhile, his dad, obviously remembering his own college days, smiled and said, "Looks like you're all settled in, son. How's the place working out for you?"

We'll let you guess whose comment drew a more defensive reaction from Larry. Obviously, when people feel evaluated, judged, or put down, they are more likely to become defensive. This is true whether the judge is a parent, a friend, a coworker, or a boss. Now you may be thinking, isn't it the boss's role to pass judgment and give feedback? And the answer, of course, is "yes." But that doesn't mean the feedback has to be delivered as a personal attack. In fact, Gibb found that the more feedback is given in an attacking manner, the lower the chances that it will be accepted. On the other hand, when feedback is delivered strictly as a description of the facts, the odds increase that the person receiving it will take it to heart and act on it.

Let us be clear about what we're saying. This does not mean that the giver of the feedback should mince words, soften the message, or attempt to be warm and fuzzy. It simply means being tough on the issue, not on the person.

For example, you remember when William brought the proposal back to Ted, he said, "Sorry, guy, this just does not cut it. You should have done more research to support your design and marketing plan." Instead of saying that the proposal "just doesn't cut it," which Ted would very likely interpret as *"You* just don't cut it," William might have said: "I think this proposal needs more work," or "I can't approve this without knowing how the retirement market will react," or "I'm unhappy with the following three things about this proposal. . . ." That way, William would have described what he did not like about the proposal and what he needed Ted to do to fix it. He would not have implied anything about Ted's character or his ability to "cut it."

Provide Freedom of Choice

Maggie was telling Richard about a problem she was having with a client who was demanding extra services. Before she could finish explaining what the client was asking for and why she was asking it, Richard interrupted her and said, "You should tell the client there are limits to what we can do, based on our client load and the level of service that she is willing to purchase. You can't let these clients push you around in the name of good customer service, Maggie. Trust me. I know what I'm talking about. I once had a customer we bent over backward for and we ended up losing a lot of money on that guy."

Maggie started to explain the extenuating circumstances in this particular case, but again, Richard interrupted her and said, "Maggie, you need to be more assertive. You ought to let Sal talk to your client. He can show you how to handle a tough conversation with a demanding customer without giving away the store."

At that point, Maggie was ready to smack Richard in the nose. It was as if he were trying to dictate answers to her without even knowing the problem. Did he think she was stupid, incompetent, or both? She finally smiled and said, "I'll sure give that some thought, Richard. Thanks." In this case, Maggie's defense mechanism of *avoidance* was probably a healthy one, since it appears that arguing with Mr. Know-It-All Richard would have been fruitless.

But think of how much more effective the conversation would have been if, instead, Richard had replied to her dilemma with questions like:

- "Are there any special circumstances that would make it worth giving this customer what she wants?"
- "How have you handled customers like this in the past?"
- "What did they say when you tried to limit their demands?"
- "How would you like this problem to get resolved?"
- "Would you be interested in seeing how someone else has handled similar problems?"

Notice that with each question, Richard is helping Maggie figure out the answer to her own problem instead of trying to take control and tell her what she *should* do. He is treating her like an adult rather than a child. When that happens, defensiveness diminishes and truth emerges.

Beware the Curse of "Should"

Going back to the example of William and Ted, William told Ted what he *should* have done, rather than suggesting what he (William) "needed" to have done. He was practically begging Ted to recoil into a defensive posture. As a general rule, we adults *hate* to be told what we *should* or *should not* do. "Shoulds" take us back to our childhoods where our parents were constantly "shoulding on us." As young adults, the essence of our declaration of independence from them was to claim the right to determine our own "shoulds," and as adults, we resent others trying to usurp that right.

The exception to this rule is when we *choose* to grant other individuals the right to tell us what to do. For example, when you hire a golf pro to teach you to improve your swing, you have *chosen* to give her permission to tell you what you *should* do. It's part of your contract with her.

So you may ask, "Doesn't the same principle apply to an employment contract? If a person consents to take a job, doesn't that imply that she agrees to give her boss permission to tell her what she *should* and *should* not do?"

We would say, "Not necessarily."

Remember our discussion of the *six forms of power*? When we accept an employment contract, we grant our employer the right to set performance standards, negotiate our deliverables, set the ground rules for behavior inside and outside the organization, and wield *reward power* over us: We produce results and the organization pays us for our efforts. The organization may also have the ability to wield *coercive power* over us—our employer can give us a difficult time, dock our pay, or fire us—but that power is not willingly given to him, and if it becomes unbearable, we can leave. The remaining four forms of power, however, *legitimate, referent, expert,* and *representative* remain in our hands, to grant at our discretion.

For example, a mentor whom you respect may be able to tell you what you *should* do because you have granted her the *expert power* to do so. On the other hand, your immediate supervisor, whom you don't respect as an expert in his field, could not tell you what you *should* do without incurring your disdain. He can only tell you what he wants you to do. This may seem like a fine distinction, but within the politics of your relationship with him, it's an important one. He hasn't earned the right to use the word "should" with you.

The permission to deliver "shoulds" is always granted or not granted by the receiver. It is *never* the right of the giver to claim as his own. The manager who hands out "shoulds" without explicit or implicit permission from the receiver is venturing into dangerous territory. On the other hand, if the manager simply describes what he needs, asks questions to clarify issues, makes suggestions for the receiver to consider, and outlines the consequences of nonperformance, he will send the same message without the risk of driving her into a defensive posture.

If you want to minimize defensive reactions in others, we suggest banning the word *should* from your vocabulary. You really don't need it to influence people or to get your needs met, and using "shoulds" runs the needless risk of pushing others into defensiveness.

If we had been there, we would have suggested to William that he replace his "should" statement to Ted with this, "Hey, Ted, I didn't see an analysis of how this product will sell in the retirement market. If I'm going to approve this thing, I'll need to see data that covers that market segment. Have you got anything along those lines?"

We think this kind of descriptive, rather than evaluative, response would have minimized the chances that Ted would react in the defensive manner that he did. Of course, we would never tell William that he *should* do it that way. He's an adult. He can choose to do so or not. We can only describe the rewards and consequences of either choice.

Bridge the Gap in Power Differences

A woman who works in a government organization told Larry that she didn't like, nor did she trust, the organization's director. When he asked why, she said that the director didn't like her. Since she worked several levels below the director, Larry asked how she knew he didn't like her. "I see him in the hall every day. He has yet to say 'good morning' to me or acknowledge that I'm on the face of the earth," she replied. When Larry asked if she had ever said "good morning" to him, she exclaimed, "Of course not, he's the director. You just can't go up and introduce yourself!"

This story may seem bizarre if you are the kind of person who feels comfortable when you are in the presence of those with more power than you, but for many people, being in the presence of the "big boss" can be a very intimidating experience. If you are that "big boss," expecting people to always tell you the truth, especially if the truth is not what you want to hear, means expecting them to act well beyond their comfort zones. And you don't have to be the CEO or top dog to be perceived by others as intimidating. Simply having the title of supervisor or being in a position to influence decisions can place you there in the minds of those with less power than you.

You can reduce that tension by taking the time to build rapport with employees. By recognizing them through the use of common courtesies, small talk, and genuine inquiry about their jobs, their families, and their opinions, you will go a long way toward helping them relax, open up, and feel comfortable enough to be honest and open with you. Only genuine interest, however, will elicit genuine responses.

Another government executive we know made sure he took the time and made the effort to do just that. As director of the City of Phoenix's Division of Solid Waste Collection, Harry Kelman was responsible for a 500-person organization whose mission was to pick up and dispose of all the garbage that the ninth largest city in the United States could produce.

Although it wasn't necessary for him to do so, Harry made a point of arriving at a different service center at 4:15 A.M. each day, just to sit and have coffee with the drivers before they started their routes at 5:00. Since there were ten centers, that meant every sanitation employee had a chance to chat informally with the "big boss" once every ten days.

Consequently, when something was wrong, Harry often heard about it first. He knew the condition of the trucks as well as the drivers did, got wind of citizen complaints that were never officially filed, and was familiar with inefficiencies in route scheduling. Harry told Larry that his morning coffee routine was one of the main reasons that the Division of Solid Waste Collection was nationally recognized so often during his directorship.

REMOVING THE GREAT WALL

Creating a culture of absolute honesty involves more than speaking the truth because speaking is only half of the communication process. Even if we feel free to speak our minds, to tell the truth in every situation, and to risk our pride and our security by revealing unpopular opinions, we are at the mercy of those who listen to us. They may not want to hear our truth. They may feel threatened or insulted by our opinions. If our honesty produces a great wall of defensiveness, communication fails. Constructive confrontation stumbles. Absolute honesty slips away.

Each of us has two responsibilities in this process: to speak and to listen. In both cases, we must watch for situations that trigger defensiveness. Defensiveness is honesty's enemy. If we mount personal attacks when we mean to criticize a decision or action, we inspire people to hide behind the great wall. If we interpret criticism of our decisions or actions as personal attacks, we slip behind our own great walls. In either case, effective communication ends and dysfunctional relationships grow.

We understand that responding defensively is a natural reaction to a perceived threat. It is part of our genetic code and it has served us well. However, that doesn't mean it's the best course of action in the workplace. We need to resist the urge to fight or flee in the face of verbal challenges. The best way to do that is to be aware of the four common areas that trigger defensiveness and to be prepared for the great walls that suddenly appear in those situations. We need to recognize the nine defensive mechanisms as they appear in others and as they surface in ourselves, acknowledge them, and move past them to more constructive dialogue. We can use the eight steps presented in this chapter to switch from attack mode to problem solving.

In the end, awareness becomes the battering ram with which we lay the great wall to waste. Be aware of the words that incite defensiveness. Avoid enlisting them for personal attacks. Recognize them in criticism from others and set them aside. The goal is to clarify, discuss, and solve problems—to communicate. By chipping away at the great wall of defensiveness, we remove one more obstacle to a culture of absolute honesty.

CHAPTER 7

Absolute Honesty Law #5:

Reward the Messenger

"You can't handle the TRUTH!"

—*JACK NICHOLSON SPEAKING TO TOM CRUISE IN* A FEW GOOD MEN

IN THE SPRING OF 2002, ELIZABETH JOICE, AN ENGLISH TEACHER in Peoria, Arizona (a suburb of Phoenix), decided to take a stand. One of her senior students had failed Ms. Joice's required course and, consequently, was not going to graduate with her class. The student's parents hired a lawyer who threatened to sue Ms. Joice and the district if she didn't let the student take a special makeup exam no one else had been allowed to take. Ms. Joice stood her ground. She felt that if she made an exception for this student, it would be a breach of standards and inherently unfair to the students who had passed the course.[1]

The school board chose a different course: It allowed the

student to take a special makeup test and to graduate. For this action, the board and the school district were justly scorched in the Phoenix press. In contrast, Ms. Joice was praised by the media and gets our vote for Teacher of the Year—not only for the sheer guts she showed but also for the example she set for the other students.

It probably wasn't easy for her to take this stand. Telling the truth and doing the right thing can be tough. Making it even harder was the lack of support from her management and the school board. We can only imagine what the effect was on the rest of the faculty as they observed the process. How many of them will stand up for their principles in the future, knowing what happened to Ms. Joice?

We define "killing a messenger" as intentionally or unintentionally punishing someone for telling the truth or doing the right thing. Our guess is that Ms. Joice felt punished for doing the right thing, whether the board meant to punish her or not. Perhaps she'll think twice before taking a similar stand. We hope not. Of more concern is how the other teachers will react in similar circumstances now that they've seen what happened to her. The chances that they will repeat Ms. Joice's act of bravery have surely diminished.

During the Enron investigations, Sherron Watkins said that when CFO Andrew S. Fastow learned she had written her famous memo to Ken Lay, he "wanted to have me fired."[2] In an NPR interview, C. Fred Alford, author of *Whistleblowers: Broken Lives and Organizational Power,*[3] said that Watkins qualified as a whistle-blower even though her whistle-blowing was internal rather than external. (She took her findings to Enron chairman Ken Lay, rather than to the news media or the Justice Department.) He went on to point out, "Most whistleblowers get fired. Most who get fired lose their homes. Most who lose their homes eventually lose their families. It's a tough road."[4]

It's no wonder there were so few folks at Enron who spoke up.

Unfortunately, there are lots of ways to kill messengers, some intentional and some not. Our hope is that you would *never* do this intentionally, but since there are some who would, here are a couple of examples of how it is done.

BLATANT RETRIBUTION

There is an unconfirmed story floating around Washington journalistic circles that intrigued us. During the 1991 Gulf War, reporters were quizzing a White House spokesperson about that day's events, and one asked why it seemed that Saddam Hussein was able to surprise us so often. The response was, "Frankly, whenever he's surprised us, it's because he's done something so stupid that none of our military planners could see it coming."

Our impression of Saddam Hussein at the time was that he was not a stupid man. Crafty, demagogic, despotic, cruel, and evil maybe, but certainly not stupid. After all, he survived for a long time when lesser dictators would have been deposed or assassinated. Our thought is that if Hussein was making stupid moves, it was because he was getting bad information. But then, who on his team would have been willing to tell him what he did not want to hear? His brother-in-law did, and as we know, Hussein had him shot.

Of course, none of us would ever be so barbaric. But there are more civilized ways to do the same thing.

As a testing technician in a software company, Victor's job was to identify potential application interface problems prior to releasing products for shipment. After testing a product for which the company had huge hopes, Victor insisted that average computer users would not understand how to load the product onto their systems. Developers argued that he underestimated the talent of most users, but Victor pressed his case. Management eventually saw his point, but they were not thrilled about pushing back release schedules and rewriting budgets on such a high-visibility and profitable project. Soon after, when the position for quality assurance manager opened up, Victor was denied the promotion. He, along with many of his fellow employees, concluded that higher-ups were punishing him for being honest and standing up for his beliefs. From then on, most employees, including Victor, kept their mouths shut about anything that was controversial or that affected company revenues because of the fear of retribution.

Nothing kills the spirit of honest communication and healthy debate faster than the fear of retribution—the same fear that kept the emperor's subjects from pointing out that he was naked. If the perception exists that managers punish people for expressing their opinions, it is unlikely that opinions will be expressed openly. They will, however, go underground, reappearing as cynical e-mail jokes, hushed conversations in the coffee room, and, in many cases, poor performance on the job. For this reason, managers must guard against retribution in both its blatant and subtler forms.

INTENTIONAL BUT SUBTLE RETRIBUTION

When Bob was vice president of human resources for a high-technology firm, he learned of a purchasing manager who used the company's performance management process as a subtle weapon for wielding retribution against one of his purchasing agents. During an operational review, the agent had embarrassed the manager by asking why they were using a particular vendor to purchase memory chips. When the manager replied that they had a longstanding contract with the vendor, the agent argued that the contract was coming up for renewal and they should consider other vendors that could deliver products of the same quality for a fraction of the cost.

Although the manager made it clear he did not want to consider anyone else for this contract, the agent continued, showing what the savings could be and asking why the manager was so loyal to this vendor. Finally, the manager agreed to take a look at other vendors, but not before it was apparent to everyone at the meeting that the manager had never bothered to investigate the possible savings of going elsewhere.

To determine how much annual salary increase an employee would get, the company used a process that included a ranking and rating system. In this process, each manager ranked their employees against their own team and against the other managers' employees. The higher the ranking an employee achieved, the greater the possibility that the employee would receive a larger increase. This agent had always ranked in the top 20 percent against his peers. After the meeting where he confronted the manager, however, the agent's rankings never exceeded the bottom 50 percent.

The agent never complained to his manager or to the human resources department about this travesty until two years later, when he resigned to take a position with a competitor and requested a special exit interview with Bob. Unfortunately, the agent had openly discussed the manager's retribution with his colleagues. The effect was to quell any challenges the team would ever make to the status quo. As a result of the manager's behavior, how many other opportunities had the company lost to lower costs? Considering the volume of expenditures the manager controlled, a conservative estimate would be in the millions.

You're probably thinking that the reason this manager retaliated was because of kickbacks he was getting from the vendor that he didn't want exposed. Fortunately, it was nothing so sinister. As Bob discovered, the only reason the manager had punished the agent was because the manager found it embarrassing to have one of his own agents point out in public that he (the manager) was not doing his job, which was to cut costs without sacrificing quality. In other words, the manager's own vanity led to losing this agent to a competitor and eroding trust among the entire team. In this case, messenger killing came at a high price.

Of course, we're pretty sure that none of us would be so petty.

UNINTENTIONAL RETRIBUTION

Not as insidious, but just as potentially damaging, is the inadvertent "killing" of messengers. It's like Mr. Magoo driving down the wrong side of the street, happily going on his way while leaving accidents strewn behind him. Here are some examples.

Verbal Punishment

Kevin is the aggressive, Type A CEO of an insurance company with whom we did some work. In a meeting with his executive team, he discussed the implementation of a training program we were going to provide to the company's managers. We had suggested to Kevin that he be involved in each of the sessions in order to show his support for the training. Kevin was hesitant, arguing that he was too busy. We continued, saying that his presence was essential to give the program credibility in the eyes of the employees who would be participating. Finally, he slammed his fist on the table and shouted, "I've been through more #@#$$##$%$%# management training classes than anyone else around here. I just got back from a summer course at Harvard, for God's sake. I don't need to spend my time sitting through Management 101."

At this point, all the vice presidents at the table silently stared at their notebooks and their shoelaces. It was clear to us that they were used to Kevin's tirades and that it was time to move on to another topic. Later, one of the VPs took us aside and said that he would talk to Kevin offline and try to help him see the wisdom of attending the training. Two days later, the VP called us to say that Kevin had been in one of his moods, but he had now decided that his support would be needed for the management training, and he was, in fact, insisting that he attend all of the sessions.

We were curious about this 180-degree turnaround. We asked the VP how often Kevin got into these moods and how the people working with him handled them. He told us that everyone stayed away from Kevin at these times and that no one ever argued with him. He said that he was the only person who could get Kevin to see reason during these times. Like it or not, that was the way it was.

Our first thought was that Kevin should be on some kind of psychotropic medication. Barring that, however, it's sad to think that this guy had probably discouraged many truth tellers from leveling with him because of his blustering temper and childlike tantrums. Only the very brave or the very clever (like this VP) would dare give him straight answers or tell him what he didn't want to hear when he was in this state.

Later, we asked Kevin if he thought people might be afraid to tell him the truth. He replied that he knew he could be "gruff" sometimes, but everyone knew it was his "moods" and that it really didn't intimidate anyone.

That's not what nine out of the ten people who worked with him said. When we asked them if they felt comfortable telling Kevin bad news or disagreeing with him, they agreed that it was only safe to do so when he was in a good mood. When we reported this to Kevin, he was dumbfounded and said it couldn't be true.

How about you? Are there times when the people with whom you work would be afraid to tell you what you need to know because they think you might react in a less-than-rational manner or that you might need psychotropic drugs?

Defensiveness

Larry and his family visited a restaurant that advertised "authentic Italian food." The food was excellent, but when Larry asked the waiter to bring him a glass of water, the water never came. He asked again, and the waiter, who did not speak English well, indicated that he would bring it but never did. When the bill arrived, Larry put a line through the tip portion and wrote along the bottom of the credit card slip, "No water, no tip. Please call me if you'd like to discuss."

The owner of the restaurant called him the next day to find out what had happened. Bravo, thought Larry, here is a merchant who wants to hear the unvarnished truth so she can improve her service. Larry told her what had happened. Her response was to argue, telling him that since her restaurant serves authentic Italian food, they do everything to re-create the authentic Italian experience. In Italy, only wine or sparkling bottled water is served with meals, not plain water.

"But I just wanted a glass of plain water," replied Larry.

"Sir," she said in a condescending voice, "real Italian restaurants don't do that."

Larry hung up, vowing never to return. Obviously, this woman was so focused on her position that she didn't want to hear the truth. How often do we do the same thing with our people? We believe in what we are doing and when someone tries to give us a different perspective, we argue instead of listening.

You may be saying, "Yes, but isn't that engaging in a healthy debate?" Well, no, because an essential part of healthy debate is truly listening to the other person and letting him know that you heard him and are seriously considering his position. The restaurant owner never paid Larry that courtesy.

Of course, if you see an issue one way and your subordinate sees it another, you should be able to candidly express your opinion. Just remember that within the power structure of most organizations, if you are the boss, you have the "big retribution stick" to punish this person if you choose to—and he knows it.

If you have established a healthy environment where candid discussion is encouraged and people know it's safe to speak up, then by all means, argue to your heart's content. Do you remember the story of Lisa, the System Cop/Wicked Witch of the West and her boss, Tom, from Chapter 2? In that situation, Tom could argue vehemently about any subject he wished and his crew would never feel intimidated. He and everyone else on the team could state their positions openly and directly because he'd established a nonintimidating working environment where they knew he would never punish them for being honest and forthright.

Do your people have that same trust in you? If you're not sure, go easy on the pushback until you've established an environment in which people know it is safe to level with you.

DISCONFIRMING MESSAGES

We've all had the experience of talking to people with whom we feel closely connected. The person listens to you, seems highly interested in what you have to say, asks you relevant questions, laughs at your jokes, expresses concern at the sad parts, connects with the personal parts, and adds more information to contribute to both of your understandings of the subject being discussed. It is likely that this person is sending you what communication researcher Evelyn Sieburg calls "confirming messages."[5] When you get them in a conversation, you feel valued and connected—you may even find yourself responding with, *Yes!* That's exactly what I mean," and "You better know it," and "You got it." High fives are not far behind.

Sieburg also found that conversations can contain "disconfirming messages" that will have the opposite effect on the receiver. Disconfirming messages push people away. They devalue the worth of the other person and can be interpreted as so punishing that the receiver feels like a slain messenger, even when you didn't mean for that to happen. Disconfirming messages can take many forms.

Nonresponsiveness

If you've ever left a phone message or sent an e-mail and received no reply, you've been given a nonresponse message. In other words, you tried to connect with the person and you got a clear message in return saying that the person did not want to communicate with you.

Of course, it's possible that the person never got the message, the e-mail disappeared into cyberspace, or the person didn't realize you wanted a return answer. You may make several more attempts but still receive no response. At some point, you usually assume that the person does not want to talk to you. You may feel devalued and even insulted. This is why so many aspiring salespeople fail at cold calling. Unless you have a thick hide, nonresponses can hurt.

In a face-to-face conversation, nonresponsiveness translates into "no interest is expressed by the receiver."

At a monthly staff meeting, Laura, a shy, soft-spoken bookkeeper for a small manufacturing company, wanted to discuss some irregularities that she had noticed during a routine audit. When she brought the subject up, it was at the end of a conversation about how the local basketball team had played the night before.

Just as she said, "There were some items in last week's audit that concerned me," Ben, a loud, boisterous, sales manager, cried out, "Man, did you see that final shot? It was awesome." The conversation refocused on the basketball game, and Laura sat quietly as the rest of the group recounted the game for the fourth time. Finally, Gil, the group manager chairing the meeting, looked at his watch and cried out, "Hey, I've got an appointment in five minutes. Was there any other business?" No one said anything and the meeting ended.

Now you may say, "That wasn't Gil's fault. It was Laura's. She should have spoken up and insisted that they address her concerns." And you would be right. But remember, Laura was shy and, more than likely, oversensitive. She may have felt uncomfortable bringing up the irregularities in the first place. Regardless of whose fault it was, if it was important to Gil to discuss and resolve problems before they became Enronesque in size, then it would behoove him to refocus the meeting on Laura's issue. As it was, continuing the discussion of the basketball game sent an unintended, disconfirming message to Laura: "We just don't want to hear it, lady." So Laura let it go.

Gil does this at his, and the company's, peril. The truth that should have been discussed may remain bottled up in Laura until she is subpoenaed before a grand jury.

Interruption

This behavior is not only rude, but it sends a message that says, "I know better than you, so listen up and hear the truth—which is that you are too stupid to figure out the truth yourself."

That may not have been the message you intended to send. If you are used to moving fast, talking faster, and making even quicker decisions, you may fall into the trap of interrupting people without realizing it simply because they talk or think slower than you do. Consequently, when you act on your own impatience, you may be inadvertently sending a message that the person you interrupted thinks is, "I don't want to hear what you're saying, so shut up." That message translates into a subtle form of "kill the messenger," whether you intended it or not.

Patronization

Let's assume that Laura was able to overcome her sense of being disconfirmed in the meeting and makes an appointment with Rob to discuss the imbalances. He responds with, "Laura, don't worry your pretty little head about it. There are extenuating circumstances that you need not worry about. But I truly appreciate your bringing this to my attention, and I'll look into it. By the way, you do great work. Keep it up; I know you will go far here."

Take a moment now to calm that gagging reflex. In addition to being sexist, the message Rob sent to Laura was that she didn't have the intelligence or perspective to understand what she had seen. Unless Laura is not very bright, she's likely to interpret his real message as, "Mind your own business if you know what's good for you"—a pretty powerful "kill the messenger" statement.

Disconnected Responses

When someone responds with statements that are totally unrelated to the topic being raised, the disconnected response sends a subtle signal that the topic raised should not be brought up again:

Rick: *Rachel, I've got some concerns about the truth in lending statements that we're using. They don't really reflect the terms of the loans we are now making.*

Rachel: *Hey, those last customers who were in here were something, weren't they? I've never seen such bad credit. And they think they can buy a house with no down payment. Give me a break.*

Ambiguity

When the responder sends more than one meaning with her response, it confuses the issue and sends a message that this issue may not be all that important. In the example above, an ambiguous response from Rachel might be:

"Yea, we'll have to get around to looking into that one of these days."

This can be confusing for Rick. Is Rachel saying that she will look into it because it's important? Or, by using the phrases, "get around to" and "one of these days," is she saying, "It's no big deal, but I might get around to checking on it?" Or is she saying, "Drop it. It's not worth fooling with?" This confusion can lead Rick to wonder if it's worth bringing things like this to Rachel's attention. In any case, the confused messenger is mauled, if not murdered.

One-Upmanship

Have you ever been in a social situation where the topic of vacations came up with someone you just met? You're in the middle of telling him about your trip to Aruba when he interrupts to tell you about his vacation—making sure you understand that his trip was more exotic, more exciting, more expensive, more adventuresome, and all around better than yours? He never says so, but the message is clear: "I'm not interested in your piddling little experience, but you should be interested in mine because I am far more interesting than you."

Pretty soon, you just don't care so you ease your way out of the conversation and move on. Of course, in a social situation like that, the only casualty was the potential relationship you might have developed.

In a business setting, the cost can be much higher. The most common example of one-upmanship is the boss who responds to your concerns with stories about how much worse things were in "the good old days." You quickly get the picture that you are being discounted and pretty soon, you just don't want to tell her anything that will put her into that mode. It wastes your time and you don't like the feeling you get when you talk to her. She may not have killed the messenger in this case, but she's slapped you around with a strong enough discounting message that you don't want to come back.

Inaction

During the 1980s many companies introduced quality-improvement programs under such names as quality circles, process improvement teams, and TQM. The idea was to improve efficiency and productivity by empowering teams of employees to analyze processes and make recommendations for improvement. By the mid-1990s, many of these programs had failed or simply faded away. In the majority of cases, the programs disappeared because the recommendations submitted by the teams were never acted upon. People simply started to lose interest.

We all have a powerful need to contribute to something worthwhile. When we see our ideas and suggestions fall on unfertile ground time and time again, we eventually get disheartened and give up.

The same thing will happen if your employees risk speaking their minds or telling you about a problem, and then see no action or response. This doesn't mean that every complaint is valid or that you have to implement every suggestion submitted. It just means that people need to know that they have been heard and their thoughts have been seriously considered. The biggest sin you can commit is to hear a complaint or receive a suggestion and then never respond with a straight answer or a valid reason for not implementing the suggestion.

PERCEPTION CAN BE REALITY

As several of these examples show, unintentional retribution can have the same effect as blatant retribution. Perception can be as debilitating as reality. For example, Victor, the testing technician we mentioned earlier in this chapter, may *not* have been qualified for the managerial position he wanted. However, if it *looks* as if he didn't get the promotion because he played the devil's advocate, that perception can become reality in people's minds.

Larry witnessed the destructive power of perceived retribution when he helped install a continuous improvement process for a county government. County employees believed that anyone who suggested improvements risked being demoted. They based their perception on an employee who had proposed a better way to assign work duties. Within a week, that employee had been transferred to the county landfill. Nobody wanted to risk such retribution, so ideas for improvement ceased. Since the employees did not know that the transferred employee had *requested* the switch, they drew their own conclusions and acted accordingly.

Considering the level of mistrust and dislike with which most employees viewed management, it's not surprising that the rumor mill had distorted the story to imply that the transfer had occurred against his will. As psychologists tell us, when human beings believe that a certain set of circumstances exist and they receive little or no information to the contrary, they will imagine circumstances that support their belief.

SLEAZY, WACKO, BIZARRE MANAGEMENT PRACTICES

A key factor to consider in the case just discussed was the level of mistrust that existed within the organization. Given the negative perception of their own management, people were quite willing to accept that a messenger execution had occurred when nothing of the sort had happened.

Jessica was an engineering manager who had a reputation for being extremely unpredictable. If she approved a proposal created by one of her subordinates and upper management later criticized the proposal, she would claim to have not seen it in its entirety. Otherwise, she would never have let it get by her. She would then chew out the employee who created it.

On the other hand, if her superiors praised the proposal, she was the first to take credit for putting it together.

Her employees quickly grasped that she was the kind of manager who could not be trusted to support them or to represent their best interests. Consequently, when the economy was up and jobs were plentiful, they left in droves. When the economy slowed and jobs were scarce, they simply did the minimum required to get along and stayed out of her way.

Worse, *no one* was willing to be straight with her or give her any news they thought might upset her because they didn't know how she would react or whom she would blame. Even though she had never actually punished anyone for being honest, her unpredictability and history of back stabbing had created the perception that telling her the truth was a risky move for the messenger.

People will only risk telling uncomfortable truths when they perceive that it is safe to do so. Both blatant and subtle executions of messengers will destroy this sense of safety, but they are not the only ways to inhibit honesty. Inconsistent management will also do the trick. It's like riding in a taxicab with a crazy driver. He hasn't threatened to kill you, but you can see from his behavior that the chances increase at every turn.

If you want to establish an environment where trust is high and people feel safe expressing themselves, you must be consistent. Put another way, a CEO of a successful marketing firm told us, "I'm so predictable, I'm boring—but that's why my people trust me. They know 99 percent of the time how I will come down on an issue before I ever say a word. They know what's important to me, they know what I will and won't put up with, and they know that I'm not erratic." You would never call him sleazy, wacko, or bizarre—and such predictability creates trust, which is the breeding ground for absolute honesty.

Now we're not telling you that you should be boring in your thinking, or see the world like everyone else does—quite the contrary. Effective leaders usually think differently than others, which is part of what makes them good leaders. Steve Jobs saw the potential of graphical user interface (GUI) when few others could, and that unique perspective enabled him to shepherd Apple into creating the Macintosh. As far as creative thinking goes, he was quite unpredictable. On the other hand, anyone who worked with Jobs will tell you that he was *very* predictable when it came to certain core values, such as the value that Apple would produce the best personal computers on the planet. Our advice: If you want to be an effective leader and/or manager, be unpredictable in your thinking, but predictable in your core values.

MANAGER'S CODE OF CONDUCT

For over ten years, Larry asked participants in his management seminars to list words that described their worst and best managers. We combined those responses with our own observations to develop what we call the Manager's Code of Conduct, a prescription for building trust and motivating people to do their best. The ingredients in our prescription are:

▲ Trust others to the degree you would like them to trust you.

▲ Be a great listener.

▲ Clarify expectations.

▲ Create a milieu of honesty.

▲ Lead by example.

▲ Treat everyone like a customer.

Trust Others to the Degree You Would Like Them to Trust You

After checking into a Marriott Hotel after midnight, Larry asked the desk clerk if anything was available to eat. The clerk apologized and said that the kitchen had closed at 10:00 P.M. When the clerk saw the look of disappointment on Larry's face, he said, "Just a minute, I'll see what I can do."

Shortly, he returned with a platter stacked high with turkey, roast beef, salad makings, bread, a slice of pie, a piece of fruit, a cup of coffee, and a glass of milk. "Is this okay?" he asked. "*Wow!*" was Larry's reply. Larry then asked where the clerk had gotten the food and with a sly grin, the clerk pulled out a ring of keys and said, "I've got a key to the kitchen."

Larry was so impressed with this remarkable act of customer service that he decided to report it to hotel management. "Uh-oh," you're probably thinking, "Larry's going to get this guy fired." Larry realized the risk, but he wanted to do something for the fellow, who wouldn't even take a tip for his efforts. Before telling the hotel manager the next day about the incident, Larry made the manager promise that the clerk would not get in trouble.

When Larry finished telling the story, the manager assured him the clerk would not get in trouble, that the clerk would get a written commendation in his file, and that his team would get bonus points.

"But didn't he break the rules?" Larry asked.

"You bet he did," replied the manager, "but here at Marriott our people are encouraged to break the rules if it's for the right reasons. All we ask is that they use good judgment." He then told Larry that he'd already heard about the incident because the clerk had reported it to him that morning.

Isn't it interesting that the clerk was so willing to report that he'd broken a rule? Chances are he knew he wouldn't get in trouble because he had done it for the right reason.

Encouraging and rewarding people for taking such actions is often referred to as "empowerment," a term so overused in the 1990s it became a bit shopworn. Nevertheless, creating an atmosphere of trust, where people will share information openly, is certainly reinforced by trusting people to make the right decisions for your customers.

We think an even more effective approach is to trust people with information traditionally hoarded by management. Known as open-book management,[6] the idea is to share the production and financial numbers with all employees at least quarterly, if not monthly or weekly, so they can see where and how their efforts fit into the company's profit picture.

This can be scary because of the possibility that an employee might divulge those numbers to your competitors, and heaven forbid they should know your operating costs, scrap rates, losses, and gains. The problem is, if you won't trust the people who work for you with this information, you can't expect them to trust you enough to share anything they don't absolutely have to. Trust is always a two-way street.

The ultimate way to open this door of trust and open communication through open-book management is to give your employees a piece of the action. Let them become partner/owners with you so they have a vested interest in all aspects of the company's operations and profits. This raises the odds they will not let the company get into trouble by making sure its executives don't engage in shady shenanigans, by not ignoring loading dock managers who take kickbacks from trucking companies, and by catching employees who steal equipment from the stockroom. Speaking out, confronting wrongdoing, and blowing the whistle become acts of self-protection.

Be a Great Listener

Sheila Paxton runs a leading-edge, sixty-five employee online training company based in Boulder, Colorado. Sheila started the company in 1998 with a vision of creating cost-effective, computer-driven training solutions for corporations. We asked her what she attributed her success to and she pointed to the loyalty and productivity of her highly talented workforce. When asked why they were so loyal, she said that the one thing she does that seems to make a difference is that she listens to every employee in a way that sends a message to the person that he or she is the most important person on the planet. During a conversation with any staff member, she *never* takes a call or allows an interruption. She asks loads of questions to make sure she understands what the person's spoken and unspoken concerns might be. And she *always* keeps her word if she must get back to the person with an answer. If she's preparing for a meeting with a major client, expecting a call from a board member, or having a severe migraine, and she can't give her full attention to the employee, she levels with him and sets up another time to meet when she will be better able to listen and engage.[7]

It gets back to what Robert Townsend, the Avis CEO, said about listening. All people really need to know is that you are willing to listen to them and take them seriously. Active listening sets the stage for honesty and truth telling.

Clarify Expectations

Researchers Markus Buckingham and Curt Coffman studied more than one million employee surveys.[8] They found that the number one factor controlled by managers that positively or negatively affects productivity, profitability, employee turnover, and customer satisfaction ratings was how well employees understand what is expected of them.

This is not only a matter of making sure people know what their jobs are and what they are expected to produce. It is also about making sure people know how they will be judged and whether that judgment will be done fairly and honestly. That way, there are no surprises. Because of differences in style or personality, your staff may not like you, but if they know what you expect of them and that you will judge them fairly against clear criteria, you become predictable and, consequently, easier to trust.

Clarifying expectations also means being clear about honesty and ethical practice. It helps if you and your staff have a formalized set of standards upon which to base decisions and behaviors. We discuss how to create one in Chapter 9. We also think it's important to simply tell people on a regular basis what you expect. The best way to do that is to establish a milieu where honesty and the open expression of opinions are common practice.

Create a Milieu of Honesty

Larry's parents were educated professionals of British and German descent. The atmosphere in his household was formal with little or no open conflict. He and his sister were taught to not argue or fight and to settle things "civilly." Voices were always subdued at the dinner table and certain subjects, like sex or neighborhood gossip, were never discussed.

Larry will never forget the culture shock when, at the age of eight, his best friend, Joey, invited him to dinner. Joey was one of nine children from a first-generation Italian family. The meal was a boisterous, noisy affair, with people shouting at each other from opposite ends of the table. There was chiding, loud disagreements, laughter, and one shouting match between Joey's older sister and her father about the sister's new boyfriend.

Of the two families, in which one would you guess people would feel freer to tell the truth? Our guess is that the Italians would win, hands down. The culture and attitudes of the family created a milieu of honesty.

In Chapter 2, we described two methods you can use to create such a milieu: Jack Welch–style Work-Outs and the U.S. Army's AARs (After Action Reviews). A manager at a highly successful manufacturing plant insists that his line supervisors hold Friday morning meetings with their workers. All the production and financial numbers are shared for the week, and then three questions are posed, discussed, and answered:

1. What did we do right?
2. What do we need to stop doing?
3. What do we need to keep doing but change how we do it?

If a problem has been brewing during the week, it's likely to come up during these discussions. The manager holds the same kind of meetings with his supervisors Friday afternoons so they can address any of the problems that came up in the morning meetings, and by Monday morning, the COO knows about any issues that weren't resolved at the lower levels.

This same plant manager practices an open-door policy that says, if you are not completely satisfied with an answer or solution that emerged from your Friday morning meeting, you will be positively rewarded by bringing it directly to him or to the COO. No one is ever punished for complaining or saying what he or she thinks is the truth. The only "punishment" occurred when it came to light that a supervisor had told an employee that "he'd be sorry" if the employee told the plant manager that the supervisor had fudged on some production numbers. Although it turned out that the supervisor had not falsified the numbers, he was fired for threatening the employee.

If you want honesty, you can't tolerate even the threat of retribution.

Lead by Example

In the 1980s, a famous athlete was arrested for using cocaine. Although it became common practice for many athletes after that, he was one of the first. When the media asked him how he could justify using cocaine when so many young people looked up to him as a role model, he said, "I didn't sign a contract to be a role model for anyone. I signed a contract to play football." *Au contraire*. He was a famous athlete in a sport that appealed to children. Whether he liked it or not, he was a role model.

The same can be said of managers. When you take on that responsibility, you become a "famous person." People will watch you. There will be many dinnertime conversations about you. What you do and say will announce to everyone what is acceptable and what is not. If you want people to be honest and not cheat, you must be honest and not cheat. If you want people to tell the truth openly, then tell the truth openly yourself and never punish anyone for doing the same. If you value ethical behavior on the job, don't promote someone who stabs people in the back to get ahead or cuts corners to make sales, even if he is the top producer.

Remember, everything you do has meaning—and people are watching.

Treat Everyone Like a Customer

We have a friend whose wife recently left him. We had seen it coming for a while because every time we got together with this couple, we noticed that he was rarely very nice to her. He'd interrupt her when she was talking. He'd roll his eyes if she said something he didn't agree with. He'd snap at her if she said or did something that irritated him. He rarely offered kind words or public displays of affection. Meanwhile, she seemed to adore him at first, but over time, her responses to him appeared to grow more and more distant.

He was devastated when she asked for the divorce. He later confided to us that he was aware he could be grouchy with her from time to time, but he never thought she'd leave him over it.

In their classic study on leadership, Warren Bennis and Burt Nanus[9] found that one of the common characteristics of great leaders was that they treated *everyone* with the same courtesy you would normally reserve for strangers. Is it possible that you could treat someone who works for you or with you with less courtesy than you would a stranger? How about someone you live with and love?

It's not that familiarity breeds contempt as much as it breeds an attitude that says, "I can take you for granted."

We've found that the best managers regularly take the time and make the effort to celebrate and acknowledge those who work for them. They remember to greet them in the halls and to send them cards on their birthdays. They take them into consideration when making decisions. They shy away from thinking of people as "resources," which to our minds conjures up images of cattle or lumber or computer equipment. They see them as people who are essential to the heart and soul of the corporation, and they treat them accordingly.

Thinking of employees as customers can also help you apply an approach we've developed for handling employee complaints and suggestions. In the service industry, only 4 percent of customers who are unhappy with the service they receive will ever tell the establish-

ment's management about it.[10] In their book *A Complaint Is a Gift,*
Janelle Barlow and Claus Moller make the point that when customers complain, they are doing you and your company a huge favor
because if they don't tell you, they will usually tell someone else.[11]
Meanwhile, you don't get vital information to improve your products
and service.

The reluctance to complain is understandable. People are not
naturally assertive in such situations. For example, as we discussed
in Chapter 5, in a restaurant they'd rather eat an unsatisfactory meal
than cause a fuss. Many fear that sending back the food might result
in the cook spitting on it. So they suffer in silence and even lie when
the waiter asks them at the end of the meal, "How was it?" Looking
him right in the eye, they say, "Fine." And then they never come
back.

Employees who have concerns or complaints often feel the same
way. They don't want to make a fuss. To make matters worse, you
have a lot more power to punish them than a restaurant does. We
suggest that you treat employee complaints and concerns the same
way you should treat customer complaints, starting with the realiza-
tion that, when employees tell you something is not right, they're
doing you a huge favor.

From there, it's a matter of handling the complaint in a way that
encourages them to tell you the truth and to do it more often. Yes,
that's right: Encourage employees to *complain more often.* If you want
to hear the truth frequently and in franker form, create an environment where people are encouraged to say what's on their minds,
and that includes complaints. The only difference with employees,
as opposed to customers, is that you can insist they bring you solutions and be willing to take some responsibility for implementing
them.

We suggest the TARGET-K approach for handling employee
complaints or suggestions:

T	*Thank the person.* Although he may be bringing you infor-
mation you don't want to hear, he is doing you a huge

favor. When your goal is to create a culture where people will be straight with you, thanking them for doing so increases the odds it will happen.

"Ed, thanks for bringing this situation to my attention. I didn't realize that you and the other analysts were being pressured to recommend stocks you don't believe in."

A   *Ask questions to clarify the situation.* "When did this happen?" "How did it happen?" "What did you do in response?" "What would you like to see done to correct the situation?"

R   *Reassure the person that you are willing to listen and do what you can to fix the problem or address the issue.* "Ed, this is a serious matter. I want you to know I will get to the bottom of it."

G   *Give your perception of the situation and what you plan to do about it—include what you expect from him.* "Ed, I'm going to discuss it with our CEO tomorrow. I may want you to join us. I will need you to be ready with the facts and what you'd like to see done to change the situation."

E   *Encourage and reinforce the behavior.* "Ed, I know this wasn't easy for you to bring forward. I appreciate your doing so. It's the best way we can make sure we're running a clean ship."

T   *Take action to correct the situation and do the right thing.* This does not mean that every complaint is valid or requires action. Let's face it, there are some employees who complain about *everything,* and chasing down every issue they bring up would be a great waste of time and resources. It does mean, however, that you must do something, even if it is learning the circumstances behind the complaint and getting back to him with an answer.

K   *Keep the person informed of all actions you are taking, decisions made, and progress toward a solution.* If there is no progress, let him know and explain why. If a decision is made to not do what he suggests, tell him why. If there will be a delay in solving the problem, let him know the reason, and when he can reasonably expect an answer. The bottom line here is to not let an information vacuum develop in which the messenger feels like he's been ignored. Such vacuums are the breeding grounds of paranoid speculation, hostile rumors, and a sense on his part that he's become a punished, if not murdered, messenger.

If the owner of the restaurant that served authentic Italian food had applied the TARGET-K approach when Larry complained, Larry and his family might have returned—provided, of course, that she started serving water. What if the leaders at Enron, WorldCom, Tyco, and other troubled companies had followed the TARGET-K approach when employees expressed concerns about financial mismanagement? Is it possible that the ethical meltdown of 2002 might have been averted?—Assuming they were willing to stop the creative accounting practices, bloated compensation schemes, and downright theft they probably knew was happening anyway. Well, it's a nice thought.

TRUTH ON A NAPKIN

The Manager's Code of Conduct must reflect a personal, deep-seated desire to create a culture of absolute honesty. It springs from a sincere trust and belief in people that compels you to encourage and reward those who tell the truth.

Early in 1991, eight leaders of Wainwright Industries, a small Missouri company that manufactures stamped and machined parts, were listening to an IBM vice president talk about his facility's culture. The speaker noted that it thrived because it had a sincere trust and belief in people. One of the leaders wrote this phrase on a napkin above the question "What is it?" and passed it around the table. Someone else wrote, "I don't know. Do we have it at Wainwright?" Everyone at the table, including CEO Don Wainwright, read it. Rather than kill the messengers, he recognized the truth and acted on it.

After three months of dialogue about what that truth meant to the company, the leaders shut down the plant for an all-employee meeting at which Don Wainwright said, "I failed you. I thought the best way to provide job security was to let the owners and managers who had all the information make all the decisions, but we can't grow and provide security if we continue like this. We failed. It's up to you to do your own job. We sincerely trust and believe in you. We'll provide the training and support you need to do your job."[12]

The truth energized employees. Over the next few years Wainwright's delivery performance improved from 59 percent to 99.7 percent. Sales jumped from $20 million to $28 million. Employee satisfaction rose from 79 percent to 95 percent with a parallel boost in customer satisfaction from 84 percent to 98 percent. And in a testament to its culture of "sincere trust and belief in people," the number of implemented suggestions reached 1.25 *per employee per week*!

Such is the power of a cultural shift from retribution to rewards. The Manager's Code of Conduct provides a course of action your organization's leaders can follow daily to build a culture where ideas—and people—flourish.

CHAPTER 8

Absolute Honesty Law #6:

Build a Platform of Integrity

"The time is always right to do what is right."

—*MARTIN LUTHER KING JR.*

CHARLIE IS IN THE CONSTRUCTION BUSINESS. WHEN HE STARTED, back in the seventies, he and his crew worked with various general contractors, framing walls and roofs on tract housing. One of these contractors had a reputation for shoddy work; intolerable working conditions; and an ethic that said get every house done in the least amount of time, at the lowest cost possible, even if you have to cut corners to do it. When Charlie and his crew had an opportunity to work for this guy, Charlie was hesitant—but it was 1974, the year of the oil embargo. The economy was in the pits, construction work was scarce, and Charlie was hungry. So he took the job.

He soon noticed that the builder had earned his reputation. The fellow constantly pushed his crews and subcontractors to cut costs and reduce time spent on each house. He was fond of yelling phrases like, "Why use two nails when one will do?" and "Time is money—you're costing me a bundle, so get your butt in gear," and other maxims too vulgar to mention. One day Charlie's crew was sheathing a roof with 4 x 8 foot plywood sheets, nailing across the roof trusses, which were laid out every two feet. As they moved across the roof, they came to a four-foot gap between trusses. Charlie called the builder over and pointed out the gap. The builder replied, "Oh, yeah, they ran short on trusses yesterday. Just lay the plywood across the four-foot span. No one's going to notice."

"Probably not," Charlie pointed out, "but in six months, the roof is going to sag there."

"Not our problem," was the reply.

"What about the building inspector?" Charlie asked.

"Not your problem. We've got him covered."

At that point, Charlie pulled his crew off the job and left.

We asked Charlie if he had done anything further to expose this fraud—report it to the building department or tell the story to the newspapers. He sheepishly said that he would now, but he didn't at the time because he was young, just starting out, and didn't want to make a fuss. He did note, however, that the builder went bankrupt the following year because of huge losses resulting from "internal shrinkage." That's right: His own people were stealing materials from him.

The thievery supports the point we made earlier in this book about mutual reciprocity and, we think, a more accurate maxim: What goes around, comes around. This builder certainly got what he deserved. More than that, he illustrated a key principle of leadership: Like it or not, leaders lead—even bad ones.

Steve Rayner, the author of *Team Traps,*[1] talks about watching his twin sons play in their first Little League game. Every time one of the kids from the opposing team would make a mistake, their coach would yell from the sidelines, deriding the boys and even calling them names like "dummy" and "stupid." Pretty soon all the kids were using the same language and harsh critical tone with each other—including those on Steve's sons' team who had never acted that way before and had never seen that coach before. Scary.

Looking at Charlie's behavior, we applaud him for his courage in walking off the job when he discovered that the general contractor was dishonest. Certainly, Charlie could have done more. As his years of experience have taught him, he should have done something to protect the public from this unscrupulous contractor and the inspector he seemed to have in his pocket. Even so, he tried to do the right thing when the situation called for it, setting an example for the people who worked for him.

Taking the high moral road is seldom easy. Consider Sir Thomas More. A devout Catholic, More was chancellor of England under Henry VIII. He fell into disfavor with Henry when the king declared himself head of the Church of England in order to ignore the Catholic Church's ban against divorce so he could divorce Catherine of Aragon and marry Ann Boleyn. More refused to accept Henry's claim and continued to support the pope's authority in England. He also refused to attend the king's marriage to Ann Boleyn.

More was beheaded on Tower Hill in 1535 and was canonized four centuries later. Never to be the disloyal employee, his last words were, "I am the king's good servant, but God's first."[2]

Doing the right thing is always the right thing to do. Fortunately, it seldom carries the consequences Sir Thomas More suffered. Instead, it establishes you as someone people can trust. The fact that it helps you sleep at night is certainly a benefit. Moreover, when you make a practice of doing the right thing, you exemplify the person you want to be, the person you want your employees to imitate, your children to become, and society to reflect.

Larry's daughter Meagan remembers going to the store with her father when she was six years old. The clerk undercharged Larry a dollar. When he realized the mistake, he brought it to the clerk's attention. Meagan says that to this day, twenty-five years later, she remembers that experience when she faces ethical decisions from declaring all her income on her taxes to making sure that she doesn't overcharge her clients, even when she could get away with it. Unlike his daughter, Larry doesn't remember the event, but he claims that giving up a dollar must have been an easy test of his honesty.

None of us would ever want to be the kind of leader who models behavior we do not want our employees to imitate. Yet there are leaders who do just that. The sins committed by Arthur Andersen at Enron in 2002 and before were not isolated events; they were symptomatic of a plague that had spread throughout the entire organization. Such plagues usually start with leadership. What is allowed is what occurs. What is modeled is what people imitate. The plague of unethical behavior spreads despite the leader's best intentions because the leader loses his focus on what is right. Loss of focus is often caused by leaders who are too concerned about the company's bottom line and their own individual wealth and not concerned enough about the survival and growth of their business.

In June 1992, Sears, Roebuck and Company, an organization with a longstanding reputation for honesty and reliability, was devastated by a series of sting operations. Sears Auto Centers from California to New Jersey were caught overcharging customers for unneeded parts, repairs, front-end alignments, and brake jobs. As a result of a class action suit brought by forty-four state attorneys general, Sears paid $27 million in damages and provided reparations in the form of $50 coupons to thousands of customers it had bilked. At the time, Sears Auto Centers had close to $3 billion in revenues, so it was a minor penalty, but the business it lost by damaging public confidence in Sears was immeasurable.

Given the national extent of the problem, the overcharging was obviously the work of more than a few rogue mechanics.[3] It was as if Sears had enacted a corporatewide policy that said, "Cheat the customer every chance you get." Lacking any smoking-gun memo or policy instructing the centers to do that, the question is, What happened?

According to Lynn Sharp Paine, author of *Cases in Leadership,*

Ethics, and Organizational Integrity: A Strategic Perspective,[4] the culprit was the pressure corporate officers placed on each Sears Auto Center to turn a greater profit. At the time, Sears was losing market share to Wal-Mart and was under tremendous pressure from Wall Street to improve performance. Auto Center advisers and mechanics faced enormous pressure to overcharge: (1) they were paid commissions to sell certain services and products—the more brake jobs, front-end alignments, and batteries they sold, the more they made; and (2) if they didn't meet specific sales quotas on these items, they were punished by transfer, reduction of hours, and dismissals. The pressure reinforced the behavior. No wonder customers were being ripped off.

There is nothing inherently wrong with offering more opportunities for customers to get value from their purchases. When you order a book online from Amazon.com, you are offered a list of other books bought by people who purchased the book you selected. That can truly add value to your purchase—and it increases revenue for Amazon.com.

Nor is there anything wrong with encouraging employees to offer more to customers—a practice known as "up-selling." When you place an order at McDonald's, the associate will always ask you if you want a "Value Meal" or if you want to make it a jumbo order of fries and a large drink with it. Bank tellers will offer information about other bank services that will make your banking experience more helpful. The salesperson at Nordstrom will always suggest a tie and belt to go with that shirt. In each case, you can bet the company encouraged their employees to offer those extras, trained them to make the offers, rewarded them with commissions when customers bought more, and even punished them when customers did not spend as much as possible.

So when does up-selling become corporate sin rather than healthy sales policy? We will try to answer that in a little bit, but first, imagine you were the CEO of Sears. What would you have done differently to avoid that PR disaster?

Here's what we would have done.

FOCUS ON WHAT'S IMPORTANT

We are reminded of a story told by marketing expert Thom Winninger.[5] Early in his career, Thom helped McDonald's with its marketing efforts. After spending time watching carloads of families drive up to the window to pick up their orders, he had an epiphany. The cars were usually full of screaming children in the backseat and frazzled parents in the front who just wanted to get their kids fed and go home. It dawned on Thom that McDonald's was not in the fast-food business—McDonald's was in the "parent hassle-relief business"—the "Happy Meal" business. Playground equipment at the restaurants was not far behind.

As baby boomers, we can remember growing up in families devoted to Sears. We can remember our fathers saying, "You may have to pay a little more for a Diehard battery, a Craftsman tool, or a Kenmore appliance, but you can rely on it being a quality product. And if there's a problem, Sears will stand behind it 100 percent." (As early as 1905 Sears implemented a policy of ensuring accurate catalog descriptions and top-quality merchandise.[6]) So everything in our homes came from Sears: the furniture, the drapes, the bedding, even that avocado-green shag carpet our mothers thought was so stylish. In our minds, Sears was never in the "merchandise-selling" business. Sears was in the "reliability business." Consequently, most of our generation and our parents' generation were flabbergasted when Sears was caught bilking its customers in the automotive scandal. More than that, we were heartbroken. Sears had betrayed us.

This was especially true because the mechanics were professionals who knew the consequences of the advice they offered. Most of us have no way of knowing if we need new brakes or not, so when our family's safety is at stake, and the mechanic says we need them, we must be able to trust that it's the truth. It's not the same as offering us fries with the hamburger or accessories with a clothing item where we can trust our own judgment.

The same thinking can be applied to doctors, plumbers, priests, accountants, or stock analysts. They are the experts and we are but laypersons who must follow their lead. In such relationships, TRUST IS EVERYTHING. In addition, the responsibility for maintaining that trust lies not only with the practitioners. It also falls to the leaders of the organizations in which they practice. The executives of the brokerage houses who winked and encouraged their stock analysts to publicly tout stocks they privately disparaged bear this responsibility. The hospital administrators who ignore surgeons who perform unneeded surgeries bear this responsibility. The Catholic bishops who placed the church's reputation ahead of the welfare of its children by transferring child-molesting priests to other parishes where they could continue to prey on the innocent bear this responsibility. The leaders of Sears, too, bear this responsibility because they pressured their mechanics to take advantage of unsuspecting customers, and do so they did.

Shortly after the scandal broke, Sears CEO Edward Brennan admitted that he and his management team had "created an environment in which mistakes did occur."[7] It's nice to admit a mistake, but imagine if Mr. Brennan had been guided by a commitment never to betray the customer's trust. Would he ever have approved a scheme that pressured the mechanics and service writers to sell unknowing customers what they didn't need? We think not.

IT STARTS WITH LEADERSHIP

In the summer of 1954, Ray Kroc, an entrepreneurial genius from Oak Park, Illinois, owned the U.S. rights to sell a five-spindle, restaurant-grade milkshake machine called the Multimixer. He noticed that one of his customers, a hamburger stand in San Bernardino, California, was buying five times more Multimixers from his West Coast salesman than any of his largest customers. He flew out to California to find out why and was so impressed with the restaurant's high-speed process for making hamburgers that he begged the owners to let him franchise it.

Having tried and failed to franchise a few years earlier, Maurice and Richard McDonald were hesitant to try again, but Kroc was a convincing salesman. He had seen and eaten at a lot of "fast food" places and he knew that most were sorely lacking in what he considered the three essential elements to a successful dining experience. He called them QSC, which stood for:

Quality:

A hot, 100 percent beef hamburger served on a fresh bun with crispy French fries, and a cold, refreshing milk shake

Service:

Consistently friendly and fast—provided by people you would not mind taking the food from

Cleanliness:

Floors, walls, tables, restrooms, and parking lot all sparkling

Kroc convinced the brothers that he could build a chain of highly successful restaurants by combining their formula for high-speed production with his formula (QSC) for managing the process. The ensuing proliferation of "golden arches" proved Kroc right.[8]

What we find interesting about this story is that, regardless of how long it's been since former McDonald's employees have worked there, they can usually still define QSC if asked, which speaks for Kroc's ability as a leader. He was able to inculcate (some would say brainwash) legions of young people with the essence of his vision and to do it so thoroughly that they can recite it word for word years later. We have asked employees who worked there forty years ago, and they can still easily reel off the definitions of QSC, including Kroc's favorite phrase, "If you've got time to lean, you've got time to clean."[9]

Kroc was the essence of a leader who did the right things to make a dream a reality. In our work with hundreds of different leaders of companies and organizations in the private and public sectors, we've noticed that the best leaders tend to exhibit some common characteristics, all of which Kroc had:

- Clarity of a vision based on values
- Passion for the vision
- An ability to communicate the vision
- Leading by example
- Standing up for what's important

Clarity and Passion for a Vision Based on Values

The best leaders know where they want to take the organization and are excited, almost obsessed, about getting there. Kroc was clear about his vision of what a McDonald's restaurant chain would look like, how it would function, what its products would look like, and even who would work at its facilities. For example, he originally refused to allow any McDonald's franchise to hire women—not because he was a sexist, but because he had seen the kind of "undesirable" male traffic that young female carhops attracted to drive-ins of the 1950s. He wanted McDonald's to be a family restaurant, not a teen-age hangout.[10] Today, of course, McDonald's is an equal opportunity employer.

Most of all, Kroc's vision rested firmly on a set of well-defined values: QSC. His passion for these values was renowned throughout the McDonald's system. It was said he could bring an audience to tears with a speech about the quality of beef that went into a Big Mac.

Kroc's vision and actions never wavered, demonstrating a consistent behavior to his employees. We believe that a vision does not last long without such consistent reinforcement by leaders.

An Ability to Communicate the Vision

By summing up his vision in an easy-to-understand formula, Kroc was able to crystallize the essence of where the organization needed to focus its efforts. QSC was then communicated to everyone, every day, in a thousand different ways through discussions, meetings, corporate communications, training, and revival-like pep rallies. In 2002, Larry worked with McDonald's as it launched a companywide campaign to focus its efforts once again on QSC, almost forty-eight years after Kroc instituted it and eighteen years after his death, proving that great visions are worth keeping alive, and great leadership will outlive the leader.

Leading by Example

There was no doubt where Kroc stood on any issue, especially as it related to QSC. He clarified his stance with every action he took, demonstrating to everyone the true meaning of his visionary formula. For example, in the early days, Kroc would come in on weekends to be the clean-up man for the McDonald's in Des Plaines, Illinois. He would hose down the parking lots, clean trashcans, and scrape gum from the bottom of seats. One Saturday he spent the entire afternoon cleaning the holes in the mop squeezer with a toothbrush. And he was the boss![11] Based on his actions, no one could misinterpret how he felt about cleanliness.

On another occasion, during a surprise inspection of a company-owned store, it was said that Kroc discovered a dead fly floating in the french fryer. He fired the entire crew on the spot and closed the restaurant. His behavior shouted that cleanliness was essential to McDonald's success.[12]

Standing Up for What's Important

One of Kroc's trademark traits was his obsession with perfection. It was reflected in everything he did. For example, one of the products that has differentiated McDonald's from its competitors is its french fries. Most people who like fast food will tell you that McDonald's fries are the best: just crisp enough outside, just soft enough inside, just the right amount of goldenness, and just the perfect amount of salt. This was no accident. When Kroc partnered with the McDonald brothers, the fries were mediocre at best. They only became perfect after spending $3 million (not a small amount in the 1950s) and ten years of research and development time. Kroc's perfectionism drove this effort.

Can you imagine if Ray Kroc had been running Sears in 1992, and his passion was nurturing the trust of Sears's customers? We have no doubt he would *never* have approved the scheme to pressure those mechanics. In fact, he might have had anyone who suggested it "drawn and quarter-pounded."

LEADERSHIP OBSESSION = ORGANIZATIONAL INFECTION

When the leader is obsessed with a concept or focus, the organization tends to become infected with that obsession. This applies to creating a culture of absolute honesty, straight talk, and integrity as much as it does to quality, customer service, or the pursuit of market dominance. A study by Gary R. Weaver of Fortune 500 companies and their ethics programs bears this out. Weaver found that companies that have executives who are serious about ethics tend to be more likely to have formal ethics programs in place and be less likely to encounter ethical problems.[13]

Well, duh! What else would you expect?

Credit Suisse First Boston (CSFB) was immersed in the 2002 Crisis of Ethics in Business USA. With a history of accusations of IPO kickbacks and of pressuring analysts to promote the stocks of investment bank clients,[14] CSFB exemplified everything that was wrong with the investment-banking industry at the turn of the twenty-first century. In July 2001, John Mack replaced CEO Allen Wheat. To right CSFB's financially disastrous and ethically shaky course, Mack implemented a host of cost-cutting measures designed to bring spending in line, gaining him the moniker of "Mack the Knife."[15] More important, he launched a companywide effort to restore ethical behavior and recoup client trust.

To help in the effort, he:

▲ Established a set of narrowly defined guidelines to prevent conflicts of interest and unethical behavior

▲ Conducted ongoing meetings to inform and educate employees about the new standards of behavior

▲ Hired former SEC officials and lawyers to oversee compliance[16]

As of this writing, CSFB is not out of the woods, but there is little doubt among those inside CSFB that Mack's obsession with restoring trust and returning to a solid financial and ethical basis will drive any substantial recovery.

CREATE A PLATFORM OF INTEGRITY

We have to wonder why some of Sears's service writers and mechanics didn't object to the pressure and complain to their managers, district supervisors, or someone in the Sears Tower. Why didn't they practice some absolute honesty?

Right!

Our guess is that, if there were any brave souls who actually spoke up or pushed back, they were figuratively burned at the stake. The pressure to sell was enormous, and bucking it would have been very difficult. We are not talking about people like Jeffery Wigand at Brown and Williamson or Sherron Watkins at Enron, both of whom were vice presidents. These folks at Sears were relatively powerless. And even if there were those who were brave enough to speak up, what could they base their arguments on—ethics?

If people are going to risk expressing controversial viewpoints, especially when challenging the ethical nature of decisions made by their own organization, it helps if they have a set of guidelines on which to base their opinions. We call such guidelines "platforms of integrity."

In 1935, three years after taking control of the bandage company his father had founded in 1885, Robert Wood Johnson published a pamphlet, "Try Reality," in which he urged his fellow industrialists to embrace what he termed "a new industrial philosophy." Johnson defined this as the corporation's responsibility to customers, employees, the community, and stockholders. Eight years later, in 1943, he published his Credo, which has been Johnson & Johnson's platform of integrity ever since. The Credo was the basis upon which J&J made every decision that guided it through the Tylenol crisis of 1982,[17] which we discussed in Chapter 1. The J&J Credo is:

Our Credo

We believe our first responsibility is to the doctors, nurses and patients, to mothers and fathers and all others who use our products and services. In meeting their needs, everything we do must be of high quality. We must constantly strive to reduce our costs in order to maintain reasonable prices. Customers' orders must be serviced promptly and accurately. Our suppliers and distributors must have an opportunity to make a fair profit.

We are responsible to our employees, the men and women who work with us throughout the world. Everyone must be considered as an individual. We must respect their dignity and recognize their merit. They must have a sense of security in their jobs. Compensation must be fair and adequate, and working conditions clean, orderly and safe. We must be mindful of ways to help our employees fulfill their family responsibilities. Employees must feel free to make suggestions and complaints. There must be equal opportunity for employment, development and advancement for those qualified. We must provide competent management, and their actions must be just and ethical.

We are responsible to the communities in which we live and work and to the world community as well. We must be good citizens—support good works and charities and bear our fair share of taxes. We must encourage civic improvements and better health and education. We must maintain in good order the property we are privileged to use, protecting the environment and natural resources.

Our final responsibility is to our stockholders. Business must make a sound profit. We must experiment with new ideas. Research must be carried on, innovative programs developed and mistakes paid for. New equipment must be purchased, new facilities provided and new products launched. Reserves must be created to provide for adverse times.

When we operate according to these principles, the stockholders should realize a fair return.[18]

Notice the order in which the major four concerns of the Credo are discussed: customers, employees, the community, and profitability/shareholder value. While Johnson had a concern for profitability and shareholder value, this came *after* his concerns for customers, employees, and the communities in which they resided. Consequently, when faced with the Tylenol crisis, every manager, spokesperson, and decision maker was able to steer a clear course that saved lives in the short run and the company in the long. To us, the order is correct in that if you are practicing the first three, number four will happen. If only Sears, Enron, and Arthur Andersen had stayed true to similar platforms of integrity, they might not have betrayed us as they did.

BUILD YOUR PLATFORM ON ETHICAL TENETS

There are those who would argue that the term *ethics* is obsolete, especially in business. They say ethics is, at best, a relative term; what matters are the laws of nature and the marketplace. These laws are often summed up by clichés like "Survival of the fittest is the only survival that matters"; "It's not how you play the game, it's who wins that counts"; and, to quote Gordon Gecko, Michael Douglas's ruthless character in the movie *Wall Street,* "Greed is good."

These modern-day cynics claim that winning is everything and that you only engage in quaint acts like being honest, keeping your word, and treating others well because doing so serves your own purposes. For example, if you run a small business, you know that if you cheat your customers, they might find out about it and leave you. You don't want to lose them, so as a matter of practicality, you don't cheat them—unless, of course, you can do it without getting caught. This is what business ethics researchers Dennis P. Quinn and Thomas M. Jones call "instrumental ethics," ethics that appear to be worthwhile and may even achieve good outcomes but are based on strategic considerations alone.[19]

It reminds us of the young bachelor who has learned that he can be more successful in his conquests by pretending to be a "good listener" with his dates. He's practicing "instrumental listening." It may make him seem appealing, especially to women who are hungry to be listened to, and it may get him what he wants, but in the long run, his relationships are likely to ring hollow and lack trust.

Not that there is anything inherently wrong with instrumentality itself. The Disney Company, for example, insists that its theme park employees smile and greet customers whether or not they feel like it. That's instrumental friendliness. Larry had a German exchange student live with his family. Sascha told him that he had read an editorial in his local newspaper that referred to the "viscous friendliness" they encountered when visiting Disney World.[20] They objected to clerks in the shops who were "friendly" just to get customers to spend more money.

And they are right, to a degree. It may be phony, depending on the individual delivering the smile, but where is the harm? From a consumer's point of view, the friendliness certainly makes the transaction more pleasant. Unless you have the social sophistication of a potato, you know that the friendliness is strategic, not genuine. No one is harmed by it except, perhaps, theme parks that lose business to Disney because the Disney staff is so much friendlier.

While instrumental listening and instrumental friendliness may be beneficial, applying instrumentality to ethics is a bad idea. Webster's defines ethics as (a) a set of moral principles or values; (b) a theory or system of moral values; (c) the principles of conduct governing an individual or a group; and (d) a guiding philosophy.[21]

If we accept this definition, then the term *instrumental ethics* becomes an oxymoron, like "jumbo shrimp." How can you have a guiding philosophy or a set of governing principles if those principles change with the whims of the business environment or the mood of your manager? It would be like using a compass that only locks on north when it's convenient for it to do so. It would be useless because you would never know whether or not to believe what it tells you.

For example, a doctor is sworn by the Hippocratic oath to not harm others. That is an ethic we certainly applaud. But does that mean that if he is a plastic surgeon and a patient wants a fourth face lift where the risk is high that the patient will emerge looking freakish, the surgeon should agree to do it?

The doctor practicing instrumental ethics might rationalize a decision to do the surgery by saying to himself, "Well, it's what my patient really wants. I tried to talk him out of it, and when he insisted, I informed him of the risks, so it's his choice. Besides, if I don't do it, someone else will." (We won't mention the nice fat fee the surgery will produce.)

In this example, notice how the ethics that guided the doctor's actions changed to fit the strategic outcome he desired. All of his rationalizations were true, but he still ended up violating a principle he swore to uphold. He also violated the trust placed in him to do what is in his patient's best interest.

Our guess is that the folks at Enron who brought the company down in 2002 probably applied instrumental ethics—if they applied any ethics at all. "Gee, it's my job to create corporate value for the stockholders. I can't let the stock go down by reporting actual losses, so it's okay to set up shadow partnerships to keep Wall Street in the dark about our true financial condition. If our stockholders benefit, I must be doing the right thing."

NONINSTRUMENTAL ETHICS

Noninstrumentality means there is no strategic purpose or hidden agenda tied to a behavior or decision. It is done because of its own merits. The young man on the date who is practicing noninstrumental listening listens because he is truly interested in hearing what his date has to say. He would not go out with her if he were not. There is no deception, and any relationship that develops from the date will reflect a level of authenticity that instrumental listening never could.

The surgeon practicing what Quinn and Jones call "noninstru-mental ethics" would weigh the decision to operate or not against a set of predetermined, unchanging ethical guidelines, and then make the call, regardless of what the patient desires—or how much the surgeon wants the fee.

Likewise, an investment bank practicing noninstrumental ethics might aggressively pursue a lucrative deal to issue an IPO but would never allow its analysts to make public statements that would falsely inflate the value of the IPO's stock—regardless of any pressure the client might bring to bear. It would do this because it subscribes to established guidelines that prohibit such practices. In the short run, this may cause the bank to lose the client to an unscrupulous compet-itor who would offer such service. In the long run, however, the bank's reputation for trustworthiness rises and its officers stay out of the headlines and out of jail.

WHY NONINSTRUMENTAL ETHICS?

Whether you are a CEO, a middle manager, a first-line supervisor, a practicing professional, or a person who's just trying to do your job, basing your decisions and behaviors on a clear and worthy set of noninstrumental ethics and values will always pay off. Here's why:

You Keep Good People

In 1997, Walker Information surveyed more than 1,600 corporate employees and found a strong correlation between employees' opin-ions of their company's ethics and their commitment to their compa-nies.[22] In other words, the better people feel about the ethical behavior of their organizations, the less chance they will leave.

You Avoid Public Ire

The scandals of 2002 fueled public interest in the entire question of ethical behavior in business. By behaving unethically, a few companies caused the SEC and Congress to tighten the laws concerning corporate behavior and governance, imposing a new set of potentially irksome and costly rules. Self-policing and prevention are usually cheaper and less painful than public exorcism, but as business has learned, when you lose the trust of the public, you will pay.

People Trust You More

Obviously, people will trust you when they know that you base your behavior and your decisions on a set of predetermined guidelines or ethics, whether they agree with those ethics or not. Ethical people are predictable people. Predictable people tend to be trustworthy, simply because you can anticipate what they will do and know it will be the right thing. As we said earlier, Ray Kroc was consistent in his behavior, and that behavior held true to a stated set of principles (QSC). Consequently, he was trusted by his customers and his employees.

You Tend to Be More Profitable

According to an analysis in *The Economist*, companies that publish and practice a commitment to ethical practices tend to perform better. Ethical salespeople tend to sell more over the long haul than unethical ones. In contrast, the value of company stock declines when unethical practices have been exposed.[23]

You Avoid Stupid Risks

If you run a shipping company, you could boost shareholder value tremendously by smuggling drugs in addition to your regular freight. But only for a while. In time, the risk would catch up with you and the organization would suffer. On the other hand, if you operate by an ethic that says you and your company will *never* engage in any activity that brings harm to others or breaks the law, then smuggling drugs is obviously out of the question. You may miss some opportunities for quick profits, but in the long run, you and your organization will benefit.

You Sleep Better

Regardless of what you have or have not done, if you follow a set of worthy principles, you will be healthier and happier because you never have to worry about the rightness of your actions. This is no guarantee that you will not suffer when you stand up for what you believe in. Doing the right thing simply makes things clearer and simpler, not necessarily easier, with one exception: Waking up in the morning and looking at the person in the mirror becomes an easier task.

Tough Decisions Become Easier

The choices faced by managers, regardless of their position, are not always as obvious as deciding whether or not to smuggle drugs. For example, what do you do if:

- You have a customer who is threatening to leave you if you do not make concessions on product price that go beyond your published guidelines—guidelines that your other customers have been told are inviolable?
- You learn that your best researcher, a brilliant scientist who has created enormous value for the company, is moonlighting on a project that is in direct conflict with the noncompete clause in the contracts of all your researchers?
- You have an opportunity to hire a promising engineer, but it will mean laying off an older employee whose performance is

satisfactory but who hasn't kept his software development skills current?

▲ You learn you can avoid reporting the losses of a division in your quarterly earnings report by shifting the loss to capital expenditures, thus creating an inflated stock value?

▲ A customer wants you to invoice him at one price and kick back a percentage so he can bill his customer at a higher rate?

In each case the question is, "What is the right thing for the organization, the shareholders, the employees, yourself, and the community?" Guidance from a clear set of noninstrumental ethics can help clarify the answer.

For example, Larry was asked by one of the partner/owners of a motorcycle dealership what she should do about an employee who had stolen a valuable set of motorcycle parts from the dealership. She said that this fellow was an absolute whiz mechanic. He was dependable, his work was accurate, he worked fast, the customers liked him, and he was one of the most knowledgeable technicians she had ever known.

In addition, finding someone to replace him would be extremely difficult. The dealership is located in a rural area, and mechanics of his caliber in that area are rare. Her inclination was to fire the mechanic, regardless of his virtues, because of the example it would set for the other employees. Her husband and co-owner of the dealership wanted to give the fellow another chance.

After some discussion with her husband, they decided to take the moral high ground and let the mechanic go. It wasn't an easy decision, but it turned out to be the right one. She recently told us that shortly after they fired him, one of their less-experienced mechanics stepped into the vacuum and became a shop leader. After a few months, production was back to normal and the customers barely noticed that the dishonest mechanic was gone. You will remember that in Chapter 3, we identified "fear of paying the price" as a major reason we avoid telling the truth, and that you usually discover it's not as painful as you think. That certainly turned out to be true for the owners of the motorcycle dealership.

ESTABLISH AN ETHICAL FOUNDATION

While advising the owners of the motorcycle dealership, Larry asked the woman if she and her husband had established any kind of basic ethics or values upon which they ran their business. "Not specifically," she said, "we just try to do what's right."

Unfortunately, each of us has a different perception of what it means to do "what's right." Larry suggested to her, and we suggest to you, that you establish a set of ethical tenets that spell out what you consider to be right and wrong.

There are many variations of basic ethical tenets. Every religion on earth has developed its own brand, though they all have a certain commonality. We have identified five that we think have universal appeal. They were confirmed by the work of Quinn and Jones[24] that we mentioned earlier. We call them the Five Tenets of Ethical Behavior:

1. Tell the truth. Don't lie.
2. Keep your word, always.
3. Respect the rights of others.
4. Avoid harming others.
5. Don't break the law.

Tell the Truth. Don't Lie

Telling the truth renders the walls of your life and your business transparent. It's like living in a glass house: You keep a cleaner house.

You don't want anyone to see the unmade bed and the dirty dishes. You make it a habit to keep things neat and clean, and you insist that everyone else in your organization do the same. The result is a very clean organization. As we stated earlier, if you don't lie, you never have to worry about trying to remember exactly what you said.

Keep Your Word, Always

This tenet is an extension of telling the truth. If you agree to do something, and then do not do it, you have retroactively told a lie. Trust evaporates. Business becomes impossible when a person's word means nothing. Life becomes very difficult when we cannot count on people or organizations to do what they say they will do. By insisting that everyone in your organization abide by this tenet, your business functions better by eliminating the excuses for nonperformance from person to person and department to department. Your customers are happier because either they get what they were promised or they are not given the promise in the first place. And your stockholders are happier because you deliver what you promised within an ethical framework that ensures honest and accurate financial results.

Respect the Rights of Others

Since criminality almost always starts with failing to respect the rights of others, clinging steadfastly to this tenet reduces the chances your organization will do wrong. Dennis Kozlowski, CEO of Tyco, who allegedly raided corporate coffers to build mansions, throw million-dollar parties, and buy a $6,000 shower curtain, could do so because he didn't respect his own stockholders. The employer who discriminates in promotions on the basis of race, color, creed, age, gender, religious preference, or sexual orientation totally disregards this tenet, as does the employee who calls in sick when he's well, earning wages for work that could be, but isn't, done.

Avoid Harming Others

Whether you liked him or not, President Clinton's legacy will be forever tarnished by the Paula Jones/Monica Lewinsky scandals. As we pointed out earlier, had the president just told the truth, he would have avoided a lot of self-inflicted pain. He also violated the tenet to "avoid harming others," which is far more distressing. President Clinton allowed people who trusted and loved him, including Mrs. Clinton, to publicly support his lies. When he was finally forced to tell the truth, his loyal supporters were the casualties of his selfish efforts to save himself. You may be thinking, "How about my competitors? Should I not try to harm them?" We think not. Healthy competition is not about destroying your competition; it is about improving your own capabilities to be the best in the marketplace. Competition creates the arena in which all ships rise by getting better. The difference with predatory business practices is that they are usually implemented to "kill" the competition, not just to outperform them. We believe that when your strategy is to destroy others using unethical practices, you have stepped over the line onto that dark road we mentioned earlier.

Consider Southwest Airlines. It has been rated the most efficient and profitable airline in the world. When Southwest moves into a new market, its competitors must lower their prices to compete, not because Southwest practices unfair or predatory pricing, but because it operates more efficiently than other airlines so it can charge less. A study on airline industry economics concluded that its competitors would have to cut their spending by $18 *billion* just to catch up to Southwest.[25] Southwest maintains a business practice that dictates it will not "overcharge" the customer. Consequently, Southwest's competitors find it difficult to undercut Southwest's prices and must instead improve the efficiency of their operations or offer better service for their higher prices. In either case, they must improve. If Southwest is your competition, attempting to harm or destroy it may sound appealing, but it will not do anyone any good, including yourself.

Improving is the only option that allows everyone, including your customers, to win.

Many of the antitrust laws in effect today responded to the predatory practices used in the early 1900s by John D. Rockefeller and other business barons of the time. They made their fortunes doing business in a way that would be considered illegal today. Unfortunately, the greed and illegal actions we saw in 2002 are not new.

Don't Break the Law

This tenet not only keeps you out of the headlines and out of jail, but it also keeps your organization in sync with the standards of the community within which you operate. Abiding by the law does not guarantee that your behavior will be honorable or ethical—you can always hire smart lawyers and accountants to figure ways around the law. But is it right?

William George, former CEO of Medtronic, describes a meeting with Tyco CEO Dennis Kozlowski, who bragged about avoiding paying U.S. taxes by locating his company headquarters in Bermuda. When George left the office, he first made sure he still had his wallet and then decided to cancel further talks with Tyco.[26]

APPLYING THE FIVE TENETS TO UP-SELLING

Earlier in this chapter we broached the question of when healthy up-selling becomes unhealthy and unethical, as it did at Sears Automotive Centers in 1992. We would apply the Five Tenets of Ethical behavior, and ask:

  ▲ Are the salespeople telling customers the truth—the whole truth—about the product, including whether the customer really needs the added item?

▲ Are the salespeople keeping their word when they promise to deliver what they say they will deliver?

▲ Does the up-selling policy respect the rights of customers to truly benefit from the extra price they will pay? Are the salespeople respecting the customer's right to make informed choices, or are they simply slamming the customer in the deal to make a buck?

▲ Does offering the customer the chance to buy a front-end alignment or a brake job cause the customer harm?

▲ Will the salespeople break any laws by exhibiting enthusiasm and attempting to up-sell the product or service?

Asking these questions—and others like them—not only helps ensure that your policies and practices are ethical, it also helps create goodwill and trust with your customers. There is nothing wrong with offering customers products and services that add value to their dealings with you. Everyone comes out a winner. It's when customers are treated like marks and sold what they don't need that trust evaporates and customers go elsewhere.

NO EASY ANSWERS

We don't mean to imply that ethical guidelines will make ethical decisions completely painless or simple. For example, in the examples listed in the Tough Decisions Become Easier section a few pages back, not giving a special price break to the customer we mentioned above will keep your promise to other customers that your guidelines are inviolable, but it may harm shareholder equity if you lose the customer. Not hiring the promising engineer will respect the contributions of the older employee, but it will cost the company in the loss of young talent. Firing the research scientist who has violated his contract will keep your promise to the other researchers, but it could also harm the company. In each case, you must weight all factors, including financial and ethical ones, and decide what's the right thing to do.

CREATE AND STICK TO A PLATFORM OF INTEGRITY

If ethics are the codes by which we should conduct our business, then integrity is the "firm adherence" to those codes. The better we define an ethical code to fit the everyday situations we all face, the easier it will be for people to "firmly adhere" to that code.

If you've watched any police shows on TV—or if you've been a guest of your local police department—you are familiar with your "rights" when you are arrested:

> You have the right to remain silent. Anything you say can and will be used against you in a court of law. You have the right to have an attorney. If you cannot afford one, an attorney will be appointed for you free of charge.

Most people think this "speech" was mandated by the Supreme Court as a result of the famous Miranda case. (In 1962, during questioning by Phoenix police for an unrelated robbery, Ernesto Miranda confessed to an unsolved kidnapping and rape case for which he was convicted and sentenced to twenty years. His attorney appealed the case to the U.S. Supreme Court, which ordered a new trial based on the premise that Miranda should have been warned that what he said could be held against him.)

What many people don't know is that the "Miranda speech" evolved from the efforts of many law enforcement agencies to create a standardized set of guidelines to help officers carry out the court's intention.[27] It is a form of what we call a "platform of integrity," a recipe for putting into action the principles the court intended. We believe that every organization should have such a platform to help its members carry out the ethical intentions of its founders and management.

BASE YOUR PLATFORM OF INTEGRITY ON SOLID ETHICS

We were not there when General Johnson wrote his Credo for Johnson & Johnson, but it seems he had some of the Five Tenets of Ethical Behavior in mind. For example, in the first line he says:

> We believe our first responsibility is to the doctors, nurses and patients, to mothers and fathers and all others who use our products and services.

It sounds like he was respecting the rights of his customers, committing to keep his word, and promising to avoid harming those he was committing to serve.

Or take the line:

> Employees must feel free to make suggestions and complaints. There must be equal opportunity for employment, development and advancement for those qualified.

The underpinnings of this section seem to be the tenet of respecting the rights of others. What makes this one remarkable is that Johnson wrote the Credo in 1943—not exactly a year known for enlightened employee empowerment and equal opportunity in the workplace.

Like J&J, Thomson Multimedia thrives with a clear platform of integrity. With sales of Euro 10.5 billion in 2001 and more than 73,000 employees in over thirty countries, Thomson Multimedia is the fourth largest supplier of consumer electronics products in the world. To guide its employees in how they conduct their business every day, the company adopted the following ten Global Business Ethics Activities as their platform of integrity:[28]

1. *Tolerate no discrimination and encourage diversity.* Thomson is located in thirty different countries. It can't afford to be anything other than inclusive of all races, religions, genders, and cultures.

2. *Promote the best working conditions; use no child or forced labor.* According to Chairman Thierry Breton, this is important not so much to avoid a Cathy Lee Gifford or Nike-like scandal, but because it makes good business sense. Better working conditions lead to improved productivity. Besides, from a noninstrumental point of view, it's the right thing to do.

3. *Support employees' development.* Thomson supports further education for all its employees through tuition reimbursement and work-study programs. Additionally, the company encourages managers to assign employees to positions outside their countries of origin to create international cross-fertilization of ideas and business knowledge. According to Chairman Breton, if you are an international company but you only hire locals, you become a fragmented conglomeration of local fiefdoms instead of an integrated international competitor.

4. *Value the company's interests first.* This doesn't mean that Thomson expects its employees to give up their families or

personal life for the good of the company. It simply means that each must be willing to do what it takes to fulfill the company's potential and goals. If you must work three weekends in a row so that one of the major television networks will have the equipment it needs to broadcast the Olympics, you do it without thinking about it.

5. *Avoid potential conflicts of interest.* Although common practice in some of the countries in which Thomson does business, giving kickbacks and special deals to vendors in order to feather one's own nest is not tolerated. Such deals are not only illegal, they make for a perception of corruption outside the organization, and they steal resources from the company.

6. *Protect people's health, safety, and the environment.* This one makes sense in any business, but especially at Thomson, which produces and sells over 16 million picture tubes annually. A picture tube is a giant glass vase weighing up to 200 pounds and filled with wires and chemicals. Picture tube factories would be very dangerous places to work if Thomson did not take this part of its business very seriously.

7. *Respect consumer and personal privacy.* In today's information age, great harm can come to anyone if his or her personal information is recklessly divulged. Thomson operates on a value that says it will cause no harm to the people with whom it does business. The company also respects individual privacy and recognizes the many legal jurisdictions it operates in that may require special care of an employee's personal information.

8. *Respect fair market competition.* You have to love this one. We've seen many companies commit to treating their customers, their employees, their communities, and their vendors fairly, but rarely do we see one publish a commitment not to take advantage of its competitors through predatory pricing or industrial espionage.

9. *Strive to be a good corporate citizen wherever we operate.* Rather than insulating itself from its communities, Thomson chooses to support them as a good corporate citizen.

10. *Respect and protect shareholder value.* Just as it respects and protects its customers, employees, and communities, Thomson respects and protects its shareholders. If you do this well, you'll never end up in the same sinking boat as Global Crossing or Enron.

If you're cynical, you can look at this list and wonder, "Aren't many of these ten planks a bit like instrumental ethics? After all, Thomson doesn't support employee development out of the goodness of its own heart. It reaps great benefits by having employees who are well trained and educated."

The answer is "Yes, but." Yes, the planks benefit Thomson, but they should. A company does not exist just to do the right thing; it exists to make a profit and chooses to do the right thing because it believes that is the best path to its goals. Remember, we said there is nothing wrong with instrumentality per se. We just think that your platform of integrity should be based on ethical values that are essentially noninstrumental—that is, created for their own merit, regardless of corporate strategy or changing markets—and that are unchanging. That way, your ethical practices don't vary with the whims of different managers and changing market conditions.

LIVE BY YOUR PLATFORM OF INTEGRITY

Going through the motions of reading a suspect his Miranda rights does not guarantee that those rights will be granted to him. An unscrupulous officer can always circumvent the spirit of the court's wishes if motivated to do so. For those honest ones not so inclined, however, having guidelines or a platform of integrity helps.

In a business setting, posting a set of guidelines or company values on the office walls or printing them in the employee handbook mean nothing if the leaders are not willing to live by them, embrace them, enforce them, and communicate them consistently as a way of doing business.

For example, Costco maintains a policy of limiting markups to 12 percent. When its purchasing department gets an unusually large discount on a purchase, rather than take the windfall, CEO James Sinegal insists on passing the savings on to customers. "The members count on us to deliver the best deal. Jim doesn't cheat on that," said Vice President John McCay.[29]

Contrast Sinegal's behavior with Enron's board of directors, who were informed about the existence and nefarious purpose of the partnerships that led to the company's downfall, and then approved moving debts off the books in order to hide losses—all clear violations of general accounting practices, and Enron's own accounting guidelines.[30] Is it any wonder that Enron got into trouble? If you're going to have guidelines, leadership must abide by them.

It also helps to have the guidelines available so people can find their own answers to the questions that inevitably arise. IBM is an example of one of the best. If you go to *http://www-1.ibm.com/partner world/pwhome.nsf/weblook/memctr_guide_chap1.html*, you will see IBM's Business Conduct Guidelines. This Web site is IBM's platform of integrity. It is organized into hundreds of possible situations that help employees make the right choice when they face an ethical dilemma. For example, if you are an IBM purchasing agent and you are not sure whether you should accept a gift from a supplier, you can go to the table of contents and click on "Bribes, gifts, and entertainment—Receiving gifts," where you will find:

> Neither you nor any member of your family may solicit or accept from a supplier or customer money or a gift that

could influence or could reasonably give the appearance of influencing IBM's business relationship with that supplier or customer.

The only way to get much clearer than that is to create scenarios where people can read about actual circumstances in which they might apply the guideline.

Northrop Grumman Corporation, an $18 billion global aerospace and defense company, does an excellent job of providing its 100,000 employees with such a reference. In addition to a statement of values from the CEO, it includes specific situations such as:

> What if you suspected a co-worker of misleading a customer in order to make a sale? What would you do? Do you ignore the problem because the sale helps the company's bottom line, or do you take action? What if you saw your supervisor harassing a co-worker? Would you keep quiet to avoid trouble with your boss or would you report the incident?
>
> In both of these cases, action should be taken. Northrop Grumman's ethics and compliance program requires all employees to report any suspected or observed wrongdoing. When we fail to report cases like this, we may think we are protecting our co-workers, our company, or ourselves. In fact, we are putting our assets and our reputation at greater risk.[31]

DEVELOPING THE TENETS AND THE PLATFORM

Scholars and practitioners have varying opinions on the best way to develop an effective platform of integrity. Some, like Robert Solomon of the University of Texas, think that the best programs are those that address the way everybody already behaves and feels. The worst, according to Solomon, are those mandated by senior managers, especially if those senior managers don't practice what they preach.[32]

Using this model, you want to incorporate as much input into your platform of integrity from as many people as possible. Create teams from all levels to brainstorm what should be the ethical standards of the organization, and then burn up reams of flip chart paper as the teams discuss, refine, and come to consensus. Finally, institutionalize the results and treat them as the law of the land. The best time and place to do this is when you create a new business plan because it can define the values and ethics you want to instill in the company from the beginning.

The Maguire Group, a firm of architects, engineers, and planners located in Providence, Rhode Island, developed its entire ethics policy through this consensus approach. In 1992, the president/majority owner was forced to resign for making improper payments to city officials in exchange for work. In response, the firm developed a comprehensive ethics policy, coordinated by its manager of human resources, Mary Rendini. To avoid creating a document "complete with legalese and complex language," the firm identified a group of twenty-seven employees drawn from all levels of the organization who volunteered to work on an ethics task force. These folks were then divided into five teams and assigned to research and write policy statements on four key issues:

▲ Gifts and gratuities
▲ Political contributions
▲ Entertainment/business development
▲ Bribes and kickbacks

It took more than eight months, but the resulting ethics policy (their platform of integrity) has served Maguire well ever since. The company even received the National Society of Professional Engineers' Professional Development Award—Honorable Mention for Private Practice for "outstanding contributions to the advancement and improvement of the engineering profession through employment policies (Ethics Program)." You can download a PDF copy of Maguire's Code of Ethics and Business Conduct Guidelines from http://www.maguiregroup.com/ethics.htm.[33]

Patrick M. Lencioni, author of *The Five Dysfunctions of a Team*,[34] offers another approach. He argues that the value statements of an organization should be created by a small team, headed by the leader and consisting of any founders still around and a few key employees.[35]

We like this approach because the resulting values incorporate the sentiments of rank-and-file employees but are strongly influenced by the values of the leader, which are paramount. Imagine Walt Disney when he was creating Disneyland back in the 1950s. Would he have tried to gain consensus among all the park employees on what the dress code should have been? If he had, our guess is that the dress code would have looked a lot like the teenage fashions of the time: poodle skirts, ducktail haircuts, and black leather jackets.

Walt had a vision of a family park that was unmistakably clean and wholesome. Creating the dress code was a matter of putting together key people to come up with one that supported Walt's vision. Once established, it became the law of the park and people were hired, promoted, and fired based, in part, on their willingness to embrace this value.

There are times when the culture of the organization dictates that consensus is a better option. At the Maguire group, leadership failed the company, putting employees in the best position to determine where they wanted the company to go. In other instances, however, leadership must take charge to pull the organization in a different direction. Lou Gerstner turned stagnating IBM in a new direction by doing a lot of listening and then exerting a top-down leadership approach that basically said, "Here's where we are going. The train is leaving the station. Get on board or get off the train."[36]

Either way, consensus or top-down, we believe that, for a platform to be relevant, the organization's leaders *must* be involved. We are reminded of something the late guru of Total Quality Management, W. Edwards Deming, said at the beginning of one of his famous four-day quality symposiums. "If your job title is quality coordinator, vice president in charge of quality, quality program director, or some other similar title—and your job is to lead the quality effort in your company—find another job!"[37]

The audience responded to Deming's comment with nervous laughter. The room was packed with 500 people with titles Deming had listed, and they obviously weren't sure how to interpret what he had said. Deming explained that the only person who can truly lead the quality effort in an organization is the person at the top. Otherwise, quality improvement becomes just another fad that will go the way of other programs—here today, forgotten tomorrow.

Deming was right. During the 1980s and 1990s, many companies tried many different programs to improve quality, with varying degrees of success. Most gave up after a few years and went on to other fads—reengineering, right-sizing, decentralization, team empowerment, and others. On the other hand, the companies whose leaders became fanatical supporters of the quality concept and led the efforts themselves were the companies that had the most success.

Jack Welch, the former CEO of General Electric, is a good example. In the late 1990s he and his executive team decided to adopt the Six Sigma approach to quality improvement that had been perfected by Motorola. He immersed himself in the effort, teaching many of the training classes himself, making Six Sigma a part of everyone's performance plan, and incorporating Six Sigma into every aspect of operations. As a result, General Electric's Six Sigma process is part of every operation worldwide and is credited with reducing costs to the point that "GE's operating margin broke the 15 percent barrier in 1997 after hovering around 10 percent for decades,"[38] saving the company hundreds of millions of dollars.

The same principle applies to establishing and living by an effective ethics program. To maximize its chances for success, the leader must be involved and committed. Period.

ETHICS AND PROFITABILITY

Leaders must build a platform of integrity because the business world is a gray world, rife with ambiguity and shaped by shifting situations. What's true today wasn't true yesterday and probably won't be true tomorrow, yet fundamental truths remain. We need an unchanging, noninstrumental platform to guide our decisions and actions in this gray world.

Some argue for situational ethics, platforms that are flexible, broad, and adaptable, that do not hamstring us with unreasonable rules. We know what's best, they declare. Let us do our thing or we cannot remain competitive and profits will fall.

Of course, the same arguments have been voiced whenever a company imposed new guidelines, whether for Total Quality Management or "green" initiatives or other cultural changes. We believe those arguments are wrong. We believe companies that develop and implement a platform of integrity will be more profitable, not less, for all the reasons we list in this chapter. People trust you more, which helps you retain customers and employees. You avoid risky decisions and actions that can cost you customers or, worse yet, your freedom. You find that tough decisions—those slippery ethical dilemmas that can be hard to distinguish in a gray world—become easier to make because you have a platform of integrity to guide you.

In Chapter 9 we explain how you can build an infrastructure that promotes ethical conduct and a culture of absolute honesty. Because in the continuum of best practices that make a company an industry leader, an ethics-based system within a culture of absolute honesty is the next great step.

TOWARD AN ETHICAL CULTURE

A sound ethical management system is one attribute of a company that knows what it is and where it's going. In our experience, evidence of such self-awareness and self-confidence can be found throughout the organization: in conversations with its leaders, in team meetings, in its dealings with customers and suppliers, and in the ways individual employees work.

The benefits of such an ethical culture cannot be underestimated:

- A *culture of integrity* prevents Enronesque disasters from occurring and builds loyalty among customers and employees.
- A *compelling brand* evolves from consistent application of ethical guidelines.
- A *competitive advantage* ensues when people feel free to speak the truth, to ask tough questions, to disagree, and to argue.
- A *productive workforce* flourishes when employees spend their time and energy on the business they need to conduct, not on destructive politics and dysfunctional relationships.
- *Consistent leadership* that makes ethical behavior an integral part of everyone's job builds unstoppable momentum for the company.
- *Positive morale* results when employees are treated and treat each other with honesty and respect.

Deciding *where* to start creating an ethical culture matters less than that you *do start*. As we've mentioned, it can take eighteen months to institutionalize ethical attitudes to the point where they become part of the culture. We have given you a number of strategies for establishing such a culture as well as Six Laws of Absolute Honesty that everyone can use to unleash the power of open communication. If you're a leader, the next step is to decide the ethical direction you want your company to take. Once you've done that, we advise you to establish an ethical platform to guide those in your organization, to train employees in what that platform means to them, and to integrate ethics into your performance management system.

If you're an employee, the next step is to learn and apply the Six Laws of Absolute Honesty. To help you with this, we have summarized the key points of each law in Chapter 10.

Whatever your position, you can influence the honest, ethical direction your organization takes because, in the end, ethical considerations are individual considerations. It's how we treat our peers, coworkers, employees, neighbors, friends, and family. Together, you can build an ethical culture where honesty, integrity, and respect thrive.

PART 3

WHERE DO WE GO

FROM HERE?

CHAPTER 9

Building an Ethical Infrastructure

Law is order, and good law is good order.

—*ARISTOTLE (384–322 B.C.)* [1]

IN HIS LANDMARK BOOK, *LEADING CHANGE*, HARVARD PROFESSOR John Kotter tells us that one of the main reasons organizational change fails is that the change is not anchored firmly to the corporate culture. He says that "change sticks only when it becomes 'the way we do things around here.'"[2] We believe that creating an infrastructure that makes ethical business practice an integral part of your organization's processes helps to create this anchor.

It clarifies for everyone what your standards are. We're not big fans of massive bureaucracy and lots of rules, however, when procedures and guidelines are in place, and people are accustomed to following them, the odds that everyone, including the leaders, will abide by them, goes up. Remember the analogy of living in a glass house. A formal ethics program raises the blinds and opens the windows of the house. There is no hiding behind the excuse of not knowing what is expected.

It makes ethical behavior part of everyone's job. When there is a formal ethical infrastructure in place, employees who want to speak up have a platform from which to do so and guidelines to tell them how to do it.

The nature of an ethical infrastructure depends on your company's needs and personality. In our experience, it should include the following elements:

1. Leadership
2. Philosophy
3. Communication
4. Training
5. Rewards and Consequences

LEADERSHIP

A new or stronger infrastructure implies a level of change that only an organization's leaders can drive. One way to do this is through a steering committee made up of the CEO and one or two senior executives, the company's legal representative, one or two middle managers, and two or three line employees. A union, if present, should be represented. This cross section of the organization will ensure that all perspectives are present.

The purpose of the steering committee, which typically meets quarterly, is to oversee the design, implementation, and operation of the company's ethics program. This includes establishing a statement of ethics and ethical guidelines. As issues arise that are not clearly defined by the guidelines, the steering committee resolves them. It also periodically audits the program to ensure it is working as planned.

If you are a top executive, you may be saying, "Wait a minute. I'm much too busy to be involved in this. Why can't I delegate it to, say, the head of human resources?" Well, you can, but then the message you send is that ethics are not as important as the other things on your plate. If that plate features finance but not ethics, the next time an employee is faced with an ethical issue that affects the bottom line, guess which one will play second fiddle?

Another important role for the steering committee is to regularly review the performance of the ethics program with the board of directors. We think semiannual formal reviews raise the odds that the organization will stay focused on the value of ethical business practices.

Some companies drive an ethical culture by creating the position of corporate ethics officer. The officer, who is a member of the steering committee, coordinates the activities of the committee and monitors ethical activities within the organization. To remain current with ethical standards and thinking, we recommend that the corporate ethics officer be involved in the Ethics Officers Association (http://www.eoa.org).

PHILOSOPHY

An ethical infrastructure stands on a philosophical foundation that defines what the company believes. This may include a statement of ethical tenets like the five recommended in Chapter 8. It may include a platform of integrity based on the tenets that capture the organization's values and desired behavioral outcomes. It may also include *business conduct guidelines* that address specific situations, like those we described at IBM and Northrop Grumman.

One of the best examples of a strong ethical foundation can be found at Weyerhaeuser, an international forest products company that employs 58,000 people in eighteen countries. Weyerhaeuser generated $14.5 billion in sales in 2001 and has been ranked first in its industry in social responsibility by *Fortune* magazine for seven years.

According to its Business Conduct Office (*http://www.weyer haeuser.com/citizenship/businessconduct/busconductoffice.asp*), the company's Business Conduct Vision is: "Ethics at the core of every Weyerhaeuser decision." Its mission is to "provide leadership on standards of business conduct, educate on ethical decision making, and ensure adherence to laws, company policies, and guidelines."[3]

Under Weyerhaeuser's business conduct program, which was started in 1976, every employee receives the company's code of ethics and business conduct, takes regular ethics training, and is expected to model and promote ethical behavior. Weyerhaeuser revises the code of ethics and business conduct every three years and makes it available to customers, contractors, suppliers, and the public. Topics covered by the code include safety, antitrust, conflict of interest, environmental responsibility, gifts and entertainment, and international business conduct.

The Business Conduct Office comprises full-time professionals who report to the committee chair and the CEO. The absence of a direct reporting relationship with any business or department means the office can be an objective resource for employees.

COMMUNICATION

Disseminating the ethics code, as Weyerhaeuser does through regular communication and training, is key to making it part of your company's culture, but that is only half the communication battle. You also need a communication system that encourages employees to ask ethical questions and to anonymously report ethics violations. For example, Northrop Grumman includes the following in its ethics policy statement:

> If for any reason you feel that you must report an incident anonymously, you can do so through our Open-Line process by phone at 410-xxx-xxxx or toll-free at 1-800-xxx-xxxx.

TRAINING

The best way to promote consistent application of your ethics code is through a training program that reaches all employees through an orientation class for new employees and introductory and refresher courses for existing employees.

This required training program covers the meaning and application of the company's:

▲ Ethical tenets/vision/mission
▲ Platform of integrity
▲ Business conduct guidelines

To be effective, the training must be more than a philosophical wish list. The best ethics training features real-life examples of ethical issues that employees have encountered, case studies of ethical dilemmas employees may face, and discussion about possible ethical solutions in these situations. The training should also touch upon those unique situations that cannot be covered by the written code.

Through this training, employees will be able to think for themselves within the framework and expectations of the organization.

REWARDS AND CONSEQUENCES

If you've taken Psychology 101—or if you've raised children—you are aware of three basic principles of behaviorism:

1. Reinforced behavior is more likely to be repeated.
2. Punished behavior will clarify boundary lines.
3. Rewards work better than punishment.

We think these principles should be a part of a comprehensive ethics infrastructure.

Reinforced Behavior Is More Likely to Be Repeated

If we are rewarded for doing something, we are more likely to do it again. Bob worked with a company that gives every employee a bank of points at the beginning of the year that can be traded for merchandise at the company store. Employees are encouraged to award these points to their cohorts when they "catch them doing something right." Employees cannot spend their own points, only those that have been awarded to them by others. There are no restrictions on how or why each employee doles out his points, only that the giver specifically describes the act that he is rewarding. The whole idea is to get "caught in the act" of doing something positive.

If you're cynical, you might wonder why people don't conspire to beat the system by just trading points. Since the specific acts are also published in the company's online newsletter, that hasn't been a problem.

Punished Behavior Will Clarify Boundary Lines

It is human nature to pursue pleasure and avoid pain. Punishment is the application of pain to change behavior. Of course, it is the threat and not the actual punishment that discourages most from doing wrong, and it can be a very effective tool. You are less likely to commit insider trading if you fear the pain of getting caught, having your face splashed across the headlines, and doing jail time. So it clarifies the boundary line over which you must not cross.

On the downside, threatening punishment is expensive because you must monitor and police potential violations for it to work. In addition, if people consider themselves untouchable because of their positions in life, the threat of punishment does no good. Leona Helmsley once said that only the "little people" pay taxes. Threat of punishment did not dissuade her because she obviously thought she was above the law. You have to believe you may get caught for the threat of punishment to be effective.

Don't get us wrong: We are not saying that you shouldn't include punishment in your ethics program because it is costly to monitor or because some people will figure ways around it. We think a good ethics program *must* include severe penalties for violation of the rules in order to make a strong statement to everyone in the company, as well as to the outside world, that ethics are important.

We just think an effective ethics program should include more than a set of penalties for crossing the integrity line. In our experience, that means there are better alternatives.

Rewards Work Better Than Punishment

When Gordon Bethune took the reigns of Continental Airlines, its on-time arrival record was the worst in the industry. In 1995, he offered employees a $65 bonus for every month the company landed in the top five as measured by the U.S. Department of Transportation. The first month they moved from last to seventh. The second month, they landed in the top five. They completed the year finishing in the top five eight out of twelve months.[4]

We're not suggesting that you should offer to pay everyone $65 for every month your company doesn't come under fire from the SEC or your industry ethics group. But you can use the same reward systems you would use to celebrate and reward outstanding performance to encourage people to do the right thing. For example, Para-Med Health Services, a Canadian home health service runs heart-warming stories about its staff who go out of their way to provide special services for their homebound patients while off the clock.[5]

In addition, we suggest that you include adherence to strict ethical standards in the contract and feedback phases of your performance management system. That way, every time an employee receives a review of performance and participates in the planning of future performance, ethical issues can be revisited. If more executives had had their ethical performance evaluated in 2002 during their performance reviews, perhaps the scandals would have been avoided.

SMALL BUSINESSES TOO

If you are part of a small business or organization, you may be asking, "Gee, do we need this much of an institutionalized approach?"

Well, yes and no. No, it doesn't have to be as elaborate as the five elements we just described, but, yes, all five elements should be present. They serve to ensure that the people in your organization behave honestly and ethically. You don't have to be Sears to mistakenly pressure your salespeople to cheat customers; it can be done in a car dealership that employs sixty or in a dress store that employs ten. In companies that don't need an elaborate performance management process, you can still set goals and objectives with your employees that define "how" they get their work done as well as "what" you want them to accomplish.

If you're in a smaller company, you will want to modify the formula. For example, no matter what the size of your organization, a statement of your ethical tenets and a platform of integrity are essential so that people know where you and the company stand on ethical issues. Having a committee to monitor ethical activity is probably overkill; an ethics leader can fill that role. Communication systems can take the form of an open-door policy to hear complaints or a voice-mail system that allows people to leave anonymous messages, or both. No matter what size your organization is, ethics training should be mandatory. In a small company, however, it can simply be a part of the agenda of your monthly or quarterly meetings. Finally, including this stuff in your performance management system is no different than in a large company since performance management plans are tailored to individuals, not groups.

DON'T FORGET GOOD JUDGMENT

CJ, the branch manager of a mortgage company, told us about a loan officer we'll call Jane who resigned after working for CJ for three years. Six months later, the home office payroll manager called CJ to inquire about the status of a deduction on Jane's paycheck. When CJ told him that Jane had resigned six months ago, he replied that she was still receiving and cashing a regular paycheck. After some investigation, CJ discovered that the company had mistakenly failed to take Jane off the payroll and had continued to send her check to CJ's office every two weeks. CJ's secretary, whose job included receiving and distributing the paychecks, had been sending checks on to Jane without saying anything to CJ or anyone else.

Jane and the secretary were friends, which meant the secretary could not claim that she didn't know Jane no longer worked there. CJ fired the secretary and the company sued Jane for return of the ill-gotten paychecks. The secretary sued for lost wages, claiming that Jane had told her that the payroll checks were a part of her 401(k) distribution. The secretary also stated that she was unfairly judged because there were no guidelines to tell her what she should do in such a situation.

The court ruled for the company, noting that it is impossible to write guidelines for every possible scenario. Sometimes, you simply have to use good ethical judgment. That's why it is so important to develop detailed ethical guidelines (platforms of integrity) built on a core set of ethics (like the Five Tenets of Ethics). That way, whether or not your Business Conduct Guidelines contain a specific reference to a particular situation, an employee can use good judgment, based on the Five Tenets, to make the right choice.

NO GUARANTEE, BUT . . .

An organization's ethical infrastructure is strongest when its leaders believe in it and behave as if they do; when its underlying philosophy rests on a strong moral and ethical sense of right and wrong; when systems are in place that allow for open communication and straight talk to occur; when there is ongoing, relevant training; and when the rewards and compensation systems support it.

Of course, having such an infrastructure is no guarantee. Many of the companies that sent us all reeling with shocking revelations of dishonesty, manipulation, and silent complicity in 2002 contained some elements of such an infrastructure. Having one in place only makes it easier for committed leaders to ensure that the right things are done throughout the organization. But it always starts with committed leaders—so take heed.

CHAPTER 10

Key Points to Help Your Implementation Efforts

LEARNING THEORISTS TELL US THAT LEARNING IS A FOUR-STAGE process:

1. *Awareness.* You read about it, hear about it, watch it, or experience it.
2. *Awkwardness.* You try it and find it is difficult and awkward because you haven't done it before.
3. *Skill.* You can do it, but you've got to think consciously about it when you do it.
4. *Habit.* You've done it so often that neural pathways have been established so you can do it and do it well without thinking about it.

If you've ever learned to ski, you probably followed this model. On the first day, the instructor showed you how to snow plow, to turn, to fall down, and to get up. Then you tried it and, except for the falling down, which comes pretty naturally, it was all dreadfully awkward. But if you messed with it and messed with it, you eventually got to where you could get on and off the lift, and then ski down the mountain, albeit on the easy runs, and do it with a minimum of falls. At that point, you were moving from awkwardness into the lower levels of skill. You could do it, but you had to think about it. The moment you lost your concentration, you'd cross your skis or catch a tip and down you'd go. The skill stage is quite long, but if you went skiing a lot, there came a time when you slipped into the fourth stage, and you were able to whip down the mountain without thinking about what you were doing. Of course, you still had to keep an eye on where you were going.

Learning to practice and implement everything we've discussed in this book is a lot like learning to ski. You'll have to go through the four-stage learning curve. Hopefully, much of the task will have been made easier because you already practice honesty, straight talking, and ethical behavior with unwavering integrity. If not, welcome to the world of awkwardness.

But first, let's make sure the awareness stage is fully locked in place. The learning theorists also tell us that this is a good idea. It's called review, and it's bound to turn up a nugget or two that was missed on the first pass. So here we go.

THE NAKED TRUTH

There are many reasons to practice absolute honesty and to establish it as a way of doing business in your organization. Absolute honesty:

Contributes to a culture of integrity. Everyone is more likely to do the right thing. Although there were doubtless many honest people at Andersen, the culture was such that dishonest practices were more than a onetime event.

Creates compelling brands. Johnson & Johnson survived the Tylenol crisis because it did the right thing. Jack in the Box almost didn't survive its crisis because it at first did not do the right thing and then ultimately did. Today, both are doing well. Doing the ethically responsible thing builds customer trust and loyalty.

Enhances competitive advantage. We should all be using a Xerox operating system instead of Windows, Linux, or Macintosh. Having a stronger culture of absolute honesty might not have saved Xerox from its blunder of ignoring the potential of graphical user interface, but it might have helped. According to Andy Grove of Intel, healthy debate and honest discussions are essential to identifying and embracing such strategic inflection points.

Increases workforce productivity. *I Love Lucy*-type tricks lead to dishonest relationships. A culture where dishonesty is rampant leads to wasting energy protecting oneself. The more energy, time, and focus an organization spends on internal politics, deceptive practices, and back watching, the less it has to spend on serving its customers, developing better products, and succeeding in the marketplace.

Establishes consistent leadership. When you can count on someone to always be straight with you, your level of trust in them rises, even if you don't like them. Therefore, when leaders practice straight talk and conduct themselves with integrity, people trust them more and they, in turn, are more effective in leading their organizations.

Creates positive morale. Although the behavioral scientists tell us that people will repeat what is rewarded and avoid what is punished, and can therefore be controlled like rats in a laboratory, the reality is that people are much more complicated than rats. When your leader is honest and trustworthy, your attitude about her tends to be positive. When she's dishonest, lies, or is a downright crook, warm and fuzzy are not how you typically feel toward her or her organization.

When a company is perceived as an honest business, the result is better decisions, improved customer ratings, greater profits, and higher employee loyalty.

A CULTURE OF ABSOLUTE HONESTY

The story of the *USS Greenville* made the point that the culture on the submarine was such that the captain could do no wrong. Consequently, when the fire control technician suspected that another ship was in the area, he hesitated to say anything, assuming that the captain must have known what he was doing.

Corporate culture is like the water in the fish tank. If you change it improperly or too quickly, you can kill the fish. There are three aspects of corporate culture that a leader should assess and attend to if he is going to transition it to one of absolute honesty, straight talk, and integrity: common behavior patterns, organizational values and beliefs, and personal attitudes and assumptions.

Common Behavior Patterns

From promptness, or lack of it, to formality versus informality, various organizations exhibit patterns of behavior that reflect its culture. Here are some questions to ask about your organization to determine its cultural patterns of straight talk, honesty, and willingness to confront tough issues.

- When differences of opinion regarding business issues arise, are people in your company more likely to express those differences openly, or do they tend to wait and see which way the wind is blowing?
- If an employee is asked by her manager to do something immoral or illegal, would she object or refuse? Would she report it to the appropriate person or department in your organization?
- When a team member has a habit that bothers others—such as holding the floor during meetings, interrupting frequently, or consistently failing to meet deadlines—does someone on

the team usually confront him, or do people just wish he would change while complaining to others about his behavior?

▲ When the boss expresses an opinion that others disagree with, do people respond by falling into an uncomfortable silence and discreetly rolling their eyes, or do they enter into a lively discussion and debate?

▲ When an employee is underperforming, is she likely to be informed by her supervisor in a direct and clear manner, or will she get broadsided with the news at her next performance review?

▲ When an employee sees a colleague engaging in an illegal or unethical act, is she likely to mention it to her manager?

▲ When a work process is flawed, do people make suggestions for improvement, or do they just gripe to their coworkers about the company's "stupidity" for doing things that way?

▲ Do suggestion boxes collect complaints and innovative ideas, or do they fill up with candy wrappers and clutter?

▲ Do people let their supervisors know when they don't like a new policy, or do they gather in the break room to moan about what "they" (i.e., management) are going to do next?

▲ In meetings, do people with strong personalities always hold the floor and get their way, or does everyone get a chance to speak, with all positions considered?

Organizational Values and Beliefs

Every leader hopes that the values and beliefs of their organizations match those printed on the poster hanging in the lobby of the home office. The reality is often far different. The real values and beliefs of an organization are reflected in the behaviors of the leaders.

Here are some questions to help you assess how your organization values straight talk and confrontation:

⚠ Does your organization have a set of values or behavioral norms that is published and displayed?

⚠ Does your own behavior and that of other employees reflect those values?

⚠ Does your organization have a written code of ethics based on stated values that influences or drives decisions?

⚠ Do you have a code of conduct based on your code of ethics that if violated could lead to termination?

And regarding the extent of open communication and healthy debate:

⚠ Does top management publicly support the honest expression of ideas?

⚠ Do top managers' actions reflect these values? That is, do they openly express themselves and encourage others to do the same?

⚠ Are suggestions for changing the status quo actively solicited from employees and responded to openly and quickly?

⚠ Are people punished for expressing unpopular views or disagreeing with superiors?

⚠ Does the organization tend to hire people who are outspoken and opinionated?

⚠ Has management installed systems to establish and reward the practice of open communication and healthy debate?

⚠ If the situation with Lisa and Tom (see p. 32) had played out with your team, would the person in question have confronted you as Lisa did with Tom? Would your reaction have been as gracious as Tom's? How would the team have reacted?

Personal Attitudes and Assumptions

Finally, the general perspective of people who make up an organization can affect the culture. An accounting firm will have more left brain number crunchers and fewer creative types than a graphic design studio. A prosecutor's office will probably have more people willing to be confrontational than a social service agency. For our purposes, the question is: Do the people in your organization, in general, tend to be open and honest and call things like they see them? Here are some questions to help you make that assessment:

- Does your organization have a specific focus that naturally draws people from certain backgrounds or professions or with certain worldviews?
- Do the majority of people in your organization fall into a certain age group (twenty-something, over forty)? If so, what attitudes or behaviors can you attribute to that group?
- If homogeneity in personal attitudes and behaviors exists, what aspects of those attitudes and behaviors support a culture of honesty and which detract from it?
- If more diversity exists in terms of individual attitudes and behaviors, are you presenting your organization's value system in such a way that employees can internalize and cultivate the key values within themselves?

Embarking on the Transformation

A useful formula for managing the pain of change is $P1 + P2 > P3$. When P1 (the pain of continuing with the old way) plus P2 (the pain of not having the new way) is greater than P3 (the pain of transitioning from the old way to the new way), then change will occur. Here are some tips on how to change the culture:

- *Create and publish a set of conduct guidelines and ethical standards that are clear to everyone and are practiced rigorously by you and your management team.*
- *When hiring new people, consider assertiveness and willingness to speak up as positive attributes.* You get what you pay for.

▲ *Clearly state and publish what you want.* If you want people to be candid and forthright, let them know that's what you want.

▲ *Open your ears and aggressively listen to people.* If you want people to express their opinions, start asking for them.

▲ *Take people seriously, even if you think they are crazy.* The idea is to encourage people to speak up and be honest. Their perception of reality will not always match yours.

▲ *Create an infrastructure to support open communication, confrontation, and ethical behavior.* This will provide the organizational mechanisms for people to make their opinions known and to do the right thing. More important, it sends a message to everyone that says, "The organization *wants* to hear what you have to say and for you to behave with integrity."

▲ *Establish, publish, reward, and practice the Six Laws of Absolute Honesty.*
   1. Tell the Truth
   2. Tackle the Problem
   3. Disagree and Commit
   4. Welcome Honesty
   5. Reward the Messenger
   6. Build a Platform of Integrity

ABSOLUTE HONESTY LAW #1: TELL THE TRUTH

Gary Condit's lying about his relationship with Chandra Levy impeached his credibility and lost him the election. It also taught us that lying doesn't pay and the truth is always a better route to take because by telling the truth, you:

Create trust with others. If your mechanic has the chance to take advantage of you and doesn't, your trust in him soars. When you always tell the truth, people begin to count on it. The more you do it, the more they trust you. It's not rocket science.

Do the right thing. Once it stopped denying responsibility and told the truth, Jack in the Box followed on with righting the situation. Truth and doing the right thing go hand in hand.

Discover it's rarely as painful as you think. Like fessing up when you did wrong as a kid, once you've done it, you usually discover that it isn't so bad after all. Telling uncomfortable truths is no different.

Avoid paying the higher price of lying. Lying may save you pain in the short run, but for the long haul, telling the truth is the better investment. Richard Nixon and Bill Clinton discovered that harsh reality when they lied. McDonald's confirmed this wisdom when it told the truth about the "Who Wants to Be a Millionaire?" game

Get it behind you. Try to practice "real-time honesty," which requires vigilance and the willingness to deal with uncomfortable situations as they occur. Real-time honesty is not for the faint of heart. But remember, you get the situation behind you, and it's rarely as bad as you think it will be.

Keep things simple. If you lie, you have to remember what you said and to whom. Pretty soon, the variations on the truth that you have produced get hard to keep track of. Some people can pull it off, but few of us are that smart.

Of course, telling the truth in difficult circumstances is easier said than done. It is usually our fears that keep us from doing it, such as:

Fear of retribution. Dr. Jeffery Wigand of Brown & Williamson discovered that being a whistle-blower can be fraught with danger, and, indeed, this fear can be real. For managers, this is one to guard against at all costs. If you want the truth to be spoken freely in your organization, you want more, not fewer, Jeffery Wigands running around.

Fear of hurting other people's feelings. When we think that the truth will hurt a person's feelings, we hesitate to say it. Sometimes, that's appropriate. There's no reason telling someone his dog is ugly—unless you are judging a dog show. Then it's your job, and not telling the truth betrays your responsibility and confuses the other person. Managers are guilty of this one more than any other. They often don't have the guts to bite the bullet and give people who work for them honest feedback. Consequently, the people don't change and the organization suffers.

Fear of change. Success can be our worst enemy. When things have gone well in the past, we don't want to change, and it's hard to discuss the realities that prove change is necessary. So we put our heads in the sand and pretend they aren't there.

Fear of being disliked. Sometimes people are afraid to speak up when they disagree because they are afraid of being disliked. Here are three steps to help overcome fear and raise the odds that a difficult conversation will go smoothly:

1. Lower the emotional temperature—don't attack, just describe.

2. Give the other person an out—everyone needs to save face.

3. Do it in private—it eliminates the chance of embarrassment in front of others.

Fear of losing support. Big organizations, along with many government entities, lose lots of good managers because of the insurmountable bureaucratic hurdles that they place in the way of those managers doing their jobs. If you're in that position, there may be little you can do to change the situation. We encourage you, however, to continue to express your opinions openly, and to do what you think is right. You may lose lots of battles, but at least you can look at yourself in the mirror and be proud of what you see. And who knows, you may actually change the system!

Fear of paying the price. If you can't do the time, don't do the crime. Often those who do the crimes don't start out intending to be criminals. It's more like an incremental progression than an intentional leap. Justifying one immoral act leads to another, and pretty soon, you're heading down a dark road. If you fear paying the price of telling the truth, don't do things that will require you to pay that price.

Fear of losing competitive advantage. Competition and the value of proprietary information require us to maintain secrets from time to time. You don't want your competition to get the designs for a new computer chip you will be releasing or know what your marketing strategy will be for next year's widget model. On the other hand, secrecy can be carried to the point of not trusting anyone, even the people who work in your own organization. And when you don't trust them, how do you think they feel about trusting you? Besides, your fears are usually unfounded. The lesson here is, when in doubt, it's probably not worth keeping a secret.

Fear of losing face. Philosopher William James said that we all have a powerful need to be accepted by others and he was right. We will go to great lengths to avoid embarrassment. The irony is that the convoluted conniving that we engage in to avoid that embarrassment usually causes us more harm than facing the situation in the first place.

There is no magic answer for overcoming these fears. Like the little boy or girl on the high diving board, the only trick to it is to summon up your courage and do what you've feared doing.

ABSOLUTE HONESTY LAW #2: TACKLE THE PROBLEM

One way to make sure you keep it professional, not personal, while encouraging lively debate, disputing, and downright arguing, is to establish some ground rules for the debates. We suggest constructive confrontation. A term first coined by Andy Grove of Intel, it's a process by which people can confront each other on tough issues while minimizing damage to their relationships. The cardinal rule is, "Attack problems, not people." Here is a six-step model to carry this out:

1. Do your homework, consisting of:
   ▲ Identifying the issue
   ▲ Deciding if the issue is worth confronting
   ▲ Identifying the desired outcome
   ▲ Seeing the situation from the other person's perspective

2. Open the debate by describing the problem or issue as you see it. Be sure to use "I" language and stay in the present as much as possible. Discussions that focus on the past increase people's defensiveness and avoid creating solutions for the future.

3. Open your ears to truly hear what the other person has to say about the issue. Two key concepts we covered here were:
   ▲ *Mutual reciprocity*—the idea that what goes around, comes around. If you want people to listen to your point of view, you've got to listen to theirs first.
   ▲ *Go signals*—comments that the other person will make that indicate that they are ready to hear your point of view.

4. Open your mouth and describe the situation or solution from your perspective. Here's your chance to express your opinion firmly and articulately.

5. Open your mind—work with the other person to find a solution that is best for the organization and, if possible, all concerned.

6. Close the deal—by assigning ARs (Action Required) to everyone involved, and establishing a follow-up date.

We offer this caution. Searching for a win/win solution is better than pursuing a win/lose; however, the first goal should be to achieve the best solution for the organization and that it is ethically and legally sound. In a divorce, achieving a win/win solution for the parents isn't necessarily the best solution for the children. A win/win solution for two warring departments may make the department heads happy, but is it the right answer for the company?

ABSOLUTE HONESTY LAW #3: DISAGREE AND COMMIT

When you don't agree with something or you think something's not right, you have an obligation to speak up and say so. You also have an obligation to support whatever the decision is, once it's made. This is called "disagree and commit."

Of course, it's easier said than done to disagree with what your team wants to do, or what your boss has done. Unless the culture encourages such behavior, it can be downright scary. If you're struggling with doing this, we suggest the following:

Express your feelings offline. Doing so can be safer and it avoids a public scene, which might embarrass your boss or other wielder of power. Sherron Watkins followed this course of action when she presented her observations to Ken Lay at Enron.

Get in the habit. Straight talk comes naturally to some people. For the rest of us, it takes some practice, so try to express yourself openly every day, just to get in the habit. Also, get used to taking a "risk a day." It strengthens your risk muscles and gets you used to being out of your comfort zone.

Ask yourself, "What's the worst that can happen?" Many of us have a tendency to engage in catastrophic chaining. We take a simple fear and blow it out of proportion. Asking yourself this question helps to control the chaining.

Create a discussion tree. A discussion tree is a plan for anticipating how a difficult discussion might progress. It's a map that will help you find your way though a difficult conversation.

Figure 10-1. Discussion Tree.

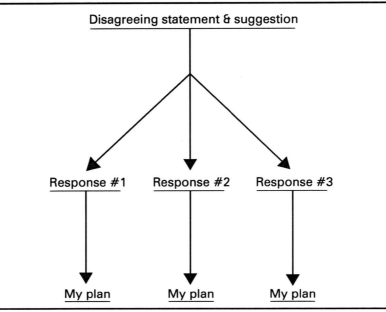

Here, then, are some things you, as a manager, can do to encourage your people to speak up and tell the truth:

▲ *Insist on candor.* If you want candor, tell people you want it.

▲ *Restrain your own brilliance.* There's a reason you are the boss. You're smart, articulate, and maybe you're good-looking too. But whatever the reason, your position and abilities can be intimidating to others.

▲ *Listen intensely.* We can't say this enough. People are more likely to speak up when they have a truly interested audience to hear their thoughts.

▲ *Play the devil's advocate.* In discussion, take the opposing point of view and argue it. Be sure to let others know you are doing so as an exercise in pursuing the best answer, not to be obnoxious or because you think they are wrong. Sure, they may be wrong, but this kind of exercise will help them arrive at that conclusion themselves.

▲ *Create debate groups and reverse roles.* Now the discussion becomes a game and is less threatening. Arguing for a point of view they don't agree with will help people to see the issue from a more global perspective.

▲ *Reward truth tellers.* This means including candor and honesty in their performance management programs.

Stop Whining and Commit. The other side of the "disagree and commit" formula is commit. When people agree to something, and then later bad-mouth it or sabotage it, we call that *lipotage: giving lip service and then sabotaging it.* There are lots of reasons why people will engage in this behavior. They perceive that there was dishonorable intent, or that the process of coming to the decision was unfair; or they think the process by which they were asked for their opinions was a sham; or they suffer from a sense of powerlessness over the situation.

You have three healthy options when you are faced with a situation you don't like or agree with:

P = Positive change—can you make an effort to change what you disagree with?

A = Acceptance or embracing—if you can't change it, can you accept it without whining or committing *lipotage*?

L = Leaving—no one is holding you captive. Sometimes the best solution is to move on.

You are never powerless—you always have a choice.

ABSOLUTE HONESTY LAW #4: WELCOME THE TRUTH

Our ancestors passed along to us the tendency to flee from danger or stick it with a spear. In today's organizational world, sticking someone with a spear when you feel threatened is not acceptable, so we have learned to employ various defense mechanisms to guard against losing face, as well as our jobs. Unfortunately, it is difficult to have an authentic conversation, or to express the truth freely, when one or more parties are being defensive. For example, if an employee tells you that one of your best salespeople is engaging in illegal activities, it is tempting to avoid the situation by denying that anything like that could ever happen on your watch, which is one of the nine major defense mechanisms most of us will employ in a threatening situation:

1. Avoidance

2. Verbal aggression

3. Sarcasm

4. Rationalization

5. Compensation

6. Regression

7. Repression

8. Apathy

9. Displacement

Of course, the dangers of today are different than they were in our ancestors' time. There are no saber-toothed tigers, but there are still dangers. Four categories that tend to make people feel threatened and cause them to be defensive are:

1. Power clashes

2. Colliding personal styles

3. Differing points of view

4. Actual attacks

Power clashes. There are various forms of power working in any organization. Experts have identified six basics:[1] coercive, reward, legitimate, referent, expert, and representative power. When these forms of power clash, defensiveness is usually not far behind. For example, the insecure manager who wields coercive and reward power by virtue of his position may become defensive when one of his employees with a high level of expert power corrects his assessment of a technical problem. Creating a meritocracy where people are celebrated and rewarded for their legitimate, referent, expert, and representative powers goes a long way toward reducing these power clashes.

Colliding personal styles. Different people have different strengths, which translates into signature styles. We identified four general styles: director, analyzer, harmonizer, and energizer. These different styles can cause conflict and defensiveness when they clash but can create great synergy when they complement one another. The trick is to be aware of your own style tendencies and to respect the style tendencies of others. When there is conflict between the styles, learning to adapt your approach with the other person to better match his or her style is an effective strategy for reducing tension, conflict, and the chances of defensiveness rearing its ugly head.

Differing points of view. The expression of differing points of view is the lifeblood of creativity and growth in any organization. On the other hand, when you feel strongly about a position or a point of view, it's difficult to see things from another perspective. You get locked into your own reality. When this reality is threatened, it is tempting to become defensive and verbally attack others by accusing them of being narrow-minded.

Actual attacks. As Henry Kissinger said, "Even paranoids have enemies." Sometimes people actually do attack us verbally. Our advice is to keep a cool head. Instead of becoming defensive, you can sidestep the attack with these techniques:

1. *Take a breath and assess:* If you respond immediately, you lose control and the other person now has you like a puppet on a string.

2. *Apply the ABC technique:* Control your belief about the activating event so you can take charge of the consequence.

3. *Ask for clarification:* So you can make a proper judgment of the criticism.

4. *Rephrase the criticism:* So you and the other person are in agreement as to what was said and intended.

5. *Consider the criticism fairly:* You would certainly want her to do the same for you

6. *Acknowledge the truth:* After all, the criticizer may be right.

7. *Describe why you don't agree with the untrue parts.*

8. *Ask for and offer suggestions to resolve the situation.*

Minimizing Defensiveness in Others

From the work of communications expert Jack Gibb, we've extracted the following suggestions to minimize the chances that others will become defensive with you:

▲ *Illuminate, don't evaluate.* Evaluative language like "you're wrong" and "why didn't you" automatically puts people on the defensive.

▲ *Provide freedom of choice.* There's an old saying about unsolicited advice. "Most don't need it, and those who do won't heed it." Most of us don't like to be told what to do unless we ask for it. Even then, the teller is on dangerous ground, because if she tells us what we don't want to hear, we'll make excuses or argue. If that's not defensiveness, we don't know what is.

- *Beware the curse of "should."* When we were children, we were told what to do and not to do. We were given a set of "shoulds" that our parents wanted us to incorporate into our lives. As adults, we automatically resent having someone else tell us what we "should" do or not do.

- *Bridge the gap in power differences.* Power distorts the communication channels between people. When there is a big difference between you and another person's power level, the chances increase that the person in the subordinate position will misinterpret what you say or do. Be careful.

ABSOLUTE HONESTY LAW #5: REWARD THE MESSENGER

The best way to create an environment where people will speak the truth and behave with integrity is to reward those who do, and punish those who don't. Unfortunately, more often than not, the opposite is true. Punishment for telling, which we call "killing the messenger," comes in many shapes and sizes.

Hopefully you aren't looking for ways to do it intentionally. If you are, you've wasted your time reading this book. There are, however, many ways you can kill a messenger without really meaning to:

Verbal punishment. Most of us have known an excitable person in a leadership role who would yell and scream when he disagreed with someone. Most people find this kind of behavior intimidating and, consequently, won't tell the person what he needs to know.

Defensiveness. When we are highly invested in something, and someone criticizes it, we tend to defend our investment. The bearer of bad news doesn't know this. All she sees is that when she tried to give you feedback, you argued with her.

Disconfirming messages. Communications researcher Evelyn Sieburg identified "confirming messages" in most conversations. A simple nod of the head and a smile can be enormously confirming, encouraging the person to continue speaking. Sieburg also found that conversations can contain "disconfirming messages," which will have the opposite effect on the receiver. Disconfirming messages push people away. They devalue the worth of the other person, and they can be interpreted as so punishing that the receiver feels like a slain messenger, even when you didn't mean for that to happen. Disconfirming messages include nonresponsiveness, interruptions, patronization, disconnected responses, ambiguity, and one-upmanship.

Inaction. Simply not acting on what someone tells you can be extremely discouraging for the person telling you a truth, especially if he considers it important. It sends a message that says, "Your efforts are wasted. Keep your mouth shut. I don't want to hear it." Unfortunately, you may have just forgotten to get back to the person. Noncommunication communicates a lot, whether it's intentional or not.

Regardless of your intentions, if the messenger feels that he was punished for bringing you bad news, it's the same as if it actually happened. Sometimes, the messenger may feel fine about how he was treated, but circumstances surrounding the situation can create a perception that there has been a messenger execution. Further, people will not come forward with vital information or speak their minds freely if they don't trust their manager. Managers don't have to kill messengers for this to happen. They only need to be unpredictable or untrustworthy. Think about the worst manager you ever had in your life. Regardless of whether this person discouraged sharing information or not, would you freely tell him about problems in his operation, or that someone in the organization is being dishonest, or that you disagree with his favorite operational program? Likely not.

You might want to adopt a manager's code of conduct—a list of prescriptions to help managers create an environment around them where people will feel okay about telling them the truth. It includes:

▲ *Trust others to the degree you would like them to trust you.* Trust is a two-way street. To what degree do you trust your people to make decisions, handle problems, adjust procedures, or spend money?

▲ *Be a great listener.* Nothing encourages open communication like a welcome ear. Nothing discourages it like one that is closed. Give all your attention to those who talk to you and they will want to tell you everything they know.

▲ *Clarify expectations.* Research by the Gallup organization showed that the number one factor that affects employee productivity, profitability, turnover, and customer satisfaction is the clarity of expectations people have about their jobs. This also applies to being forthright, candid, and ethical.

▲ *Create a milieu of honesty.* Like a noisy family who likes to talk around the dinner table, managers must create places where people can exchange ideas, argue, and come to agreement. Jack Welch created Work-Outs at GE. The army created AARs. Create your own Milieu of Honesty so straight talk can flourish.

▲ *Lead by example.* When you take on the leadership mantle, you become a "famous person." People will watch you. If you want people to be honest and not cheat, it behooves you to be honest and not cheat. If you want people to tell the truth openly, then tell the truth openly yourself and never, never punish anyone for doing the same.

▲ *Treat everyone like a customer.* In their classic study on leadership, Warren Bennis and Burt Nanus[2] found that one of the common characteristics of great leaders was that they treated *everyone* with the courtesy that would normally be reserved for strangers. We've found that the best managers take the time and make the effort to regularly celebrate and acknowledge those who work for them. They treat their employees the same way they treat their customers.

This is particularly important when employees complain to you or tell you things you'd rather not hear. Just like customer complaints, employee complaints are gifts that you should treasure. We suggest the TARGET-K approach:

T	Thank the person for bringing the problem to your attention.
A	Ask questions to clarify the situation.
R	Reassure the person that you are willing to listen and do what you can to fix the problem.
G	Give your perception of the situation
E	Encourage and reinforce the behavior.
T	Take action to correct the situation and do the right thing.
K	Keep the person informed of all actions you are taking.

ABSOLUTE HONESTY LAW #6: BUILD A PLATFORM OF INTEGRITY

Doing the right thing pays off in many ways: People trust you, you can sleep better, and your business will be better. We also note that it can be tough. Witness the plight of Sir Thomas More. But he was a saint, and for us mortals, it's rarely so difficult that you must lose your head over it the way he did.

When your organization has no ethical foundation, or when you have lost touch with the one you have, you risk making decisions that can get your company into serious trouble. Strong leadership, based on clear values, is the key to making sure the organization does the right thing for the right reasons. We offer a five-part leadership model that Ray Kroc of McDonald's followed:

- Clarity of a vision based on values
- Passion for the vision
- An ability to communicate the vision
- Leading by example
- Standing up for what's important

You might want to keep in mind the formula that Leadership Obsession = Organizational Infection, and that this principle applies to establishing a code of ethical behavior as much as it applies to building empires, creating shareholder value, or dominating a market. To establish this code, we suggest creating a platform of integrity, based on a solid ethical foundation. Based on the work of ethics researchers Dennis P. Quinn and Thomas M. Jones,[3] we suggest five basic tenets:

1. Tell the truth. Don't lie.
2. Keep your word, always.
3. Respect the rights of others.
4. Avoid harming others.
5. Don't break the law.

These tenets provide the foundation upon which to build a platform of integrity, like Johnson & Johnson's Credo. Once this platform is in place, you can create a set of business conduct guidelines–specific answers to various situations that people can use to make the right choices. We suggest you look at those published online by the Maguire Group at http://www.maguiregroup.com/ethics.htm and those published by IBM at http://www1.ibm.com/partnerworld/pwhome.nsf/weblook/memctr_guide_chap1.html.

We cannot reiterate too strongly that doing the right, ethical thing is always the best thing to do, and as a leader, it is your responsibility to put into place a system that will ensure that everyone does the right, ethical thing.

Did reading this book make you think of an example or situation that you would like to share with us? We want to hear it! Please e-mail your story to *stories@absolutehonesty.com*.

Notes

CHAPTER 1

1. H. Josef Hebert, "Enron Executive Says Lay Was Duped," Associated Press, published in the *North County Times*, 15 February 2002, http://www.nctimes.net/news/2002/20020215/62843.html.
2. House Energy and Commerce Committee proceedings, 14 February 2002, http://energycommerce.house.gov/107/hearings/02142002Hearing489/hearing.htm
3. Jennifer Frey, "An American Hero," *Washington Post*, 5 January 2002, http://www.apfn.org/enron/Sherron_watkins.htm.
4. David Schepp, "Andersen Faces Another Trial," *BBC News Online*, 30 April 2002.
5. Terry Green Sterling, "Arthur Andersen and the Baptists," *Salon.com*, 7 February 2002.
6. Larry Dignan, *CNET News.com*, 17 June 2002.
7. Jerry Knight, "Tylenol's Maker Shows How to Respond to Crisis," *Washington Post*, 11 October 1982.
8. Tamara Kaplan, "The Story of the Tylenol Poisonings," *tbk108@psu.edu*, 1998.
9. Knight, "Tylenol's Maker Shows How to Respond to Crisis."
10. *Seattle Post Intelligencer*, 31 October 1997, http://www.marlerclark.com/news-jitb.htm.
11. Ibid.
12. R. R. Ulmer and T. L. Sellnow, "Consistent Questions of Ambiguity in Organizational Crisis Communication: Jack in the Box as a Case Study," *Journal of Business Ethics* 25 (2000): 143–155.
13. T. W. Coombs, "Choosing the Right Words: The Development of Guidelines for the Selection of the 'Appropriate' Crisis-Response Strategies," *Management Communication Quarterly* 8, 4 (1995): 447–476.
14. Elaine Porterfield and Adam Berliant, *The News Tribune*, Tacoma, Washington, 16 June 1995, http://www.marlerclark.com.
15. *Triumph of the Nerds: An Irreverent History of the PC Industry*, Video Documentary, Ambrose Video Publishing, 1996.
16. Abraham Maslow, Robert Frager, and James Fadiman, *Motivation and Personality* (New York: Addison Wesley, 1987).
17. Patrick M. Lencioni, "Make Your Values Mean Something," *Harvard Business Review*, July 2002. All Rights Reserved.
18. Leonard L. Berry, *Discovering the Soul of Service, The Nine Drivers of Sustainable Business Success* (New York: The Free Press, 1999).

CHAPTER 2

1. CNN.com./U.S., 9 March 2001, Web posted at: 9:27 A.M. EST (1427).
2. Josh Peters, University Wire 04-10-2001, reporting on the military inquiry into the sinking of the *Ehime Maru.*
3. Laura Lee, "Forecasts That Missed by a Mile." Originally published in the September/October 2000 issue of *The Futurist,* pp. 20–25. Used with permission from the World Future Society, 7910 Woodmont Avenue, Suite 450, Bethesda, MD 20814. Telephone: 301/656-8274; Fax: 301/951-0394; http://www.wfs.org.
4. Reprinted by permission of *Harvard Business Review,* Noel M. Tichy and Ram Charan, "Speed, Simplicity, and Self-Confidence: An Interview with Jack Welch," September/October 1989. All Rights Reserved.
5. David H. Garvin, *Learning in Action: A Guide to Putting the Learning Organization to Work* (Boston: Harvard Business School Press, 2000). All Rights Reserved.
6. John Kotter, *Leading Change* (Boston: Harvard Business School Press, 1996). All Rights Reserved.
7. Michael Abrashoff, "Retention Through Redemption," *Harvard Business Review,* January/February, 2001. All Rights Reserved. Michael Abrashoff has also written a book, *It's Your Ship,* published by Warner Books, May 2002.
8. IBM.com Web site: http://www.ibm.com/lvg/bio.phtml, August 2001.
9. Betsy Morris, "Lou Gerstner, the Holy Terror Who's Saving IBM," *Fortune,* 14 April 1997.
10. Michael D. Abrashoff, Speech to JPMorgan/Chase Human Resources Conference, Houston, TX, 3 May 2001.
11. Robert Townsend. *Up the Organization* (New York: Knopf, 1970).

CHAPTER 3

1. *Seattle Post Intelligencer,* 31 October 1997, http://www.marlerclark.com/news-jitb.htm.
2. See http://www.jackinthebox.com/aboutourco/history.php.
3. Meagan Johnson, "Stop Me Before I Strangle Someone," http://www.zapthe gap.com.
4. Lou Carlozo, "Masters of Disaster," *Chicago Tribune,* 29 January 2002.
5. Marie Brenner, "The Man Who Knew Too Much," *Vanity Fair Magazine,* May 1996.
6. www.jeffreywigand.com.
7. Harles Cone, Ph.D., psychologist, speaker, trainer.
8. James M. Utterback, *Mastering the Dynamics of Innovation* (Harvard Business School Press, Cambridge, Mass., September 1994). All Rights Reserved.
9. http://www.aligned-agility.com/Inspirations/inspirations.html#Tudor.

10. Guy Kowasaki, *Rules for Revolutionaries,* HarperBusiness, New York, April 25, 2000.
11. William James, *Principles of Psychology,* Volumes 1 and 2 (Harvard University Press, 1983).
12. Del Jones, "Many CEOs Bend the Rules (of Golf)." *USA Today,* 25 June 2002.
13. M. Scott Peck, *People of the Lie: The Hope for Healing Human Evil* (New York: Simon & Schuster, 1983).
14. Stella Ting-Toomey, "Cross-Cultural Face-Negotiation: An Analytical Overview," DLC Pacific Region Forum, Simon Fraser University at Harbour Centre, presented 15 April 1992.
15. Mike France, "25 Ideas for a Changing World—Corporation : 2: The Mea Culpa Defense," *Business Week,* 8 August 2002.
16. Lynn Sharp Paine, "Managing for Organizational Integrity," *Harvard Business Review,* March 1994.

CHAPTER 4

1. Joseph Joubert, *Pensées,* quoted in *The International Thesaurus of Quotations,* compiled by Rhoda Thomas Tripp (New York: Crowell, 1970), p. 52.
2. Marcus Buckingham and Curt Coffman, *First Break All the Rules: What the World's Greatest Managers Do Differently* (New York: Simon & Schuster, 1999).
3. This term was coined by Dr. Harles Cone and is used with his permission. Dr. Cone can be reached by e-mail at harlescone@kc.rr.com.
4. Stephen Covey, *The 7 Habits of Highly Effective People: Restoring the Character Ethic* (New York: Simon & Schuster, 1990).
5. David Garvin and Michael A. Roberto, "What You Don't Know About Making Decisions," *Harvard Business Review,* September 2001. All Rights Reserved.

CHAPTER 5

1. Reprinted with permission from *Harvard Business Review,* Noel M. Tichy and Ram Charan, "Speed, Simplicity, Self-Confidence: An Interview with Jack Welch," September/October 1989. All Rights Reserved.
2. Janet Lowe, compiler, *Jack Welch Speaks: Wisdom from the World's Greatest Business Leader* (New York: Wiley, 1998), p. 43.
3. David A. Garvin, *Learning in Action: A Guide to Putting the Learning Organization to Work* (Boston: Harvard Business School Press, 2000), p. 198. All Rights Reserved.
4. David A. Garvin and Michael A. Roberto, "What You Don't Know About Making Decisions," *Harvard Business Review,* September 2001. All Rights Reserved.

5. Reprinted by permission of *Harvard Business Review*, Noel M. Tichy and Ram Charan, "Speed, Simplicity, and Self-Confidence: An Interview with Jack Welch," September/October 1989. All Rights Reserved.
6. W. Chan Kim and Renee Mauborgne, "Fair Process: Managing in the Knowledge Economy," *Harvard Business Review*, July–August 1997. All Rights Reserved.
7. Garvin and Roberto, "What You Don't Know About Making Decisions."
8. Ronald A. Heifetz, *Leadership Without Easy Answers* (Cambridge, MA: The Belknap Press of Harvard University Press, 1994), p. 121. All Rights Reserved. For a complete discussion of decision-making modes and their applications, see Victor Vroom and Authur Jago, *The New Leadership: Managing Participation in Organizations* (Englewood-Cliffs, NJ: Prentice-Hall, 1992).
9. Garvin and Roberto, "What You Don't Know About Making Decisions."
10. Kurt Eichenwald, "He Blew the Whistle and Health Giants Quaked," *New York Times,* 18 October 1998.
11. Kurt Eichenwald, "Big Hospital Manager to Pay a Fraud Settlement of $95 Million," *New York Times,* 3 October 2000.
12. Eichenwald, "He Blew the Whistle and Health Giants Quaked."
13. Thomas J. Watson, *A Business and Its Beliefs: The Ideas That Helped Build IBM* (New York: Columbia University Press, 1963), pp. 5–6, 72–73. This quote was taken from James C. Collins and Jerry I. Porras, *Built to Last: Successful Habits of Visionary Companies* (New York: HarperBusiness, 1994), pp. 73–74.
14. Safetyforum.com, http://www.safetyforum.com/fordfuelfires/.
15. New York Fasteners Leadership Code. Used by permission of Doreen Remmen, VP, NYF.
16. Jim Collins, *Good to Great: Why Some Companies Make the Leap—And Others Don't* (New York: HarperBusiness, 2001), pp. 83–87.

CHAPTER 6

1. R. D. Laing, *Knots* (New York: Pantheon, 1970), p. 56.
2. Ronald B. Adler and Neil Towne, *Looking Out, Looking In: Interpersonal Communication,* 5th ed. (Holt, Rinehart, & Winston, 1987), pp. 376–379.
3. William James, *Principles of Psychology,* Volumes 1 and 2 (Cambridge, MA, Harvard University Press, 1983).
4. Adler and Towne, *Looking Out, Looking In,* pp. 376–379.
5. Karen Horney, quoted in Adler and Towne, *Looking Out, Looking In,* pp. 376–379.
6. Terry Green Sterling, "Arthur Andersen and the Baptists," *Salon.com,* 7 February 2002, http://www.salon.com/tech/feature/2002/02/07/arthur_andersen.
7. J. R. P. French and B. H. Raven, "The Basis of Social Power," in Dorwin Cartwright, ed., *Studies in Social Power* (Ann Arbor: University of Michigan Press, 1959).
8. http://www1.excite.com/home/careers/company_profile/0,15623,1221,00.html.

9. David Merril and Roger Reid, *Personal Styles & Effective Performance* (Radnor, Pa.: Chilton Books, 1981).

10. Arie de Geus, *The Living Company* (Boston: Harvard Business School Press, 1997), p. 31. All Rights Reserved.

11. Stephen Covey, *The 7 Habits of Highly Effective People: Restoring the Character Ethic* (New York: Simon & Schuster, 1990), pp. 28–29.

12. Albert Ellis and Robert A. Harper, *A Revised Guide to Rational Living* (North Hollywood, CA: Wilshire Book Company, 1997), pp. 119–121.

13. Jack M. Gibb, "Defensive Communication," *Journal of Communication* 11 (September 1961).

CHAPTER 7

1. Monica Alonzo-Dunsmoor, "Graduation Problems? Just Call In An Attorney— West Valley Teacher Threatened with Suit," *The Arizona Republic*, 10 June 2002.

2. U.S. Congressional Hearing Record, 14 February 2002, Serial #107–89.

3. C. Fred Alford, *Whistleblowers: Broken Lives and Organizational Power* (Ithaca, NY: Cornell University Press, 2001).

4. Lisa Simone, interview with C. Fred Alford, who talks about his book *Whistleblowers: Broken Lives and Organizational Power*. (NPR, Weekend Edition, Sunday, 1-20-2002).

5. Evelyn Sieburg, "Interpersonal Confirmation: A Paradigm for Conceptualization and Measurement," San Diego, United States International University (ERIC Document Reproduction Service No. ED 098 634), 1975.

6. For an in-depth look at how to implement an open-book management system, read these two books: *The Power of Open Book Management: Releasing the True Potential of People's Minds, Hearts and Hands*, by John P. Schuster, Patricia Kane, and Jill Carpenter, (New York: Wiley, 1996); and *The Great Game of Business: Unlocking the Power and Profitability of Open-Book Management*, by Jack Stack, edited by Bo Burlingham, (New York: Doubleday Currency, 1992).

7. Telephone interview with Sheila Paxton, September 15, 2002.

8. Marcus Buckingham and Curt Coffman, *First Break All the Rules: What the World's Greatest Managers Do Differently* (New York: Simon & Schuster, 1999).

9. Warren Bennis and Burt Nanus, *Leaders, Strategies for Taking Charge,* 2nd ed. (New York: Harper Business, 1997), p. 66.

10. Technical Assistance Research Programs (TARP), "Consumer Complaint Handling in America: Final Report," White House Office of Consumer Affairs, 1980.

11. Janelle Barlow and Claus Moller, A *Complaint Is a Gift: Using Customer Feedback As a Strategic Tool* (San Francisco: Berret-Koehler, 1996).

12. Stephen George, *Uncommon Sense: Creating Business Excellence in Your Organization* (New York: Wiley, 1997), pp. 34–35.

CHAPTER 8

1. Steven R. Rayner, *Team Traps: Survival Stories and Lessons from Team Disasters, Near-Misses, Mishaps and other Near-Death Experiences,* (New York: Wiley, 1996).
2. *New Advent Catholic Encyclopedia,* http://www.newadvent.org/cathen/14689c. htm.
3. Lynn Sharp Paine, "Managing for Organizational Integrity," *Harvard Business Review,* March/April 1994. All rights reserved.
4. Lynn Sharp Paine, *Cases in Leadership, Ethics and Organizational Integrity: A Strategic Perspective* (New York: McGraw-Hill, 1997).
5. Thom Winninger is the author of four best-selling books on marketing. His latest, *Full Price: Competing on Value in the New Economy,* can be seen at www.winninger. com.
6. http://www.sears.com/sr/misc/sears/about/public/history/history.
7. Paine, "Managing for Organizational Integrity."
8. Interview with David Bear, co-owner of BearCo, a management company that owns ten McDonalds franchises, 21 October 2002.
9. http://www.mcdonalds.com/corporate/info/history/history2/index.html.
10. John F. Love, *McDonalds: Behind the Arches* (New York: Bantam, 1986), p. 39.
11. Ibid., pp. 27–29.
12. This is an unconfirmed story that has been repeated to us by several McDonalds employees. It may be true, or it may fall into the realm of urban legend. Either way, it speaks to the mystique surrounding Kroc and his obsession with QSC.
13. Gary R. Weaver, Linda K. Trevino, and Philip L. Cochran, "Corporate Ethics Programs as Control Systems: Influences of Executive Commitment and Environmental Factors," *Academy of Management Journal* 42 (1 February 1999), pp. 41–57.
14. Norm Alster, "Complaint Expected to Be Filed Against Credit Suisse First Boston," *New York Times,* 18 October 2002, www.your/lawyer.com/resource/news/ index.htm?story_id=2567.
15. "Credit Suisse Cuts Another 1,700 Jobs," *Reuters Business,* 8 October 2002.
16. Emily Thornton, "Can This Man Be a Wall Street Reformer?" *Business Week,* 23 September 2002.
17. http://www.jnj.com/our_company/our_credo_history/index.htm.
18. http://www.jnj.com/our_company/our_credo/index.htm.
19. Dennis P. Quinn and Thomas M. Jones, "An Agent Morality View of Business Policy," *Academy of Management Review,* January 1995.
20. The newspaper was *West-Deutsche Allgemeine,* circa 1993–1994. We were unable to locate a more specific reference.
21. http://www.m-w.com/cgi-bin/dictionary.
22. Gayle Sato Stodder, "Goodwill Hunting. (The Importance of Business Ethics)," *Entrepreneur Magazine,* 1 July 1998.
23. Author unknown, "Doing Well by Doing Good," *The Economist,* 22 April 2000.
24. Quinn and Jones, "An Agent Morality View of Business Policy."
25. Sally B. Donnelly, "One Airline's Magic," *Time* 160, 18 (28 October 2002).

26. Bruce Horovitz, "Scandals Grow out of CEO's Warped Mind-Set," *USA Today,* 10 October 2002.

27. Robert Longley, "Miranda: Rights of Silence," *U.S. Government Info/Resources;* http://usgovinfo.about.com/library/weekly/aa012300c.htm.

28. Reprinted with permission from Thomson Multimedia's *Global Ethics Charter.*

29. Nanette Byrnes, "The Good CEO," *Business Week,* 23 September 2002.

30. Kathleen Day and Peter Behr, Washington Post Staff Writers, "Enron Directors Backed Moving Debt off Books," *WashingtonPost.com,* 31 January 2002, p. A01, http: / / www.washingtonpost.com / ac2 / wp-dyn / A64820-2002Jan30?language= printer.

31. http://www.northgrum.com; "Reporting Ethics Violations" by Donna Davis, Director of Ethics and Business Conduct at the Electronic Systems Sector of Northrop Grumman Corporation; sensor.northgrum.com/ethics/Circuit/Circuit082 001.pdf.

32. Author not available, "Doing Well by Doing Good," *The Economist,* 22 April 2000.

33. Mary G. Rendini, "Team Effort at Maguire Group Leads to Ethics Policy," *HR Magazine,* 1 April 1995, p. 63.

34. Patrick M. Lencioni, *The Five Dysfunctions of a Team* (San Francisco: Jossey-Bass, 2002).

35. Patrick M. Lencioni, "Make Your Values Mean Something," *Harvard Business Review,* July 2002. All Rights Reserved.

36. Betsy Morris and Joe McGowan, "He's Smart. He's Not Nice. He's Saving Big Blue. Lou Gerstner Isn't Easy to Love, but You Have to Respect Him," *Fortune,* 14 April 1997.

37. W. Edwards Deming, Anaheim, California, 16 April 1993.

38. Kim M. Henderson and James R. Evens, "Six Sigma: Benchmarking General Electric Company," http://www.emerald-library.com, B1J, 7, 4, pp. 260–281.

CHAPTER 9

1. http://www.quotationspage.com/subjects/laws/.

2. John Kotter, *Leading Change,* (Boston: Harvard Business School Press, 1996), p. 14.

3. Weyerhaeuser Web site: http://www.weyerhaeuser.com/citizenship/businessconduct/ busiconductoffice.asp.

4. Gordon Bethune and Scott Huler, *From Worst to First: Behind the Scenes of Continental's Remarkable Comeback* (New York: Wiley, 1998).

5. Confirmed in a telephone conversation with Beverly Thompson, Para-Med Client Services System manager for Vancouver, BC.

CHAPTER 10

1. J. R. P. French and B. H. Raven, "The Basis of Social Power," In Dorwin Cartwright, ed., *Studies in Social Power* (Ann Arbor: University of Michigan Press, 1959).
2. Warren Bennis and Burt Nanus, *Leaders, Strategies for Taking Charge* (New York: HarperBusiness, 1997), p. 66.
3. Dennis P. Quinn and Thomas M. Jones, "An Agent Morality View of Business Policy," *Academy of Management Review,* January 1995.

Index

CPSIA information can be obtained
at www.ICGtesting.com
Printed in the USA
FSOW01n1624150416
19282FS